Politics, Religion and Power in the Great Lakes Region

Murindwa-Rutanga

CODESRIA

COUNCIL FOR THE DEVELOPMENT OF SOCIAL SCIENCE RESEARCH IN AFRICA DAKAR

In association with

FOUNTAIN PUBLISHERS
Kampala

CODESRIA
Avenue Cheikh Anta Diop, X Canal IV
BP 3304, CP 18524, Dakar, Senegal
E-mail: codesria@codesria.sn
Website: www.codesria.org

In association with:
Fountain Publishers
P. O. Box 488
Kampala, Uganda
E-mail: sales@fountainpublishers.co.ug
          publishing@fountainpublishers.co.ug
Website: www.fountainpublishers.co.ug

© Murindwa-Rutanga 2011
First published 2011

ISBN 978-286978-492-5 (CODESRIA)
ISBN 978-9970-25-070-7 (Fountain)

The Council for the Development of Social Science Research in Africa (CODESRIA) is an independent organisation whose principal objectives are to facilitate research, promote research-based publishing and create multiple forums geared towards the exchange of views and information among African researchers. All these are aimed at reducing the fragmentation of research in the continent through the creation of thematic research networks that cut across linguistic and regional boundaries.

CODESRIA publishes *Africa Development*, the longest standing Africa-based social science journal; *Afrika Zamani*, a journal of history; the *African Sociological Review*; the *African Journal of International Affairs*; *Africa Review of Books* and the *Journal of Higher Education in Africa*. The Council also co-publishes the *Africa Media Review*; *Identity, Culture and Politics: An Afro-Asian Dialogue*; *The African Anthropologist* and the *Afro-Arab Selections for Social Sciences*. The results of its research and other activities are also disseminated through its Working Paper Series, Green Book Series, Monograph Series, Book Series, Policy Briefs and the CODESRIA Bulletin. Select CODESRIA publications are also accessible online at www.codesria.org.

Dedication

Dedicated to all people who have been engaged in struggles against imperialist oppression, domination and exploitation in whatever form, content and magnitude.

Their rifles they deliberately broke, shouting as they died, "We will not look upon a white man, he shall not have our 'iron' but a curse!"

– Ntochibiri and his comrades

Last warning to Commander of British troops. By numerous letters, I have informed you that I consider any forward movement of your troops tantamount to an attack on our position. My force, being then in the position of lawful defence, will open fire from now, and you will take on yourself alone and entirely the heavy responsibility of the armed conflict which you are provoking!

– Telegraph from the Belgian Military Commander
at the Uganda-Rwanda-Congo border warning the
British Military Commander in the same area on
29 January 1910.

Contents

Abbreviations

ACS	Assistant Chief Secretary
ADC	Assistant District Commissioner
AFDL	Alliance of Democratic Forces for Liberation of Congo-Zaire
BCR	The 1911 Boundary Commission Report
Cap	Captain
CBR	Centre for Basic Research
CMS	Church Missionary Society
CNDP	National Congress for the Defence of the People
Co	Company
CODESRIA	Council for the Development of Social Research in Africa
CS	Chief Secretary
CSSSC	Centre for Studies in Social Sciences, Calcutta
DC	District Commissioner
DM	District Magistrate
DNA	Deoxyribonucleic Acid
D\O	Daughter of
Dr	Doctor
DRC	Democratic Republic of Congo
ENRECA	Enhancing Research Capacity
FDLR	The Rwandan Hutu Democratic Forces for Liberation
Fr	Father
GEA	German East Africa
GLR	Great Lakes Region
HM	His/Her Majesty
KAR	King's African Rifles
KDA	Kigezi District Administration
LRA	The Lord's Resistance Army

Maj	Major
MK	*Umkhonto we Sizwe* – the armed wing of the African National Congress of South Africa
NRM/A	National Resistance Movement/Army
OC	Officer in Charge
PC	Provincial Commissioner
PCWP	Provincial Commissioner Western Province
PRA	Popular Resistance Army
PWD	Public Works Department
Rev.	Reverend
RI	Rigorous Imprisonment
RPF/A	Rwanda Patriotic Front/Army
Rs	Rupees/*Rupiiha*
SE	South East
SPLM/A	Sudan People's Liberation Movement/Army
Unpub	Unpublished
UP	Uganda Protectorate
WC Ord.	Witch-craft Ordinance
WP	Western Province
WPAR	Western Province Annual Report

Preface

This book covers the political, religious and power relations in the contemporary Great Lakes States. These states include: Uganda, Rwanda, Burundi, the Democratic Republic of Congo (DRC), Tanzania, Kenya and the Sudan. The work is important because of the nexus between these countries' shared present and past: their political, socio-economic, cultural and historical aspirations. In terms of regional cooperation, they are the countries, save for the DRC and Sudan, that form the current East African Community (EAC). They share common boundaries in the Great Lakes Region and get their water from rivers flowing across the countries. They lie astride the equator and share its tropical characteristics, which define their territorial topography and resource base. These characteristics endeared them to European colonisers, who promoted their national economic interests, by pursuing a united political strategy and common objective of bringing them to colonial subjection.

The colonialists used Western Christian religion alongside Mohammedanism and *Emandwa* (a pro-establishment traditional religion) to fight and supplant the insurgent Nyabingi traditional religion, thus ensuring colonial dominance over the resistant Nyabingi Movement. This book reflects on the complex dynamics and strategies of the ensuing power struggle, bringing forth a unique set of fascinating revelations of patterns of primitive capital accumulation, resistance, human rights violations and the political compromises between traditional enemies when confronted by a common (foreign) enemy. The enmity, of course, was fostered by the unholy alliance between the English, French, Germans and Belgians in their successful conquest and colonisation of the peoples and their territories. They used religion, propaganda and territorial demarcation to segregate the same peoples speaking the same languages into different countries under different colonial administrations.

A critical analysis of this political distortion brings to light the relevance of these divisive tools on the current trends in the African countries, drawing inferences from the African Great Lakes Region (GLR). The colonial administration used indirect rule selectively at the lower levels and employed loyal local agents and deliberately destroyed lives, cultures and property.

The book is the outcome of a study based on the Kigezi region and its surroundings, and the objective is to analyse the rivalry among the three imperialist powers – Belgium, Germany and Britain, as well as the people's resistance to them. The choice of study is guided by the fact that this area constitutes the heart of the GLR and the centre of struggles in the colonial project in the GLR, for decades. The work exposes the different concessions which led to the redrawing of the colonial boundaries in the region in order to accommodate British imperialist interests. The most illustrative of these was how the British diverted the borderline and rewarded Germany with the control of Mount Kilimanjaro for Germany's recognition that Ufumbiro (Bufumbira) belonged to Britain.

The study highlights how the conflicts were finally resolved to avert a serious war, thus bringing about new reforms. Therefore, Kigezi area has continued to be the centre of conflicts, social movements and horrendous pogroms. This history is instructive to the contemporary reader because of the frequent skirmishes caused by ethnic and religious differences, political and territorial conflicts as well as resource and leadership disputes in the GLR.

There are also useful lessons concerning human and food security worth emulating. These can be drawn from the practices of both the colonial and Nyabingi strategies to ensure the people's security and constant food supplies in a pre-modern war situation. Political coercion was employed, causing human rights violations. These issues are discussed to offer contemporary lessons for human rights protection and policy making as well as make a case for reparation for the victims. This study is based on a rich collection of evidence and a knowledge generating discourse about the political, socio-cultural and religious activities of the people of the Great Lakes Region, in reaction against colonial policies in a region whose commonality of beliefs and social practices are made evident in the people's quest for a regional identity. It also exposes how the Berlin Act imposed on all the European imperialists a racist requirement for maintaining high discipline to protect their 'prestige in face of blacks'.

The book's importance also stems from the dearth of studies on the region which look at political questions from a well historicised and an adequately theorised position other than those done by Mahmood Mamdani and Dan Nabudere. It is my hope that this study will generate debate across disciplines and continents, and contribute to the understanding of the geopolitics of this politically volatile region.

Acknowledgements

I received a lot of goodwill and support during my research and the subsequent writing of the book. My first thanks go to the Council for the Development of Social Research in Africa (CODESRIA), Makerere University, Kampala; Jadavpur University, Kolkata; Lund University, Lund; Centre for Studies in Social Sciences, Calcutta (CSSSC); Centre for Basic Research (CBR), Kampala; and DANIDA through ENRECA for their intellectual and material support.

I am exceedingly grateful to my mother, the late Mukyara Asanensi Joy Kifwabusha and to my father Omwami Yosamu Rutanga, popularly known as Founder for bringing me into the world and for giving me education, for teaching me how to talk, think and apply my other faculties.

I am equally very grateful to all my teachers – principally to Professor Mahmood Mamdani for equipping me with crucial conceptual, methodological, epistemological and analytical tools. I am equally very thankful to him for initiating me into organic research The same thankfulness goes to Professors Partha Chatterjee, Gautam Kumar Basu and Amiya Kumar Bagchi, for their contributions to my intellectual growth, and their insightful review of this book.

In the same vein, I am extremely appreciative of Hon. Dr Ndugu Ruhakana-Rugunda and his family for their comradeship, encouragement and inspiration. The same appreciation goes to Hon. Bright Rwamirama and family. I can not forget Mr F.S. Lwanga and his family, for their friendship and encouragement.

Special thanks go to all my Kolkata friends and their families who welcomed me into the Bengali society. Notable among these are Mr Debashish Choudhury, Anjan Gupta and Surijit Sanyal; Drs Indra Choudhury, Shibashis Chatterjee, Partha Basu, Prabi Roy, Uttam Battacharya, Shreya Bhattacharji and Sukla Sen. Also appreciated are the Maharajas and staff of Ramakrishna Mission Institute of Culture, Gol Park, Kolkata. '*Kaj shesh! Dhanna bad!*' (Work is finished! Thank you!)

I owe a special debt of gratitude to members of the CODESRIA African scientific community, my colleagues at Makerere University and the Centre for Basic Research (CBR). Unforgettable among these are Dr Ebrima Sall, the

Executive Secretary of CODESRIA and his predecessor, Professor Adebayo Olukoshi; Professor Francis Nyamnjoh; Drs Pinkie Mekgwe, Omobolaji Olarinmoye and Richard Akum. Within the GLRs, thanks to Professors John Jean Barya, James Tumwine, Ruth Mukama, Eric Aseka Masinde, Joy C. Kwesiga and Elijah D. Mushemeza; Dr Richard Ndyomugyenyi and family, Dr Charles Bwana, Dr Lawyer Kafureeka, Dr Simon Rutabajuuka, Mr Alex Bangirana and all members of the Mukono CODESRIA Workshops for Scholarly Writing. You have all been an inspiration to me.

I am equally grateful to my uncles; Rev. Fr Dr Vincent Kanyonza, and Justice J.B. Katutsi and his family for their insights about knowledge, life and justice. The same goes to Hon. Justices Okumu Wengi and Patrick Tabaro for their varied contributions towards the realisation of this book project.

Special thanks go to members of the Frontwards Family for their different contributions. These include the Byambabazis, the Turyomurugyendos, the Rwaganikas, the Sabiitis, the Muhwezis, the Odois and the Akampumuzas. I thank them all for their invaluable contributions to my intellectual life. The same goes to the Ndarubweines for their comradeship and respect for honesty, truth and knowledge.

I equally extend a gesture of gratitude to my dear family – my wife Sarah Muzaki, for her immeasurable contributions, challenges and consolation. And to my children: Muhumuza-Busingye, Ruyooka-Tuhumwire Murindwa Jr, Rodney Lumumba Taremwa and Fanon Nkrumah Rutatiina Rutanga; Claire and Linda Bewayo.

I would like to also register my deep appreciation to all my Ugandan friends, especially those who directly facilitated my research. These include: Mr Sunday Mutabazi and family, Mr B. Muhwezi, Ms G. Kyarimpa, Ms Thabitha, Mr M. Twinomugyisha, Mr D. Byaruhanga, Mr H. Byomugisha and the late Rev. Fr M. Ahurwendeire. I am equally thankful to Prof. Emmanuel Muranga, Dr J. Natukunda and Mr Ahmed Kagwa for translating colonial documents from French and German into English for this study. The same goes to Mr Mukotani Rugyendo who edited this work. I cannot forget Mr. Charles Ndyabawe for handling the technical aspects of the work.

Above all, I am extremely thankful to all my respondents who sacrificed their valuable time to provide information for this study by answering questions which might have appeared irrelevant to them and their lives. The same goes to

Mr Ongom and other members of staff at the National Archives, Entebbe; and to the staff of the District Administration and Archives at Kabale.

My final thanks go to all my past students at Makerere University and centre for Basic Research for their persistent urge to me to write books for people to read. This book comes as an answer to their request.

1

Introduction: Tracing Politics, Religion and Power in the Great Lakes Region

One of the aims of this book is to publish in contemporary literature fresh evidence that Africa has always had a history that is worth studying. The work highlights how individuals and groups of both genders defended the continent and its values by fighting wars using various tools at their disposal. It explains why and how they were invaded, conquered, disorganised and then reorganised to serve European capitalist interests.

The conditions that influenced both their protracted resistance and subsequent defeat are analysed and documented to give the reader useful insights into those factors that define Africa's political structures, processes and destiny. The objective, of course, is to further provoke a dialogue on Africa's history to negate uncritical acceptance of imperialist justification for their invasion and plunder of Africa. The book counters the patronising claims of religious institutions, which they teach in schools and institutions of higher learning, that Africans invited the Europeans to come and colonise Africa so as to preach Christianity, 'civilise' the Africans and save them from barbarism. They argue that these were vices which had been fuelling internecine wars and that they came to stop the human tragedy characterising Africa. They cited the sacrificing of twins and other forms of infanticide, slave trade and so on.

This work contains a systematic detailing of the brutalities that were meted on Africans for resisting European enslavement of Africans on African lands.

It demonstrates that the reorganisation that was undertaken gradually deprived the inhabitants of their capacities – history, military, economy, knowledge and independence.

By exposing the literature informed and dominated by colonial propaganda through juxtaposing colonial and African perspectives, this book brings out the missing picture of an Africa founded on love, devotion and a renewed realisation of the strength and historical mission to defend it through all ways even when they are enticed by the attractions of modernity, development, industrialisation and globalising the world into a single village.

It also aims to explain why and how alien powers – the English, the Germans and the Belgians – invaded the GLR area, struggled amongst themselves over it to impose their power over it, and the resistance by the indigenous peoples and their reactions. It analyses the shortcomings of the resistances, the consequences of their defeats and the reforms that emerged from the arduous encounters.

Given its nature, this study adopted a retrospective study design. It relied heavily on historical and documentary sources and was supplemented by information from respondents. It began with a library-based research, mainly for secondary and documentary sources. This was followed by archival research both at the National Archives, Entebbe and at the District Archives in Kabale. This availed the study rich historical documents for review and analysis. This was then followed by interviews in South-Western Uganda.

This study benefited enormously from seminars and discussions at CBR, Makerere University, the University of Lund, Sweden, the Centre for Studies in Social Sciences, Kolkata, and Jadavpur University.

This study was confronted by a series of challenges. Some of these arose from incessant agrarian tensions and struggles in the research areas. Topical among these was the horrendous lynching of a rich farmer and the destruction of his property in broad daylight by a group of male peasants. The cause was the victim's implementation of a High Court ruling which was in his favour. His killers were his immediate neighbours. They, however, belonged to a different *oruganda* (lineage or clan). The resultant tensions, feuds, state repression, arrests and flight compelled the people that did not flee the area to become reticent. The timing and the prevailing circumstances made the motives of the research suspect.

There was also the challenge of broken appointments, plus the operations of different social movements. Another problem was the lack of written records by the Nyabingi[1] resistance, who were predominantly illiterate. Both the leadership

---

1   In this book, Nyabingi is variably spelt as Nabingi, Nya-bingi, Nya bingi and NyaBingi.

and the membership did not leave behind any written records about their struggles, their history, plans, actions, military encounters, views and outlooks about the Movement. This limitation forced the use of combined information from archival sources and oral sources - narratives, histories, and interviews with respondents.

The records at the National Archives were scattered and mixed up in heaps, sometimes under obscure titles, or unlabelled. This increased the time spent working through these records. It, however, enabled the researcher to come to grips with the reality of the dangers of colonialism and how the colonialists were able to hide, forever, their crimes in the colonies, as obviously, they were not ready to leave behind any incriminating records. Yet, there were very important records on the nature and magnitude of the atrocities and crimes committed in the GLR. Recently, the Bunyoro Kingdom accused Britain of massacring over two million Banyoro in the war of invasion of the 1890s.

The above created an inter-related problem of the possibility of erroneous or falsified facts in the colonial materials, to cover up and explain away the missing records since the colonialists were writing the history of the victors. These documents were written by the colonialists to inform the colonial project.

The study held on to the belief that they would not write deliberate lies for their administrative purposes and actions as their intention was to ensure the success and longevity of the colonial system and its exploitation of Africa. Though cognizant of the fact that belief implies absence of facts, still, our ground was that colonialism was a serious political, economic project which had to be founded on solid facts. As such, false records would have implied self-deception, which *ipso facto* would have meant sowing seeds for the destruction of the entire colonial system.

The researcher carefully examined the representations in the colonial texts and contexts which were highly racialised. Archival materials were combined with the responses by the respondents, the narratives and songs about these struggles and the other secondary sources.

The other major challenge revolved around the political assaults and social stigmatisation that the pre-colonial African religions had undergone since the inception of colonialism. Many respondents were not willing to talk about them freely. Some could have been under actual fear of these religions, while others, especially the formally educated, could have developed duplicity, pretence and disdain towards them.

In fact, this field research brought to light how and why many of these people lived dual or multiple religious lives. They worshipped African gods in secrecy and so on, and were Christians or Moslems openly. In other words, they found having different religions neither contradictory nor conflictual but rather empowering, and at times enabling their manoeuvrability, concealment and benefits. Thus, converting into Christianity became handy for many of them. People took on European or Arabic cultural names to show their new affiliation with the Western religions and their search for 'modernity'.

This shows the resilience and persistence of old beliefs, gods and religions in the face of concerted demonisation by the colonial authorities and their agents. It also demonstrates a crisis of identity which was created by colonialism and its ideological arms – Christianity and Muhammedanism. This issue of identity is well-handled by Castells (1997). Quoting Calhoun, he explains the locus, functions, usefulness and imperativeness of names, languages and cultures to all peoples. He argues, correctly, that names stem from and do constitute people's origins of meaning and experience. These are the ones where 'some manner of distinctions between self and other, we and they, are not made... Self-knowledge – always a construction no matter how much it feels like a discovery – is never altogether separable from claims to be known in specific ways by others.'

The book is organised into nine chapters. Chapter One deals with the introduction of the study and the theoretical perspective. It examines the various functions of religion in society at different levels of development and its roles to different social groups and classes. This is followed by Chapter Two, which attempts to reconstruct the pre-colonial setting, the existing modes of production, the forms of ownership, the social set-up, the levels of production and exchange, and the mode of politics. Chapter Three then analyses the nature of the religions, the material base of Nyabingi religion that facilitated it to gain supremacy over other institutions, its exploitative and oppressive character and the events that precipitated the Nyabingi Movement.

Chapter Four examines the colonial invasion, the complexity of the colonisation of this region – inter-colonial rivalry, on the one hand, and the anti-colonial struggles by the indigenes, on the other. It explores the factors underlying this phenomenon and its course. Chapter Five then deals with some factors underlying the Nyabingi Movement, its objectives, its course and the various phases it went through. The chapter examines part of the Nyabingi leadership, the reasons why these resistances were defeated, and the effects of these defeats on both the actors and the movement.

Based on some cases, Chapter Six analyses the role of women in these struggles, the contributions of some individual women in the leadership and the factors that led them to leadership. Chapter Seven analyses the emerging political coercion and human rights issues. It analyses the contributions and limitations of the Nyabingi Movement, and the factors that led to its decline.

Chapter Eight explores the new methods of struggle, the colonial methods to undermine the movement, and the new survival methods adopted by the Nyabingi Movement, while Chapter Nine concludes the study.

Though history is a lived experience that cannot be erased, as Tajudeen (2007) correctly observes, it however faces possible dangers of disputation, denigration, misrepresentation; or of being forgotten, mythologised or transformed into tales, stories and scares, if it is not captured and recorded by those interested in its narrative, dissemination and preservation. The varied rich histories of the people in the Great Lakes Region (GLR) seem to be headed towards that fate if intellectuals do not come forward to take on the mission of digging them out, recording them and disseminating them.

The countries of the GLR came into formation through the European colonisation of Africa. This project resulted in the Anglo-German-Belgian colonial rivalry and it was concluded diplomatically in 1910-1911 through the signing of the Anglo-German-Belgian Agreement. It was then implemented through the demarcation of the British Uganda, Belgian Congo and German East Africa. The latter later became Ruanda[2]-Urundi[3], after the World War I. They are today independent nation states under the names Rwanda and Burundi. Part of the then Belgian Congo is the DRC.

With the exception of the DRC, all the other five countries have embarked on a regional integration project politically and economically, by reviving the East African Community. This had originally been formed in 1967 by Kenya, Uganda and Tanzania but it was dismantled in 1977 because of the irreconcilable political and economic disputes amongst the political leadership of the three member states.

The GLR has been characterised by vicious, bloody and conflictual politics. These are ethnicised, social, religious or individualised differences. The most horrific and memorable one is the recent ethnic conflict in Kenya, arising from disputations over electoral malpractices and irregularities after the elections of 27 December 2007. These resulted in unprecedented ethnic cleansing.

---

2   Rwanda was variably written by the colonialists as Ruanda.

3   Burundi was also variably written by the colonialists as Urundi.

But do these conflicts have an origin? To understand their origin one requires a historicisation of the European invasion, the colonisation of Africa, and the establishment of its rule. This will provide explanations as to why and how the same peoples were divided and confined to different territories belonging to the competing imperialist powers, while at the same time combining different peoples, with differing modes of production, cultures, outlooks, organisations and politics.

This book, therefore, focuses on the European invasion of the GLR. It analyses the factors that underlay the invasion, the demarcation process that followed and the indigenous people's responses to it. What is worth noting is that most of the anti-colonial struggles in the GLR were anchored in religion. Reference is made to the Maji Maji Rebellion, the Nyabingi Movement, the Lamogi Movement, *Dini Ya Misambwa* and the different independent churches that arose in the GLR during colonialism. Even the more secular Mau Mau Movement integrated religious cultural practices in its bondings through oath taking.

The most pronounced was the Nyabingi Movement, which covered almost the whole region – Tanzania, Rwanda, Burundi, DRC and Uganda. Its modes of politics and resistance influenced the inhabitants and politics in the whole region and it forced the colonial powers to reform their *modus operandi* in the GLR. Its *abagirwa* (mediums) paralysed the colonial system as they spread their operations to different parts of the GLR. Some of them ended up being arrested and charged in kangaroo courts and within a few hours or days convicted and sentenced to imprisonment with hard labour, or fined and imprisoned, or deported. This will be demonstrated with a few cases from Tanzania. In colonial Uganda, the Nyabingi Movement covered the whole western region and spread to parts of Buganda.

This work investigates why they resisted, the nature of their resistance and the reasons why they were defeated. It explains why and how the European colonisation of this region created material conditions and seeds for the subsequent recurrent conflicts in the GLR. Cabral (1976), Fanon (1966) and Canale (1988) provide insights into the inevitable tensions and contestations between the repugnant and malignant colonial master, and the indigenous people during their encounter. Colonialism presupposes belligerency between the contending forces. On the one hand is the invading force which is struggling for occupancy and control of that space in order to impose its technologies of power, demands and hegemony. On the other hand are the inhabitants who wage arduous struggles of various forms to liberate themselves, their domain, property and rights. Right challenges might, which reproduces unending tensions and conflicts between the colonisers and the colonised.

This book is about these processes and contestations – right from the initial colonial encounter to resistances, the processes through which the colonisers established their *modus vivendi* and hegemonised it. It brings to light the causes, nature and intensity of the conflicts and military confrontations amongst the colonisers, and between them and the colonised people. It examines the diplomatic and strategic manoeuvres by the three imperialist powers - whose interests were clashing within this territory - and the methods through which the imminent possibilities of a fatal inter-imperialist war were averted. It analyses the processes through which the British imperialists outmanoeuvred and ejected Germany and Belgium out of their positions. It also examines why and how non-capitalist, non-commodity producing peoples organised themselves against a highly developed, well organised, well armed and resourced capitalist adversary, and the material conditions that facilitated religion to provide them with leadership. It exposes the socio-political programmes of this movement, its forms of mobilisation and recruitment into its membership and leadership, and the locus of gender in the movement. It examines the course of this movement, the various tendencies characterising it, the attempts to pre-empt, fight and defeat it. It analyses the internal reforms that were undertaken by the belligerent contestants and the consequences of the subsequent defeats. It demonstrates the primacy of the rights and sovereignty of a people and their mode of existence, irrespective of their level of development.

The book uncovers the different forms of conflicts – endogenous and exogenous, popular and individualised, legitimate and anti-establishment, anti-imperialist and inter-imperialist, passive and militant, benign and virulent. It brings out methods through which the belligerent imperialist powers did respond to anti-colonial movements. Anti-imperialist movements did at all times compel the rivalling imperialists to unite, suspend their conflicts or transfer them to the metropolitan centres for diplomatic transaction and resolution in order to fight their common enemy. These responses clearly demonstrated the gravity of anti-colonial movements to imperialism as compared to their inter-imperialist rivalries. They also demonstrate that whereas they had to try all diplomatic measures to contain and resolve contradictions amongst themselves so as to avert any bloodshed, they did not take any diplomatic initiatives to resolve their conflict with the indigenous peoples. Instead, they applied maximum force 'to put sense into them'. This reflected the character of the racial dictatorship that characterised colonial imperialism. The imperialists considered the peoples as primitives. The study also brings out the different colonial responses to the movement and the different forms of divisive colonial administration that were put in place. It explains how all these were conflictual seeds being sown in the GLR. It also exposes the reasons, positions, roles, costs and benefits of individuals who abandoned their people to collaborate with the invading colonialists.

Through these brutalities and processes, colonial technologies of power were instituted. Labour processes were instituted through taxation and force. This was gradually strengthened by the introduction of money. Over time, money became a social power as it became a conduit for exploiting resources from the colonies. That way, colonial imperialism was established and it would last till the 1960s.

Its demise in the GLR first came to the open with Sudan's independence in 1956. This was followed by Congo's ill-fated independence in 1960, with Patrice Lumumba as Prime Minister. This government was tragically overthrown within a few months by Kasavubu, Tshombe and Mobutu. Being the blue-eyed boy of imperialism, Mobutu soon outmanoeuvred the other two, took over power and he ruled for thirty-two years. The DRC was followed by Tanzania in 1961, Burundi, Rwanda and Uganda in 1962 and Kenya in 1963.

Thus, the time of formal occupational imperialism or the so-called colonial modernity project came to an end. Imperialism developed into a borderless, roaming predator under the self-acclaimed labels of partners in developments, agents of international development, donors, poverty alleviators and globalisation. Globalisation is known in the GLR as global lies for global pillage. Imperialism has thus taken on a new character, where occupation of physical space has become obsolete and irrelevant.

The concept, *Great Lakes Region*, was coined by the colonialists to refer to the territory in East and Central Africa. This region was endowed with a heavy concentration of large lakes and rivers. In an effort to export their history as they created their legacy, the British colonial invaders renamed four of these lakes after their English rulers. These were Lake Nalubale which became Lake Victoria - the largest lake in the world with clean water. Lake Rwitanzigye was renamed Lake Edward and Lake Katunguru became George. Another lake on the border between DRC and Uganda was renamed Lake Albert. The other big lakes in the GLR included Tanganyika, Kivu, Kyoga, Bunyonyi, Mayanja, Mutanda, Magadi, Rudolf, and so on. This is the region where the River Nile - the longest river in the world – begins. Other gigantic rivers include Congo, Kagera, Ruzizi,

Nyabarango, Kiruruma, Rwizi, Ishasha, and so on. The region is famous for its large swamps and equatorial rain forests, including some impenetrable ones.

This region is also endowed with enormous natural resources. These include precious minerals like uranium, diamond, gold, petroleum and tanzanite, columbium (niobium), cobalt, zinc, cadmium, manganese, tanzanite, nickel, limestone, tungsten, tin, iron ore, petroleum, natural gas, tantalum, cement, fertile soils, fertilizers, soda ash, salt, waters, equatorial forest resources and fertile soils, fresh waters and waterfalls, hot springs, and fishes, rains, livestock, and so on. Others include daily sunshine and excellent temperatures, equatorial rains, and equal days and nights. Yet, it is paradoxically ranked as the poorest in the world, being characterised by economic retardation, political misrule, corruption, authoritarianism, dictatorships and malpractices. It is also ranked as the region leading in non-gainful, destructive and anarchical, incessant conflicts, horrendous massacres, which in the worst cases deteriorate to genocide, and so on (Mamdani, 1991; Bayart 1993; Bayart et al, 1999).

These works are riddled with flaws (See *Sunday Vision* of 6 July 1997). Bayart's work of 1993 reduced everything in Africa simplistically to politics of the belly. His two works were all out in search of crimes and failures with no room for inclusion of anything to the contrary. Their message is that nothing good ever comes from Africa. But would Africa still exist if everything was so negative right from independence? Put differently, was Africa better off during colonialism than in the pre-colonial period and after independence? Is it a characteristic of Africa?

The GLR continues to be ranked among the most volatile regions of the world, with great possibilities of inhuman massacres and genocides. Cases in Rwanda, Burundi, DRC, Uganda and Kenya are cited as evidence of such destructive possibilities.

The persistence of all these negativities, together with low levels of education and lack of committed thinkers and nationalists have changed this region to the Great Conflicts Region.

GLR evokes and resonates varying notions and memories. These range from the different anti-colonial struggles which targeted the three contending colonial powers in the region – the Belgians, the Germans and the British – the suffering, cruelty, oppression and exploitation experienced by the colonised peoples, and the resultant conflicts, authoritarianism, dictatorship and other forms of misrule by civilians and the military elite. These were the categories which certain strands of the modernisation discourse, spearheaded by Janowitz (1964) and Huntington

(1968), had identified and heralded as the guarantors of stability and modernity in the post-colonial era. The military elite had been trained in the colonial military disciplines. Examples included Colonels Bokassa, Idi Amin, Marcius Nguema, Mobutu Sese Seko and Juvenal Habyarimana.

The GLR's continental contributions became pronounced in Tanzania under Mwalimu Nyerere. Tanzania took up a pan-African historical-political role of assisting oppressed Africans in their efforts to liberate their countries and peoples from the oppressive and exploitative yoke of colonial imperialism. Tanzania became the centre of liberation activities for Eastern and Southern Africa, Zimbabwe, Zambia, Mozambique, Namibia and Uganda. Within the GLR itself, Tanzania waged war against the military dictatorship under Idi Amin in 1978/79. She, together with Ugandan guerrilla forces which were based in Tanzania at the time – mainly Kikosi Malum and Front for National Salvation (FRONASA) – defeated the military dictatorship and flushed it out of Uganda (Museveni, 1997).

With the new developments in Tanzania, following Nyerere's exit from presidency in 1985, Uganda, under the leadership of the National Resistance Movement (NRM), from January 1986 took up the Pan-African leadership role. It provided the Southern African liberation forces with logistics and terrain to establish bases for training. It was not the first time.

In 1969, the Obote Government declared diplomatic support for the liberation of South Africa and Rhodesia from the white supremacy rule without taking any practical steps to actualise it. Idi Amin later inherited this politics of rhetoric which was specifically directed against 'Apartheid South Africa' and 'Zionist Israel'.

The difference between those two and the NRM was the level of commitment to the declaration. The NRM demonstrated practically, its commitment to this promise. After capturing state power, it allowed the Umkhonto we Sizwe (MK) – the armed wing of Africa National Congress – to establish bases in Uganda for military recruitment and training against the Apartheid South African dictatorship. It was doing this at the same time and within the same space with the Rwanda Patriotic Front (RPF/A). It is noteworthy that both of them came to power in the same year. In 1994, South Africa got independence and RPF/A captured state power in Rwanda. The RPF/A had launched its military attacks onto Rwanda from Uganda on August 1, 1990 and it used Uganda as its dependable rear base till it finally captured state power. The RPF guerrilla activities in Rwanda resulted in masses of refugees, many of whom had been involved in genocidal criminalities (Mushemeza, 2007).

It was on this ground that the founding of the Alliance of Democratic Forces for Liberation of Congo – Zaire (AFDL) under Kabila's leadership enjoyed political, military, logistical and diplomatic support from Rwanda and Uganda. This enabled the newly formed AFDL to cross the vast forests, rivers and swamps of Congo while fighting. They defeated the 32- year-old decadent Mobutu regime and captured state power in Kinshasa within seven months. This was made possible by the weaknesses of the Mobutu regime in Kinshasa. This regime was characterised by a multiplicity of vices, most of which had been cautioned against by Machiavelli. Among these was the dependence on mercenaries, and foreign assistance, violation of people's property and other rights.

Shortly after capturing state power in Kinshasa, Kabila's new government chased away the allied forces. It began by chasing away the Ugandan forces. His rule was characterised by full-time alcoholism instead of attending to the immediate reconstruction needs of the country. Kabila's tragic assassination by his bodyguards resulted in his son's ascent to power. This was neither constitutionally sanctioned nor democratically executed via an election. He chased away the Rwandan forces and opted to pursue the war option.

Today, different movements in the region have bases in the DRC. These include the anti-Batutsi Bahutu ethnic movements from Burundi and Rwanda. The defunct Rwandan forces during the late Juvenal Habyarimana's rule and the dispersed *Interahamwe* have reorganised under the Rwandan Hutu Democratic Forces for the Liberation of Rwanda (FDLR). Given their murderous history, their new name is a mockery of democracy.

Three major anti- NRM movements have been operating in the DRC and the Sudan. These include Uganda's Allied Democratic Forces (ADF), the Popular Resistance Army (PRA), and the Lord's Resistance Army (LRA). The LRA sprouted from the defeated Holy Spirit Movement of Alice Lakwena. Then, there was Sudan's SPLM/A before the Comprehensive Peace Agreement with Khartoum plus the ongoing massacres in Darfur. In addition, there have been inter-state conflicts – either directly or by proxy. These include conflicts between Uganda and Congo right from the 1960s, between Uganda and Tanzania, between Uganda and the Sudan, between Uganda and Kenya, and between Uganda and Rwanda.

New forms of movements have been emerging. These are either majorly political though they may take on religious fervour. Most of these are predominantly peasantry-based. These include The Movement for the Restoration of the Ten Commandments of God in Kanungu, Western Uganda that killed over 1,050 people, mainly peasants hailing from the GLR. The others include Dini Ya Mukaaka, the Abarangi Movement, Mungiki Movement, the Sungu Sungu and National Congress for the Defence of the People (CNDP). Other well-known ones, mainly of a political nature, include the National Resistance Movement (NRM) and the Rwanda Patriotic Front (RPF).

It is noteworthy that the GLR is the origin of humanity. As such, it is also the origin of most human constructions - socio-political, economic, physical, philosophical, scientific, meteorological, astronomical, mathematical and epistemological, and so on. Different Africanist scholars have dealt with this subject using different methodologies. These include Amadiume (1997); Ben-Jochannan (1991); Bernal (1987); Connah (1975); Davidson (1959, 1966, 1992); Diop (1966, 1974 a,b, 1989, 1978, 1981); Freund (1984); Hrbek (1988); Jackson (1970); Ki-Zerbo (1988); Lane-Poole (1990); Mokhar (1981); Ogot (1992); Sertima (1985); Tabaro (2006) and Zeleza (1997).

GLR is still the home of the apes. Notable among these are mountain gorillas, chimpanzees, monkey, and so on. All these have features, characteristics, mannerisms and practices and *Deoxyribonucleic Acid* (DNA) nearest to those of human beings. These, and other facts, attest to the fact that this is the origin of human beings. Given this enviable history, the contemporary developments in the GLR demand great attention. What explains the origins and persistence of these crises and inhuman tragic occurrences? Given that the GLR is endowed with enormous resources, why should it be one of the poorest places in the world, with minimal signs of development (Bayart, 1993, 1999)?

Another paradox stems from the differences in levels of development between the GLR and other regions of the world. The countries in the GLR got their independence about ten years after the Chinese revolution and at the same time as Cuba. But while Cuba and China have advanced economically, scientifically, industrially, educationally, socially, politically and militarily, those in the GLR have not made any significant advancements.

This work is mindful of the ravages and negative effects of the many centuries' old horrendous human resource depletion from the whole continent through violent raids and capturing of Africans, transporting them as human merchandise to other continents and selling them in the trans-Saharan slave trade (7th century), the Eastern African slave trade (12th century) and the Trans-Atlantic slave trade (15th century). The main beneficiaries from this inhuman but lucrative trade were Europeans, Americans, Arabs and Asians. This inhuman trade deprived Africa of millions of robust, productive young people; without any replenishment. It resulted in the destruction of the human socio-political, economic and physical constructions, developments and civilisation. Therein lies the origins of Africa's crises and miseries (Rodney, 1976; Freund, 1984; Suret-Canale, 1988; Thornton, 1992).

Any committed study must broaden its analytical frontiers to be able to grasp the territorialisation of European material and political interests in this region through colonisation and the institutionalisation of destructive strategy of ethnic divisions, which over time fruited into persistent conflicts. The most dominant ones are the *Abahutu-Abatutsi* ethnocentric politics in Rwanda and Burundi since independence. Rwanda's case provides a sufficient example. The ethnic conflict in Rwanda first exploded in 1959-60, then in 1963 and finally from 1990 to 1994. These climaxed into a three-month state-inspired and supervised genocide that decimated about one million people – mainly the Rwandans of *Abatutsi* ethnic grouping and the 'moderate' *Abahutu*. It was perpetrated by the *Abahutu* Rwandans, who were being driven by an anti-*Abahutu* ideology. This ideology was massively propagated in all mass media including radios and religious pulpits. It demonstrated how far the press machinery and propaganda could go in mobilising and inciting people for destructive purposes. This demonstrated the destructive capacities and efficacy of irresponsible and compromised journalism.

Historically, the long-term Rwanda crisis always overflowed the borders through the reproduction of refugees, internal displacements and finally through thousands of cadavers floating from Rwanda to Uganda through River Kagera to Lake Victoria. The conflicts in the DRC have roots in the 1960 coup in Kinshasa. Uganda has been experiencing wars since 1964. The same applies to the Sudan (Murindwa-Rutanga, 1996; Mamdani, 2001; Mushemeza, 2007; Prunier, 1995).

Congo, the largest country in the GLR has a unique history. Belgium established power over Congo and declared it Independent Congo State in 1885. Then, King Léopold II privatised it in 1908. He used cruel, brutal and atrocious rule to exploit the Congolese people and their wealth. Belgian colonial imperialism transformed Congo into a slave state. Its crude oppression and exploitation resulted in millions of deaths of the Congolese peoples of all ages, gender and groups. Its rule was characterised by forced labour, heavy taxes, naked racism, arbitrary brutal punishments and deaths. These gave rise to persistent revolts.

These resistances included the political activities of the Independent Church of Jesus Christ on Earth, which was founded in 1921 by Prophète Simon Kimbagu. Another one was the Pende Uprising in Kwilu Region in 1931 under the leadership of the Parti Solidaire Africain. This movement resulted in the death of 500 Congolese. This was followed by the strike of the Union Minière Workers in Lubumbashi in December 1941, and a mutiny by the Force Publique garisson in Kananga in February 1944. These were followed by another strike and demonstrations by dock workers at Matadi. Then, people in Kinshasa revolted on 4th January 1959. They resisted the inhuman conditions, curfews, political brutalities, and so on. All these movements were suppressed through the use of brutal force by the Belgian colonialists. However, those counter-insurgencies could not deter the movement of the Congolese people's history. Instead, all these struggles plus other pressures compelled the Belgians to grant the Congolese people their independence.

Elections were held in May 1960 and were won by Lumumba's party. He became Prime Minister. Kasa-vubu, Tshombe and Mobutu were mobilised by the foreigners to stage a coup on 5th September 1960. Patrice Lumumba, the first Prime Minister of Congo was arrested on 30th November 1960 and assassinated on 17th January 1961. These anti-nationalist activities gave rise to the first massive anti-imperialist movement in 1962. Its membership included workers, peasants, the unemployed, students, civil servants and nationalists. The leaders were Antoine Gizenga and Pierre Mulele. It was defeated by the neo-colonial forces led by US-Belgian forces on 24th November 1964. The capture of Mulele and his assassination on 3rd October 1968 marked its end. Notably, it was the first resistance against any African independent state.

Practically, the existing colonially imposed borders constitute a wall which blocks people fleeing persecution in any country. This many times results in suffering and/or untimely horrific death. These borders have also been blocking individualised solutions to famines and droughts, poverty, unemployment, lack of necessities, and so on. People have been harmed while trying to cross the borders in search of socio-economic or political solutions. Notable among these is the cross-border trade locally known as *magendo* (smuggling) and 'refugeeism'. Complications of passports and failure to speak languages of the colonial rulers – notably French and English – do constitute a major barrier to the vast majority of the peoples in this region.

The re-constitution of the East African Community, with Rwanda and Burundi joining as full members, and the ongoing engineering for political and economic unity form a pointer to a larger and more meaningful solution to many of the problems that have been afflicting the GLR. It should be noted that the Africans in the GLR have been resisting these border impediments since their demarcation. Some of the initial ones were recorded derogatorily by the colonialists in the 1911 Boundary Commission Report (BCR).

Given the expansiveness and diversity of the GLR, the scope of this book was confined to the Kigezi region and its immediate surroundings. This area is in South-Western Uganda, bordering Rwanda and the DRC. It was part of the Kivu-Mulera-Ndorwa region, which was shared amongst the three European imperialist powers through the 1911 Anglo-German-Belgian Agreement. In terms of geographical location, it is at the centre of the GLR. It has a very rich political history. It was bitterly struggled for by the three imperialist powers, while the indigenous inhabitants resisted them. It was finally shared amongst them through a long-term political, military and diplomatic process. Yet, Britain had declared its sovereignty over Uganda in 1894. This region was also the centre of various bitter anti-colonial movements. These movements spread across the borders into the DRC, Rwanda and Uganda.

Kigezi which was the centre of these inter-imperialist and anti-imperialist struggles is about 2,045 square miles, with a population of over one and half million people. *The 2002 Uganda Population and Housing Census* showed that Kigezi had a total population of 1,205,001. The British colonial authorities had estimated the population of the same region at 100,000 in 1911. Much of this population had been migrating for wage labour and resettlement in other parts of Uganda, Rwanda, Tanzania and Democratic Republic of Congo. It is presently divided into four districts - Kabale, Kanungu, Rukungiri and Kisoro.

The various indigenous peoples inhabiting Kigezi region are the Abakiga, the Abahororo, the Abafumbira, the Abanya-Butumbi, the Abahunde and the Abatwa. These are invariably collectively classified as Abanya-Kigezi (People of Kigezi). It should be noted that these ethnic groupings stretched across the borders into Rwanda and the DRC and share different characteristics - socio-cultural, linguistic, religious, economic, philosophical, demographic and morbidity.

Intermarriages, visits, entrusting one's livestock and/or fowls to the care of another person *(okuhereka)*, and other socio-economic and cultural activities and arrangements like seeking social brew or free booze *(okuvuumba)*; plus cooperatives locally known as *ebibiina*, still disregard the logic, dictates and imperatives of international borders. Seen in broader terms, these peoples have retained their larger communities despite the separatist measures by the colonial and post-colonial states. Seen from the peasants' perspectives, the post-colonial states can be said to be returning to these people's position through the resurrection of the East African Community.

In terms of physical features, the region is mainly mountainous, with variations in form of plains in the North and in the South-West. A stretch of its western part along its border with the DRC is in the Rift Valley. A lot of geological explorations for minerals are being undertaken in this region. At the time of European colonial invasion, it was largely characterised by a variety of thick, trackless, impenetrable forests, swamps and bushes. The CBR noted that most of the hill tops were over 7,000 feet in altitude, the highest being 8,500; and yet these are not bold, well defined summits, but rather giant undulations, with lakes, swamps and rivers in the valleys (Lardner, 1912; Roscoe, 1922; Philipps, 1923).

All these balanced the ecosystem, influenced climate and rainfall, health, production and life. They were sources of water, fuel and raw materials for construction, household production, medicines, salt, pasture for livestock, hunting ground, gathering and fishing. They also provided shelter and concealment for defence purposes in times of attacks and wars.[4] Wild animals in these habitats were hunted for meat, hides and skins for clothing. The forests and swamps were critical in influencing the climate and seasonality for agricultural purposes. They were sources of fish and raw materials.

Clearly, the persistent ravages and plunders by the inhuman slave trade that raged all over the continent for centuries did not leave this region free. It had negative consequences which detained this region at a low level of production.

The inception of the colonial state in Kigezi occurred with the active assistance of some locals - soldiers and chiefs. These included two authors on Kigezi: Sebalijja (1911) and Ngorogoza (1969). Forced demands were introduced; people's lands expropriated and their independence usurped (Mamdani, 1996; Murindwa-Rutanga, 1991 and 1996). All these were bitterly opposed by the indigenous peoples through armed struggles. The most persistent one was under the Nyabingi Movement. The colonial state, which started its mission with brutal and uncompromising force to suppress the resisting inhabitants, soon learnt through heavy material, human and time costs the futility of relying on naked coercion in exclusion of the involvement of the local peoples. It had to shift from that exclusionist politics to an inclusionist one.

---

4   See Captain Reid's Route Report from Kigezi to Mbarara, dated 13 February 1912; Purseglove, 1951; Roger, 1963.

Determined not to totally abandon the use of force, the colonial state began to combine political, administrative, ideological, religious, economic and educational efforts to fight these movements. The objective was to defeat them and institute their colonial rule. The agents were the missionaries, administrators, educators in schools, converts to the Western religions and the family.

The colonialists adopted the household as the smallest socio-political unit for colonial control. Political and economic headship of households was bestowed on the husband, with distributive and disciplinary powers. The man was to ensure the discipline at the household level, or experience the bitter wrath of the colonial government.

The colonialists were in *foucauldian* terms reconstituting a patriarchal form of governmentality (Burchell, 1991). At the top were the colonial chiefs who, over time, became corrupt and despotic. It was worse in Belgian territory where taxation and forced unpaid labour was demanded of both genders.

Mamdani, in his work, sidelines the class question as he shifts his analytical lenses to generalities. Jewsiewicki (1980) posits that modern European colonisation of Africa probably constituted the most extensive western attempt to build an authoritarian and technocratic state on the myth of the Welfare state. In the same line, Fether (1970) noted that the Belgians tried to *Belgicise* the colony, which was shaped in the Leopoldian traditions (Macambo, 2005).

Chatterjee brings out similar issues in the *Nation and its Fragments* (1993), and discusses how the colonial state, instead of creating a people in empty homogenous times à la Anderson, imposed capitalism with its multiplicity of demands to the political society which it had created (Chatterjee, 1993, 2004 and 2005).

The question to ask is: why did colonial invasion ignite the Nyabingi Movement. Why did it take place in the GLR? Were they able to link Nyakairima's prophesies of the invasion of people with wings to this invasion (Ngorogoza 1969, Aseka 2005)?

The Nyabingi Movement was anchored in Nyabingi religion. This was an insurgent religion which was against any established order and power. Nyabingi was assumed to be a female spirit, and a god and religion for sections of peoples in the GLR. This spirit was assumed to be living under the earth and supposedly had transformative characteristics and possibilities of personifications, malignance and virulence.

Nyabingi is said to have originated from Karagwe and spread to other parts of present-day Tanzania, Rwanda, Burundi, DRC and Uganda. The colonialists confronted it in all these territories and it tended to paralyse their activities, administrators, armed forces and missionaries. Its activities, ideology and promises influenced and inspired the thinking and rebellious potentials of other peoples within and even beyond its geographical scope. Examples included the Dini Ya Misambwa in Kenya and Uganda and the Mau Mau movement in Kenya and even Rasta and Resistance in the Caribbean (Murindwa-Rutanga, 1991; Campbell, 1987).

Colonial Facets of Domination

The invasion and defeat of a people that were at varying levels of development, largely stateless or under nascent states and the imposition of an alien belligerent state apparatus with its alien laws, demands, and so on, shaped the pace and trend of the consequent developments, notably the numerous peasant struggles. To understand these movements holistically, materially and dialectically, one needs to begin with a broader review of works on movements that have unfolded in different places and at different times.

Various people, scholars, politicians, policy makers and moralists around the world have reflected on the question of social movements and come up with different findings, positions, conclusions, proposals and/or solutions. To understand popular resistance to the capitalist seeds of conflicts in this region, its dynamics, the various responses to it, its achievements and shortcomings, it is imperative to analyse various contributions and determine which of them can provide a suitable and sufficient framework for this study.

The basic argument of this study is that the area was invaded and conquered militarily, and that the inhabitants resisted the occupation and the attendant in various ways impositions. In the process, the varied forms of resistance compelled the colonial states to shift from their high-handed militaristic approaches. Instead, they created reliable, broader social and political bases (Murindwa-Rutanga, 1991; Fanon, 1966; Rodney, 1976; and Museveni, 1975).

This study opines that it is erroneous and fallacious to confine a complete analysis within the strictures of the colonial discourse which qualifies any action by Africans as savagery, primitiveness, barbarism, conservatism, cannibalism, backwardness and averseness to change. These views came out clearly in the communiqué by the British Consulate in Congo in November 1909, part of which is reproduced below:

The native troops are nothing more or less than savages; and looking, as they do, upon the British as the only hope of salvation from the state of oppression in which they have lived for so many years, should hostilities commence the European population would be in imminent danger of being massacred. British subjects... would probably not be molested as they are regarded by the natives as their protectors but it is very difficult to foresee what might happen should these savages commence hostilities. The Congo Government would be utterly powerless to resist such a rising.

These negative notions and fixtures by the victors filled the colonial social sciences and its successor, the modernisation discourse. This book brings out these negativities and how they failed to help the colonialists understand the actual situation for long.[5] It is this position which buttressed and informed the Apartheid South Africa. An article which was attributed to former South African President Botha (*Sunday Times* of 18 August 1985; *Daily Monitor* of 28 November 2006) articulated this position very succinctly. It is beneficial to examine that article for purposes of explication to our readership. The argument was that:

The fact that blacks look like human beings and act like human beings does not necessarily make them sensible human beings. Hedgehogs are not porcupines and lizards are not crocodiles simply because they look alike. If God wanted us to be equal, he would have created us of a uniform colour and intellect. But he created us differently. Intellectually, we are superior.

The article reasoned that the white people were created to rule black people and that blacks were the raw materials for the white people. This simply meant that the Africans occupied the lower order while the Europeans occupied the higher order, and that the occupants of the lower order were meant to serve the occupants of the higher order. Europeans in South Africa were urged to unite and 'fight against this black devil'. They were asked to devise creative ways of fighting that war, and that their God would never forsake them. This religious invocation alluded to the biblical one and the ones by the leaders of the African resistances like Kinjikitile of the Maji Maji Rebellion, oath administrators for bonding in the Mau Mau, and even the Nyabingi Movement, in the Holy Spirit Lakwena Movement, and so on. The article emphasised that Blacks could never

---

5   See Kroeber (1953), Foster (1967), Redfield (1971), Gavin (1985), Purseglove (1950), and Roscoe (1922).

rule themselves because of their inherent self-destructive nature, promiscuity, polygamy, merrymaking and epicureanism:

> Give them guns and they will kill each other. They are good in nothing else but making noise, dancing, marrying many wives and indulging in sex. The black man is a *symbol of poverty, mental inferiority, laziness and emotional incompetence* (emphasis mine).

It reasoned that whereas whites from all over the world were doing the same to the blacks, only the Afrikaners had the courage to say what they were practising. The methods which the Apartheid regime employed to exterminate the 'black bug' included poisonous fertility destroyers which were aimed at stopping the increase of the black population. This was being done in hospitals, food, alcohol, and so on.

The Apartheid regime had imported into the country sex mercenary squads of white women and men from Europe and America to administer the chemical weapons while camouflaging as anti-apartheid activists. Black newborn babies were killed in maternity wards and plans were made to build more hospitals and clinics for this purpose. It ensured that blacks would never access this technology on the grounds that their retaliation could decimate the whites since many blacks were working for them.

It emphasised that the war against blacks was not of atomic bombs but of intelligence. It disclosed that the Apartheid regime had set aside a special fund for hiring experts to set black people against one another. It argued that this was possible because of the black people's greed for money, their inferior sense of morals and lack of foresight. It stated that the regime had set up a committee for inciting Africans to murder fellow Africans and that government would grant leniency to the culprits so as to encourage it into a cyclic and widespread criminality. It revealed that the state had secret plans to dividing the Africans so as to rule them. It disclosed that the Apartheid regime had long term secret plans to combat the Africans.

The article gave rise to a number of pertinent questions. Who had created the conditions of deprivation, poverty and squalor that afflicted the Africans in South Africa? Are Africans as useless, promiscuous and dangerous as the article suggests? How does that view, in 1985, differ from that held by the colonialists prior to independence? What could be expected from people whom Apartheid had caged for so long and turned into the appalling and inhuman *Bantustans*?

Is there not a likelihood of more fundamental social-economic and philosophical issues which explain their actions? Who has the right to define the Africans' priorities and development? Given the crusade for developmental projects right from the 1950s, can rights be foregone for modernisation and should popular struggles be branded 'primitive,' 'barbaric,' 'tribalistic', 'ethnic', 'sectarian', and so on? And, is every 'tribal' and 'ethnic' struggle necessarily 'anti-progress' and 'anti-people'?

The ruling discourse was doctrinal and programmatic, universalising and totalising. It was an integral part of the colonial political technology. It excluded the colonised people from the newly constructed power structures and arrangements, whereby it created two diametrically opposed though united worlds – one of the oppressors and the other of the oppressed, one of the exploiters and the other of the exploited (Fanon, 1966). Over time, it brought into formation a certain form of modernity, which Macambo et al (2005) explore at length conceptually and empirically.

Creating a new class brings into formation new outlooks, practices and struggles. New classes are racially and anthropologically mapped, politically engineered, promoted and protected. Colour becomes an ideological rationale for one group of people to dominate and rule the others. The *exclusionist* project was aimed at making the *colonised* feel desperately in need of saviours, and to hate themselves and everything that defines them - their colour, names, identities, cultures, religions, practical lives, environment, constructions, achievements, histories, rights, property, modes of production and existence, thinking, learning, practices, and so on. (Fanon, 1966; Macambo, 2005).

Illiteracy, lack of art, poetry, witchcraft and black magic became definers of the colonised peoples. On their part, the Africans rejected these labels and representations. They wanted to be left alone in their ancestral lands, without external interference. They had strong love for their land and freedom. They, therefore, resolved to struggle against everything related to the invaders, their expropriation and order. They wanted to be free from all state obligations and impositions – whether legal, political, religious, economic, and so on. They came to learn practically the brutalities, excesses, exploitation, killings and discrimination of the colonial order.

Given the variations in the levels of development and modes of politics of these peoples, they opted for different forms of resistance. Whereas colonialism at times engaged duplicity to colonise the highly developed states like Buganda, Rwanda, Nkore, and so on militarism remained its main mode of penetration.

Examples of areas where duplicity became the main mode of penetration include the kingdoms of Bunyoro, Mpororo and Buhweju.

Colonialism found a problem in areas where states were still either in their embryonic formations or non-existent. These peoples lacked organised state power to protect and defend them militarily – which is the primary function of the state. They, therefore, had no other option than to defend themselves. In these circumstances, the most readily available and interested leadership came from the existing religions.

The Changing Roles of Religion

Various studies have addressed these struggles in different areas and classes at different times. For purposes of our study, we shall begin with a review of works on religion and militancy, then works on people's struggles against different crises and, finally review works on colonial invasion and anti-colonial movements.

Religion needs to be studied concretely and contextually in each social setting. There can never be universal generalisations on religion; contrary to the tenets and claims by dominant hegemonic religions. Functions of religions are diverse in various social settings and times, depending on the concrete, historical, socio-political and economic realities. Any serious scholarship has, therefore, to analyse historically the factors that gave rise to a particular religion in a particular setting, its dynamics, and changes that it was undergoing; how it was addressing social demands; which social forces it was serving, its strengths and weaknesses, handicaps and hindrances to society, and so on.

In other words, a movement does not exist for its own sake but is a product of the prevailing conditions in a particular setting to address the concerns of a particular section of people. Neither can movements be generalised as 'purposive collective actions whose outcome, in victory as in defeat, transforms values and institutions of society', as Castells argues. Responding collectively to social problems or threats does not necessarily imply transformative intentions or potentials. That would be encumbering them to be programmatic (Castells, 1997).

Many works deal with religion and its relation to people's socio-political and economic lives, the material conditions that gave rise to it and its historical roles. In his anthropological studies on the Ik people in Uganda and Abatwa in the DRC and Uganda, Turnbull (1961, 1972) reveals how the nomadic patterns of hunters and gatherers afford them a much greater sense of security than others like peasants.

Turnbull discusses that while peasants may lose a year's inputs overnight without any replacement, the hunter and gatherer is capable of replacing what is destroyed the following day. This partly explains the rise and dominance of religion among peasant societies, unlike among the hunters: 'there tends to be little fear of supernatural malevolence among hunters; they live an open life, untroubled by the various neuroses that accompany progress.' Their mode of existence is contrary to that of the peasants.

Marx had similarly explained that peasants had a tendency of being fixed in the soil on their separate plots of land like their crops. It should be noted that the two groups of people under his study were still dependent on nature. As such, they could not produce surplus labour for appropriation and accumulation. They could not save in order to experience social mobility and any resultant class formation. So, they were still at the band level. This does not, however, absolve Turnbull of the derogatory and demeaning manner in which he projected his subjects of study, especially the *Ik*.

In concentrating on religion in developed capitalist societies, some of these works emphasise its ideological nature in class societies. These are best exemplified by Marx, Engels and Lenin (1972). The positive roles in the socio-political, economic and cultural aspects of the people is either left out or given secondary importance. These are issues that revolutionaries in former colonies like Cabral (1969); Fanon (1966); Chchachchi (1989) have tried to address.

They bring out the central role played by religion in various societies, but also demonstrate that religious movements are not necessarily conservative. Chchachchi shows the material basis of religious fundamentalism and its ideological functions, its relationship with state ideology, and women subordination in a historical context and its implications. Raising the issue of exploitation and discrimination based on gender division, she shows how women are segregated and undermined although they are the major practitioners of religion, and hence the producers of culture and tradition.

In addition to religious fundamentalism, much literature delves into the question of messianism and millenarianism; the material conditions that give rise to them, their roles and limitations. Karen discovered that millennia movements provide a new revolutionary consciousness through a vision of the overthrow of civic authority, renewed self-respect and Pan-African content; offer new organisation not based on kinship, ethnic loyalties or customary political leadership; and promote mass expectation of independence (Hill, 1981, 1986; Young, 1986; Lionel, 1987).

These studies show that one of the limitations of messianism and millenarianism was the emphasis on external saviours and the expectation of miracles. They ignored any action to liberate themselves. For instance, the leadership of the Watch Tower Movement preached that external saviours would come from America. Contrary to this inaction, the leadership of the Nyabingi Movement mobilised people and armed them politically, ideologically and militarily to resist colonialism.

Chatterjee (2004), on popular politics, explicates the political nature of such collective action. Colonialism and the collective action against it would gradually constitute the colonised peoples into political societies. Adas (1979) brings out the bases of militancy of millenarian protests against colonialism in five different regions; the social origins of the prophets, their capacity in mass mobilisation and struggles, and the reasons underlying their defeats. The main limitation of Adas' study is that it is silent on the role of women and other minorities in these struggles. Yet, as these minorities were part and parcel of these social movements, they cannot be ignored.

Comparative Perspectives and Locale of the Social Movement

Lan (1985) underscores the role of women in these anti-colonial struggles; the role of a female spirit medium, Charwe who led the 1896 rebellion against colonialism. Like the Nyabingi *abagirwa*, she was one of the last to be captured after the rebellion had failed. She maintained her defiance to the invaders even as she was being hanged.

Like Muhumuza and other *abagirwa* after their deportation till their death, Charwe left behind a promise that her bones would rise to win back freedom from the Europeans. Philosophically, the bones could have meant the young revolutionaries who would come after her to continue the struggle for independence. This thinking has roots in the African philosophy of reincarnation.

These studies show the charismatic nature of these leaders, which was characteristic of Nyabingi *abagirwa*. This, however, does not limit the study to the narrow confines of the Weberian type of charismatic movements.[6]

The Weberian approach has the possibility of causing an impasse in our search for charismatic leadership within the Nyabingi Movement. Worse still, it would leave us at a loss in the event of death, imprisonment or any other form

---

6   Weber (1978).

of unplanned, unexpected exit of the 'individuals' to whom such charismatic attributes would have relegated. That would block us from understanding the contribution of the membership, the leadership and the environment in the rise and development of the movement.

Various works have come up with important findings on different social movements all over the world and the role of particular social groups, gender, age, and so on. Take Mau Mau[7] as a case in point. Many works deal with its historical origins and development, its content, the various social groups that participated in it at various levels in membership and leadership, their motives and the role of the colonial state to suppress it (Karogo, 1987; Gakaara-wa-Wanjau, 1988; Throup, 1988). They inquire into the role of cultural bondings in the Mau Mau and their contributions to unity, solidarity, devotion, courage and determination among the masses. They contextualise and explain oath taking and other rituals of bonding and secrecy in a dictatorial situation, discussing how they are characteristic of rural protests in general, and how such practices have a longer history than these protests. Furedi (1989) explains the impossibility of compartmentalising and isolating social movements from previous trends. All these expose Carother's (1954) intellectual falsity of psychologising the causes of social movements.

Throup's main limitation arises from his focusing on the policy implementers only so as to understand the economic and social origins of the Mau Mau. In doing so, he attributes its causes mainly to one individual, the then Governor Mitchell for 'his liberal bias' which had led the frustrated educated young politicians to begin the war against the dictatorial colonial system in Kenya.

In no way can the Nyabingi Movement be conceptualised holistically within the realm of the classical collective behaviour paradigm. Neither had the peoples in and around Kigezi broken down, nor were they under any form of psychological stress (Smelser, 1962; Carothers, 1954). The causes of a social movement cannot be understood simply through a behavioural approach. Social movements cannot be explained by attributing their causes to continued anxiety among Africans, which led to 'the highest degree of unconstraint and violence, a common experience in psychiatric practice in Africa', social movements' membership being made up of 'unstable, emotional, aggressive people who are a constant menace to society due to lack of medical facilities'. It is imperative to

7   Mau Mau movement was soon embraced by the subalterns in East Africa and it adopted a broader anti-European liberating meaning: 'Mzungu Aende Ulaya, MAfrica Apate Uhuru' – that Europeans should vacate Africa so that Africans get independence.

go beyond the narrow view of Carothers that social movements in Africa were caused by African modes of thinking and by egotists for their personal ends which were 'political or often purely mercenary'.

Also, the resource mobilisation paradigm cannot singularly enable us to understand the movements. The determinant is not one variable of the availability or the absence of resources as cause of the rise of movements, and the participation in this movement, but the continuous arduous resistance by the peasants all over the region in the three neighbouring countries amidst the state's persistent repression, in counter – insurgency, backed by executions, exactions, other forms of punishments, strategic hamlets, enactments and banishments hand-in-hand with ideological propaganda. The question is: to what extent can people's response to a socio-political and/or economic threat be quantified in material incentives or profits. It would be highly inaccurate involvement or erroneous to try to attribute material interest as the motive of participation in the Nyabingi Movement. Social movements are not trading companies, corporate bodies or banks where profits can be accumulated on individuals' accounts (Oberschall, 1973; Tilly, 1978; Elster, 1985; Piven et al, 1977).

In fact, instead of being self-interested the Nyabingi resisters developed into formidable guerrilla forces, with the collective motive and commitment to free the region from 'Europeans'. However, some individuals saw opportunities for bettering their personal lot and gaining power positions through collaborating with the colonialist. This drive for personal gains and power guided such people to sell out to the colonialists. They became collaborators par excellence and helped the colonialists to fight and defeat the different anti-colonial movements.

To understand the material conditions that gave rise to the Nyabingi Movement requires we go beyond the orthodox Marxist approach of assuming the cause of social movements to be relative deprivation based on classes (Marx and Engels, 1962; Lenin, 1962, 1963, 1964). Confining this study to such a narrow framework has the possibilities of obscuring it from realising how this movement arose, developed and thrived in this area that had differing modes of production – some areas with developed class and state structures, others with classes still in their embryonic stages while others were undifferentiated.

Secondly, it would block the correct understanding of the different social movements as the Marxist approach bestows legitimacy and recognition to only one movement in any society at any single time - the workers' movement. This would cause a dilemma to us since this region had not yet experienced an intensive commoditisation process. The issue is how we are to rank and analyse these peasant movements in non-capitalist or quasi-capitalist societies. Who would take up this historical mission in the absence of the exploited, alienated and oppressed wage workers? How and to what extent can the proletarians liberate other classes?

In the same vein, this study cannot be conceptualised within Touraine's post-industrial society (Touraine, 1981, 1988). To embrace Touraine's theoretical postulations of programmed societies would create a problem of retrospectively burying the history, actions and achievements of non-capitalist societies in search of obscure futures. This process of trying to truncate the people's history from the people has enormous possibilities of denying all non-capitalist societies any meaningful history, and consequently their social movements.

This negates Touraine's premise that social life is a product of cultural achievements and social conflicts, that at the heart of society burns the fire of social movements, and that social movements lie permanently at the heart of social life. Such an approach, which is anchored in theorising on the post-industrial societies may lead to abstraction from the reality and become more ideological. The effect of this is that it ends up also being deterministic, and portrays human history as pre-planned, pre-fixed and unilinear since it claims one true movement at any given time and within the Western capitalist society model. This is a resurrection of the socialist theory of the workers' revolutionary movement. The problem confronting the Nyabingi social actors was not merely to form new social collective identities but to defend and liberate themselves and their land from the invading, uncompromising colonialists (Habermas, 1987; Melucci, 1985, 1989, 1992).

In the same way, it is vital to avoid the glorification of new social movements as 'truly social movements' or 'total social movements'. The issue of truth about movements is highly problematic and complex. What is the judgmental criterion for ascertaining truthfulness, half truths and falsity of a movement? Can any movement be objectively constructed and guided or are movements always subjectively constituted – given their causes, individual social class material bases and leadership? What measurements can be used to discern the levels or quanta of truthfulness or totality of different social movements to fit the Tourainean totalising and universalising methodology, conceptualisation and categorisation?

These questions underline the imperativeness of confining studies about societies within the exclusivity of Euro-centric lenses. Gramsci's insight on the importance of distinguishing organic movements from conjectural movements is very important for this study (Gramsci, 1988).

Using a historical materialist approach, Hobsbawn (1959, 1969 and 1973) probes into the question of social banditry in different continents, its historical origins, causes and courses as well as strengths and weaknesses. In studying the conditions that give rise to millenarianism and protest, and the conditions that will sustain them and make them grow, he is able to explain why it is not possible to have purely religious movements. Like Fanon (1966), he underscores the role of peasants in these wars; highlights the role of banditry in societal transformation; distinguishes between various forms of violence, its roles, the limitations of spontaneous peasant revolts and then exposes liberal culture which preaches submission and inaction to the oppressed and exploited masses.

There is the need to understand the various contending social forces, their objectives, achievements, and so on. It is impossible to isolate these forces or study them singularly as if they were fighting in isolation, with individual, isolated achievements. Rather, it would be beneficial to understand each of them and then analyse the total of their combined efforts and limitations. It is in this line that Hobsbawn brings out the relationship between millenarianism, social banditry and modern guerrillas. He shows possibilities of transformation of bandits into revolutionaries - those truly great apocalyptic moments - and the conditions that lead to it. He explains why and how banditry cannot constitute a social movement although it may be a surrogate for it or even its substitute.

However, one needs to go beyond this to show clearly the various social groups that were involved in these social contests. The focus has to go beyond the leadership. The membership cannot be relegated to secondary roles in the background. Hobsbawn's work is limited in that it does not show if these social bandits were organised peasants into struggles, and how. Then if these bandits remained alienated from society as saviours or Robin Hoods - robbing the rich for the poor, for how long could such a practice be carried out?

A study that stops here has the potential of presenting peasants as objects of history. It presents them as desperate, and deprives them of initiative. It negates the dialectical development process of societies. History shows that bandits do not always steal for the poor.

Also, following this approach that singularises individuals – all of them tend to originate from rich classes but emerge as social aberrations or misfits who go to liberate the poor classes - creates conceptual, practical and analytical problems. Where do organic intellectuals stem from? Must poor people always sit desperately until saviours come in from outside to liberate them? Can the poor people not have visions and conceptual clarity on their own and liberate themselves? In other words, are they objects of their own history? Are they permanent victims of their circumstances? Would this not be an adoption of an anti-dialectical methodology that negates cognitive action?

A committed study on social movements needs to go beyond idolising primitive accumulators like bank robbers and paralleling them with Robin Hood. Such romanticisation has the potential of obscuring or falsifying facts about social reality. It is vital to understand the roles played by various individuals, groups, and other sections of society in these social movements. Any serious study of social reality must come to grips with the concrete situation. This then demands contextualising the various social groups including women, youths and other minorities in the whole social movement. What we witness is marginalisation of the various contributions, support and direct participation of these social groups. This has the effect of isolating individuals from the whole movement and creating heroes of these individuals.

Attributing social struggles to individuals in the leadership leads to mythologisation. The study should be distanced from gender trappings. Each situation must be studied in its own context. Without such safeguards, one might end up like Hobsbawn, viewing men as the main supporters of peasant families. This approach divorces women, youth and children theoretically from production in peasant societies. Yet, this is contrary to the existing reality.

In a bid to halt or pre-empt these social movements, Huntington (1968) recognises the various social forces in African societies. So, he underscores the role of authority and control to avoid political decay which might lead to instability and violence. The modernisation package of increased foreign investments and creation of local allies *inter alia* was aimed at depoliticising and discouraging the whole populace. The solution goes beyond technical and reactionary solutions for modernisation. It is important to advance beyond this, not to control social reality, but to identify correctly the motive force in social movements. It is vital to understand which individuals, groups or sections of society had the capacity and willingness to lead such a movement; their motives, achievements and weaknesses. It is in this light that a committed study must understand the various social classes in these movements.

It would be misleading to consider these social classes as geographical, or to dismiss them as non-existent in pre-colonial Africa. Proponents of this view, like Nsibambi (1987), dismiss peasant struggles as merely ideological conflicts.

Nyerere, on the other hand, argues that social differentiation in Africa begins only with colonialism. Presenting past and present Africa as classless implies continental homogeneity.

This implies a uniform linear type of backwardness - a continent without dynamism. This view implicitly condones colonial invasion to unleash the forces of production and put the continent on the capitalist road. Another dimension has been to blame the current class struggles on colonialism. The tendency within this type of thinking is to advocate a return to the imagined glorious pre-colonial, pre-class society or to start on socialism (African or whatever label they may give it).

This approach raises a variety of conceptual and practical problems. Silence or trying to refute the existence of social classes in Africa and their relevance to the social movements cannot help us to come to grips with reality. It has the effect of obscuring facts on power relations in understanding social phenomena, the forms of exploitation and oppression, and social movements historically.

The blanket generalisation of continental classlessness masks people's resistance to various forces from within and from outside. This view presents them as fragmented individuals, struggling for survival against nature, animals and fellow people. This renders these people in a Hobbesian state of war against all these forces. Thus, without external saviours, life to them remains 'solitary, poor, nasty, brutish and short'.

One of the proponents of this view, Roscoe (*op. cit.*), in the Western fashion of defining the other, commends the colonial state repression for 'reducing these wild people (the inhabitants of Kigezi) to order ... any taxation is hotly resented.' In such a painted situation of 'the survival of the fittest', people are assumed to be guided by instinct. They are devoid of consciousness. Whatever relationship that develops is founded on the instinct of survival.

The intellectual efforts to salvage Africa from such Western representations have been made in the nationalist project that takes the Pan Africanist stance. These make efforts to probe far back into the origins and development of humankind with the view to locate the historical origins of all people, human production and development, formulation of epistemologies and different types of disciplines, thinking and philosophy, architectures and constructions, religions and civilisation in Africa. Although this is outside the scope of this study, one should still be mindful of the conceptual, epistemological, historical, methodological and factual contributions by Africanist scholars already dealt with at the beginning of this chapter.

The subaltern studies also make a radical departure from this approach as they focus on struggles by the marginalised against colonialism in India. In showing the peasant consciousness, peasants are portrayed not as victims of history but as its principals, with a capacity to resist and change events, and so on (Guha, 1983).

However, this school fails to delineate the different categories and social groups, genders, caste and ages. Dividing societies into 'elite' as collaborators and 'subaltern' as resisters is not sufficient categorisation. This classification leads to assumptions of homogeneity of the peasantry in pre-colonial and colonial periods. This has the potential of obscuring the dynamics within societies, the impact of colonialism, and how it shaped the colonised people to serve British capitalist interests. It is important to understand the form of transformation that these societies have undergone to serve alien capitalist interests and the new social relations that emerged.

While it is important to note that different historical and social conditions led to different social responses, it is also crucial to understand the class character of each social movement. Whereas the pre-colonial peasants responded militarily to colonial invasion, it should be noted that those who led these resistances were not the most marginalised individuals.

In other words, it is not the level of deprivation that determines the type of revolution. Hence, it is not correct that 'subaltern consciousness is inherently revolutionary'. Although there is no general rule or formula on factors leading to revolution or resistance, historical facts show that the most deprived, the most exploited and oppressed often fail to conceptualise correctly their situation and then translate it into struggle.

In no way is this an elitist view. However, it shows the objective limitations confronted in any social struggle and the need for broad alliances and unity between various social groups. Neither does this relegate peasants to secondary roles, nor does it render them inactive. Evidently, peasants do not have an independent perspective of development beyond what exists within their setting. Their outlook is broadly uninformed due to lack of contact with the world beyond their small societies due to lack of travel, massive illiteracy, and so on. It is in this regard that they tend to be rooted in the soil, on their separate plots, like their crops.

In studying peasants and their responses to social and historical conditions, it is vital to consider what type of class(es) exist in this setting. In a developed, capitalist society, the peasants operate as a class within the ideological framework of its leadership - the bourgeoisie or the working class. It lacks an outlook that can help them draw up a programme for leading other classes. However, peasants in pre-capitalist societies did respond militarily to colonial invasion. They went beyond being sacks of potatoes, took initiative and resisted relentlessly. However, it is obvious that their narrow outlook limited their struggles (Marx, 1972; Mamdani, 1986; Adas, 1979; Hobsbawm 1979). It is in this context that the role of outsiders has been found vital. They became instrumental in the organisation - ideological, political and military - of these struggles.

In military contests against a better armed, well organised superior force, a peasant leadership must, out of necessity go beyond commitments and willingness. They must have the ability to lead, organise, and plan as well as have knowledge of the enemy and his weaknesses, and so on. They must have wider experience than that of fellow peasants to be able to lead them into advanced, sustained struggles for years. An absence of that would lead to spontaneous uprisings which would lead to massacres and repression. It is thus vital to understand concretely each of these social struggles, their character, the material conditions that facilitated the various leaderships to come up, the origin and type of leadership, its ideological content, and so on.

While accepting as correct and a guide to action, Marx's dictum of violence being the midwife of any old society pregnant with a new one, is vital to study the type of violence in any social context, its character; and analyse if its objectives are popular, criminal or counter-revolutionary. One cannot understand social movements by merely looking at the forms of struggle. Violence is not synonymous with revolution.

Similarly, no individual or section of society has a monopoly of violence. Neither is violence endemic in any society. Historical evidence shows it as situational, in application to specific aims and conditions. It is vital to study the various methods of struggle. Not all situations demand the same tactics and strategies.

Despite its internal social reforms, the Nyabingi Movement aimed at defending the besieged, invaded peoples and territories. It would be far-fetched to claim that it envisaged the democratisation of this society as Cohen and Arato (1992) project part of the historical mission to be.

Giddens (1987); Rao (1984); James (1938); Scott (1990); Lindberg (1992); Slater (1994) and Werhteim (1992) provide a broader and more comprehensive framework in which to analyse and conceptualise social movements. This arises mainly from their shifting focus from the structures to the social actors and to historical analyses of the obtaining reality.

It is vital to understand that colonial invasion, oppression and exploitation called for new forms of peasants' consciousness and responses. New social and economic conditions always call for new consciousness and responses. This then calls for going beyond the subaltern school's view of continuity of subaltern consciousness from pre-colonial to colonial era. There is the need to understand the obtaining reality and reflect on what is to be done, the role of the masses, and so on (Cabral, 1969; Campbell, 1987; Wamba-Dia-Wamba, 1986).

In his recent works, Chatterjee (2004, 2005) demonstrates the importance of shifting the analytical lenses to the politics of the governed - how the different communities articulate their issues differently, respond to state demands and negotiate with it. He demonstrates that this approach will enable studies on popular politics to grasp the nature, form and course of the politics of the governed, their achievements and shortcomings.

One has to avoid making generalisations and conclusions based on findings from singular studies. Such an approach might be too expensive if one is conducting regional studies. These issues notwithstanding, Chatterjee's views of the politics of the governors and the governed tends to share commonalities with Mamdani's politics of the citizens and the subjects. They differ at the unit of analysis.

Whereas Mamdani's approach basically focuses on countries in the colonial setting, the way the subaltern paradigm focused on the colonisers and the subalterns, Chatterjee shifts his analytical lenses to popular politics in the communities, locations and settlements. Whereas the first two categories were dealing with a colonised situation which was totalising and universalising, Chatterjee is dealing with politics of subalterns in the post-Cold War era. This is politics characterised by democratic demands, threats, persuasions, coercion, bribes, deceit, resistance and authoritarianism. These have been made possible by the increasing state authoritarianism, non-compromise and lack of solutions for the increasing hardships. The nature of adulterated pillaging capitalism and neo-liberal policies are reproducing poverty massively and rapidly. The products join the existing socio-economic and political problems to the state. The state has, on the other hand, the propertied class, who happen to be the ruling class. It has to balance all these class interests. We find these approaches very important.

Through understanding the basis of colonialism, its motives and how these changed over time and space, its modes of penetration, the various resistances it encountered and how these influenced the colonial policies and practice, and the consequent developments, one is able to grasp the colonial reality. This brings in the important question of the colonial representation of the colonised.

Said (1995) explores this to a great depth. He exposes the Western invention and deployment of Orientalism, as a discourse, episteme, an intellectual style grounded on ontological and epistemological differences between the Occident and the Orient, as a career, and as a Western method to dominate, restructure and control the east. An analysis of the anti-colonial movements would benefit from examining Western thought through which the Western cultures were able to produce and manage the colonies politically, sociologically, militarily, ideologically, scientifically and imaginatively. It would have to question the Western representations of Africa and the impact of Western epistemes on African indigenous systems of thought and knowledge.

Michel Foucault brings to light the often marginalised aspects of knowledge, power and struggle. He exposes the negativities of power through repression and how they end up giving rise to movements. His argument is that power is saturated in the whole society, as permanent, repetitive, static, self-reproducing and inflexible. He underlines the need to study the character of power relations. To him, acceptance of power depends upon; *inter alia,* its productive capacity, material content, social and intellectual dimensions and epistemology. Every power relationship implies struggle, in which the two forces are not superimposed and they retain their identity (Foucault, 1977, 1978, 1984).

This *foucauldian* approach exposes the danger of universalising power and subsuming it under the state apparatus. The state functions on the basis of other power relations, which it controls. It underpins the imperativeness of violence and agreement in power relations, though these are not its basic constituents. It avers that if insubordination and recalcitrance on the part of freedom are central to power relations, then any relationship of power is bound to have ways of escape. Its situating of power in terms of governmentality and panopticon without bringing in the issue of struggles has high possibilities of leading to a partial and at times detached understanding of power. Whereas conceptually, power can be seen to be practised over free subjects, still power is in practical terms intertwined with coercion, threats, violence, struggle, incentives, rewards, and so on. The question, therefore, would be to understand how power is constituted, distributed and repelled or resisted. Preconditioning power relations to freedom has a tendency of relapsing into idealism. Power cannot be assumed to be absent in conditions of servitude, domination, subjugation, suppression and oppression.

Such would obscure any meaningful understanding of power relations in the colonial phenomenon.

It is the *gramscian* notion of power and hegemony which would be more beneficial in shedding light on the other alternative technologies of power deployed. These include ideology, dialogue, diplomacy, politics, cultural constructs, religion, rewards, promises, aspirations, lies and rumours – all of which are aimed at capturing and controlling the minds of the subalterns. It is this approach, like the proverbial *omwiru* (slave) that is used to control the other *abairu* (slaves), which would also explicate the colonial politics of indirect rule. This is the politics of exploiters using some of their victims to control and harness the rest of the victims for the oppressors' interests.

It is beneficial conceptually, methodologically, epistemologically and practically to understand the various forms of power, its loci, spheres of operation and its relationship with the other forms of power. Even the other relationships in which Foucault locates power such as economic processes, knowledge relationships and sexual relationships are produced and controlled by the privileged social forces. It is, however, impossible, whether theoretically, methodologically or practically, to reduce social movements to single variables. Various factors underlie different movements and these have to be grasped concretely. Above all, the *foucauldian* approach fails to transcend the limitations of Western knowledge systems.

Anti-Colonial Movements in the GLR

Another set of literature gives a historical account of colonial invasion and some description of people's reactions. This literature gives insights into the extent to which these peasants were not merely objects of history, but show that they bitterly resisted colonialism. It also shows forms of these struggles, the colonial repression and terror that were intended to crush them and threaten others from resisting (Report on the Anglo-German-Belgian Boundary Commission, 1911; Sebalijja, 1911; Brazier, 1968; Ngorogoza, 1969; Mishambi, 1980).

However, this set of literature leaves out vital issues about the causes, objectives and leadership of these struggles. Its other limitation is the effort to project the inevitable good mission of colonialism and its bounden duty to crush resistances so as to accomplish its project. As such, the studies are confined to the official position of the colonial state, and they justify and glorify both its actions and the role of collaborators. This arises mainly from the positions that many of them occupied in the colonial set-up. Being actively in the colonial service, they were not able to distance themselves from the whole events and processes to be able to see what was on the side of the people, the character of colonialism, its motives and dynamics, the forces it represented, how it operated, and the reasons underlying the resistances against it.

Most of these studies were carried out seeking ways to suppress and defeat resistances and to demoralise the peasants. Others bring out justifications for the continued resistances and the various transformations that they underwent. The first type presents the colonised people and their resistances to colonialism as the problem, and colonialism as the solution. Consequently, it fails to trace the origins of the crisis and to put the Nyabingi Movement in its proper context. Yet, it is vital to put these peasant struggles in their proper historical context.

Focusing on religions alone, Father de Lacger brings out vital information about religious movements in this region, in pre-colonial times and the position of the Nyabingi Movement, among them and in society. The limitation of this approach arises mainly from trying to fit all religions within the European religious framework. This assumes that all religions must develop within a pre-designed, fixed, linear pattern. There arose distortions in such attempts to reconstruct the historical origins of Nyabingi. This is a major limitation to works which are inspired by the Philipp's Report (Rwampigi, 1980; Bamunoba, 1965).

This literature is silent about the motives of colonialism, its role, dynamics, operations and the factors underlying the struggles under Nyabingi. Forges (1986), in dealing with peasant resistance under Muhumuza,[8] states that 'though short-lived it exhibited much of the complexity of composition, aims and leadership found in more stable political formations; it drew support from every rank of society, pulling in some adherents as individuals, others as blocs of kinsmen.' He shows how they attacked both local and foreign oppressors and the negative consequences of Muhumuza's failure to persuade and unite all the people against British troops. Muhumuza is exonerated of this charge by the report of one British Commissioner, E.M. Jack, which was underlining Muhumuza's anti-colonial mobilisation. He reported that on 28 August 1911, he received a letter from Captain Reid, the Acting Political Officer at Kigezi detailing anti-colonial resistance being organised by Muhumuza. It read in part:

---

8   The name Muhumuza was variably spelt by the colonialists as Mamusa, Mumusa, Muhumusa and Nyamuhumuza.

... a woman named Mumusa was preaching an anti-European Crusade and collecting a considerable following in Rukiga. Mumusa or Muhumusa is a well-known personage in Ruanda, and has formerly given a great deal of trouble to the Germans. She is one of these 'witch-doctors' who are found in this part of Africa, and who are regarded with superstitious reverence by the natives. Mumusa at one time had enormous power, and still has, I imagine, a great deal. She was doing a great deal of damage (Major Jack on 15 May 1912; and 1911 BCR).

Forges' argument that Muhumuza's forces defeated British troops twice because the latter withdrew voluntarily is value-loaded. There can never be voluntary withdrawal in military contestations. Retreating implies that the other side is having an upper hand. Inspired by Sebalijja's work, Forges aims to deny these peasants their military victory. Neither is Forges' assessment tenable that some people preferred to stay under British protection - a force which was just being imposed from outside for the first time - a view also propounded by Sebalijja et al.

Court evidence after the 1917 Nyakishenyi rebellion exposes the duplicity of this argumentation. Those peoples who refused to join the anti-colonial resistance and her leadership were not necessarily ready to embrace British, German or Belgian colonialism. While they were opposed to colonialism, their different *enganda* wanted to be led by their own leaders, *abakuru b'emiryango*, chiefs or kings but not by a woman. Many of these practised the Emandwa religion – a pro-establishment, pro-stability religion which, prior to colonial invasion, had been under threat by the insurgent Nyabingi Movement. Worse still, many of these people did not want to be led by a foreigner from Rwanda who did not have any roots in the area – whether through birth, marriage or blood relations.

The claim by Forges that Nyabingi resistance was short-lived is also a distortion of social and historical reality. The Nyabingi Movement had existed for years before Muhumuza, and it remained in existence during Muhumuza's long term deportation to Kampala, till her demise in 1944.

Philipps, a serious colonial intellectual and administrator, carried out great organic and basic researches on the Nyabingi Movement. He came out with enormous findings, conclusions and solutions for defeating this movement. He supervised their implementation and that helped to weaken the movement a great deal. After failing to defeat it, Philipps was forced to confess in 1919 that Nyabingi had been defeating military campaigns launched by successive kings in Rwanda.

Tying the Nyabingi Movement to an individual leader has the effect of condensing the whole history of the Nyabingi Movement and attribute it to Muhumuza. Through this process, all people's actions were attributed to her individual leadership qualities. This is more or less to equate the Nyabingi Movement with Muhumuza. That would historiographically confine the study to the 1911 Anglo-German-Belgian Commission Report and Sebalijja's article of 1911.

Would it then be correct to argue that the movement collapsed with the capture and resultant deportation of Muhumuza to Kampala? These are issues that Campbell (1987) addresses. His work is a major step forward in studying the links between Rasta Resistance and Nyabingi Resistance. It brings out the material conditions that gave rise to the Rasta movement, its aims, objectives, achievements and limitations. It also tries to contextualise the Nyabingi Movement historically, territorially and socially.

However, it also falls into the same problem of generalising that the Nyabingi movement was a continuous movement under Muhumuza. Attributing all the peasant resistances in Kigezi to Muhumuza's leadership obscures the various peasant struggles that ensued in the region at different times under different leaderships with varied aims, objectives, tactics and strategies. It is this problem that has to be addressed.

Aseka (2005) brings back to the centre of discussion the role of ideology, morality, religions and consciousness. He underlines their loci, centrality and importance in politics and power. He, like Chatterjee (2004) and Shiva (1989), exposes capital as an agency of neo-patriarchy in its various forms. While discussing the states in pre-colonial East Africa, Aseka leaves out the Mpororo Kingdom. Secondly, his work leaves little room for people's resistance. While it brings out low scale movements like *Dini ya Musambwa*, it offers little space for the vibrant Nyabingi Movement, which operated in the four colonial territories for decades. Its operating in the colonial territories of the Belgians, the Germans and the British demonstrated its international character. This enabled both its leadership and membership to escape snares by the colonialists in the three colonies. Thirdly, the work is greatly constrained by a high inclination to Christianity.

2

The Political Economy of the Great Lakes Region Prior to Colonialism

All able-bodied men are called upon to fight, and in such a case will wear charms, consisting small bucks horns, or small pieces of wood, round their necks. Such charms protect the wearer from death or wounds. Dances take place before the warriors set out for the scene of action and after their victorious return. Their arms are two spears, used either for throwing or stabbing, and bows and arrows. All the male prisoners are killed, and the dead have their hands and feet cut off; but women, and children who can march, are made captives... show great courage and do not hesitate to charge home in the face of rifle fire...

This chapter begins by reviewing, albeit cursorily, the pre-colonial socio-economic and political organisation of this region. The aim is to enable people to understand how this area was developing prior to colonialism, what major problems existed and peasants' solutions to them. It will provide a basis to study reasons that underlay the peasants' choice of militant resistance, the rise of the Nyabingi Movement, its recruitment of membership and leadership, the forms of struggles, their strengths and weaknesses and the forces that led to its defeat. It will also lead us to understand whether colonialism was a necessary evil, the new social formations that arose from this new encounter and the consequences.

This area was inhabited by different peoples, with varying modes of production, cultures, and so on. While the plain lands like Kamwezi, Rujumbura and Bufumbira were inhabited by pastoralists and peasant agriculturists, parts of the southern parts of Lake Bunyonyi and the surrounding forests were inhabited by *Abatwa*, a roving people. *Abatwa*[9] and *Abanyabutumbi* had no fixed homes. Their mode of existence was predominantly hunting and gathering. *Abatwa* were also feared for raiding the peasants, looting and pillaging sprees.

Within Rwanda region, *Abatutsi*[10] constituted the ruling class and they hired the *Abatwa* into their forces. Both ethnic groups constituted privileged classes, as compared to *Abahutu* peasants. So, in Rwanda, the insurgent Nyabingi religion was opposed to these two privileged classes. It then added on the colonialists who invaded the GLR – the Germans (then locally known as *Abadaaki*), Belgians (locally known as *Ababirigi*) and the British (locally known as *Abangyereza*) and their local allies. The latter included the chiefs – both the pre-colonial chiefs and the colonially appointed ones sometimes called Agents, heads of clans, converts in the foreign religions and self-interested individuals.

The rest of the region was inhabited by settled peasants, *Abakiga, Abafumbira, Abahunde* and *Abahororo*. These practised mixed farming, which involved crop husbandry, rearing cattle, goats and sheep, poultry, and so on. They supplemented these with hunting, fishing and gathering (1911 BCR). Randall in the 1942 Report noted that livestock were regarded as criteria of wealth, other than rearing cattle for sale as an economic proposition, or as a normal method of augmentation of the annual income. In Reid's account, this region was full of 'food, water, milk ... thickly inhabited, the huts in the valleys and cultivation extending to tops of hills... numerous petty clans' (Captain Reid Report, 1912).

Production in this area was mainly for use-value at household level. Their main tool was the locally made hoe. The 1911 Boundary Commission Report noted:

> The chief produce is *matama* (Sorghum), *wimbi* (millet), peas, beans (in great quantities), bananas, sweet potatoes and honey. Hoes and sickles are used in the cultivation of the crops. The iron for these is obtained from the ironstone found in large quantities in the hills and

9   The colonialists variably wrote Abatwa as Watwa.

10   The colonialists also variably wrote Abatutsi as Watussi.

smelted down by native craftsmen. The iron-ore is collected and carried to the local smithy in long wicker-work baskets.

Roscoe (1922) recounted that the fields in this region:

... looked as though they were laid out in terraces and fenced. Some were planted with peas, which were in full bloom, with blossoms of three or four colours - a sight quite new to me, as I had never seen edible peas with any but white blossom. Cattle plague had not penetrated in the district ... there was an abundance of milk ... pots of milk were presented in such quantities that I had to refuse some of it.'

In his cursory observation on Kigezi, Captain Reid in 1912 reported dense cultivation, notably in the vicinity of the long swamp, with chief crops as sorghum, millet, peas and beans, sweet potatoes and bananas further north.

This sheds light on these people's production of nutritional staple foods and instruments of production before colonisation. This is demonstrated in the table below which deals with the nutritional values of some of the precolonial staple foods in this area and the newly introduced ones, which we may call *modern foods*. The pre-colonial food crops include sorghum, millet, beans, peas and sweet potatoes. The newly introduced ones include solanum potatoes (*emondi*), bananas, and the daily intake of meat and other animal products.

Table 1:   Nutritional Values of Some of the Staple Food Crops and those
of Modernity in the GLR (Nutrient Content per 100 gm. of
Edible Portion)[11]

Crop	Calories	Protein (gm)	Fat	CHOs (gm)
Sorghum	354	10.2	2.8	72.1
Millet	346	8.7	2.9	71.2
Beans	330	19.5	1.4	60
Field Peas	330	22.4	1.4	57.0
Sweet Potatoes	116	1.3	0.3	32.8
Solanum Potatoes (*Emondi*)	75	2.0		17.0
Bananas	100	1.5	0.2	23.3
Milk	64	3.2	3.7	4.7
Beef	202	11.0	14.0	
Mutton/Goat Meat	145	16.0	9.0	
Chicken	200	20.0	12.0	

Source: *Food Consumption Tables: (Nutrition Division), Ministry of Health,
Uganda. Quoted from Export Policy Analysis Unit Food Security and Export, Vol.
I, August 1995, Page 4. The Table is adopted from Murindwa-Rutanga's PhD Thesis,
Jadavpur University, 1999).*

Modern foods have, through political machinations, modernity, imperialist push
and funding, dominated public taste. However, their nutritional status vis-à-vis
the pre-colonial staple foods remain lacking. Unlike the modern people who find
it prestigious and class-differentiating to eat different types of meat at every meal,
pre-colonial Africans ate meat on a regulated basis. The same applied to milk.

The war against the indigenous foods came into the open when children who
had been sent to colonial boarding schools became alienated from their cultures,
ways of life, foods and feeding habits. They began by despising and rejecting
their traditional foods. The first victim was local sorghum bread (*obuhemba*).

---

11   NB: This table does not include all the other food values such as vitamins and mineral
salts.

They, through their limited acquired foreign language named it derogatorily as *John kyankarata wanyiha ahabi* – meaning that *obuhemba* was an unpalatable food only eaten as a last resort by desperate people.

This war spread like wild fire among the young generation and they abandoned *obuhemba* and *enkumba*. (*Enkumba* is porridge prepared from raw sorghum.) The elite transformed the two types of food into curses. The stigmatisation of local food helped to create a reliable market for European wheat bread. And so, graduates of colonial education and modernity were pitted against African cultures and foods. This resulted in cultural conflicts and confusion. Those who ought to have saved their areas from imperialism transformed their people into haters of their own products and consumers of imported foods. This confirms the dependency discourse which argued that imperialism transformed the colonised people into producers of what they did not consume and consumers of what they did not produce.

In Kigezi, nearly every household had its own livestock. These were kept for clothing, bride price, exchange and home use. The colonial Intelligence Report of March 1911 recorded a lot of cattle of the Ankore type, goats and sheep (Intelligence Report No. 39, March 1911). Reid, *op. cit.* noted wide distribution of cattle, goats and sheep except in the Lake Edward area. Baxter noted, 'cattle and secondarily, sheep and goats are the most regarded form of wealth throughout the district'. Lardner noted that they worked hard at their crops, producing peas, spinach, potatoes, and maize.

In anticipation of the peasants' resistance, Captain Reid's strategy and praxis was to '...seize all cattle and stock as the natives are loathe to part with their cattle and to requisition them would be to alienate the natives'. The value of livestock to the natives, was affirmed seventeen years later by the DC in a correspondence to the PCWP about the loss of cows which the indigenous people were incurring through forced milk contributions to the individual missionaries of CMS. He stated succinctly that '... the loss of a cow to a Mukiga[12] is equivalent to the loss by fire, to a poor European who has neither income nor bank balance, of his house and all its contents ... uninsured!' He concluded, 'A cow to a Mukiga frequently represents the savings of a lifetime.' (DC to the PCWP on 28 September 1928).

Despite their self-sufficiency in household and societal requirements in form of food, tools of production, livestock, women, defence, entertainment,

---

12   A Mukiga is an indigene of southern Kigezi. Its plural was Abakiga. The colonialists variably spelt it as Mkiga.

sports, art, religion, and so on, they were still at a low level of harnessing their environment. Communication was mainly by land and water. Travelling on foot and human porterage was the mode of transportation on land while canoes and swimming constituted the mode of travel on water, mainly lakes and rivers. Reid *op. cit.* recorded 60 canoes on Lake Edward, 20-30 canoes on Lake Bunyonyi and others on lakes in Bufumbira. Canoes on Bunyonyi were commended for military purposes because of their superiority and stability. All these demonstrate the peasants' resemblance to Alavi's category:

> ... relatively unstratified, 'segmentary', communities of independent small peasants; their economy centred primarily on the domestic households, their political system involved wider groupings like lineages and clans or the village community. ...relatively egalitarian, the peasant farm as an economic unit was reproduced generationally ... produced primarily for self-consumption, virtually self-sufficient, ordinarily self-governing and relatively undifferentiated and free from exploitation by other class (Hamza, 1987).

What needs to be noted is that Kigezi was not homogenous. Social differentiation was taking place amongst the large scale cattle owning communities. These were, however, scanty and scattered. They lived side by side with agricultural peasants, hunters and gatherers. Other classes which had emerged revolved around professionals and skilled households whose products or services were required by members of the society. This put them in positions where they accumulated wealth, by providing the required products or services. These included *abaheesi* (smiths), *ababuumbi* (potters), *ababaizi* (carpenters, carvers), *abacuruuzi/abashuubuzi* (traders), *abafumu* (medicine people), *abavubi* (rain makers), *abaibiki* (apiarists), *abambari/abagirwa* (priests and priestesses) and *abaraguzi* (prophets, prophetesses, prognosticators).

The most famous *muraguzi* was and still is Nyakeirima Ka Muzoora. He foretold *inter alia* the impending colonial invasion, the form of the invaders, their behaviours, their objectives, their technologies of power, their negativities, invincibility and the long term consequences of this invasion (Ngorogoza, 1969; Aseka, 2005).

Forms of Property Ownership and the Labour Process

Property ownership was basically at household level. Cap. Philipps (*op. cit*) described it as:

...the system by which each valley or hill is occupied solely by a solid block of people consisting each of a different clan... They do not admit or understand the private ownership of land, which is held by the tribe sub-divided into the clan, for the benefit of the family or community. They consider land, as the birds, the water, and the air, to be the attributes of mother earth to provide a sufficiency for the direct maintenance of all.

In his study of Kigezi, half a century after Britain had carved out Uganda and declared it its colony, Purseglove was able to grasp property ownership in land. He explained that a man owned as much land as he could cultivate and defend with the assistance of his clansmen. His explanation leaves out women, children, dependants and *abatendezi* – poor men who came to work in order to be rewarded with wives for their long term services. These too had certain property rights in land and other agrarian property, and those rights were enforced and protected by culture and members of society. They applied shifting cultivation with the use of as much land as the household could cultivate in a season, together with the fallow land that they had cultivated in the past (File District Book, KDA; Okumu-Wengi, 1997). There is the need to appreciate the scientific and practical value of this form of agriculture. It prevented soil exhaustion and degradation, soil erosion, invasion of pests and vermin, maintained soil fertility, and balanced the ecosystem. As it insured against environmental destruction, it also ensured continuity for the peasants' economic, military and social needs.

While men seemed to have the main control over land, production decisions in agriculture were made mainly by women. The same applied to matters related to feeding plans. Individuals and households owned property in form of land, shelter, granaries, livestock, utensils, clothing and ornaments, beehives, instruments of production, weapons, canoes and troughs, and so on.

Governing the people in this region was a responsibility of members of households together with *oruganda.* Though children were collectively attributed to the entire *oruganda,* still, the individual households and *enganda* were responsible for their birth, rearing, moulding, discipline, training, protection and initiation into adulthood. However, the role of caring for households was shared. Security at household level was principally the responsibility of men and elderly people. In the absence of men, women and youths took charge.

Being physical minorities, children together with the disabled people were given utmost attention and protection. It was a societal requirement for adult males to ensure that children and women were never allowed to straggle. This applied to all, irrespective of whether the relationship was consanguinity or matrimony. It was everyone's collective responsibility to ensure their security until their safe arrival to their destination or where their security would be guaranteed. The saying was that children and women belonged to the *oruganda* (the community).

Similarly, tradition demanded that everyone had to be provided with sufficient food and drink wherever he or she was. It was a cultural imperative to offer food and beverages to whoever came to the compound. Requesting for a drink implied asking for food and beverage – normally *obushera* (sorghum/millet porridge) or *omuramba* (a potent brew from sorghum). It was taboo to deny these to anyone. Cultural sanctions to violation of this included pouring away all the food that a guest would have left in the house after taking his fill. It was feared that eating such food would cause the stomach to bulge (*obwijuranda*) and result in painful death. This has parallels with the Hindu deification and ranking of guests as the fourth god after the mother, the father and the teacher.

Likewise, it was taboo to bypass friends' homesteads without calling on them to inquire about their health. In case of haste, one would have to throw some small stones in the homestead of friends before moving on.

Nyineeka (head of household) was the overall controller of household property. When he/she died, his/her property would be divided amongst his/her family. This was known as *okubagana*. The brother to the deceased or his eldest son would normally take over the economic, political and social responsibilities of the deceased. In case the responsibilities were bestowed on the son, assumption of those responsibilities would accord him chance to get the greatest share of the property.

Women who had not established their hegemony in society through bearing and rearing of children to maturity did not normally have substantive ownership rights to the livestock, even to those attached to their households. However, they had the user rights and other residual rights to the livestock which would be attached to their households. They would be entitled to products of these livestock like milk, hides and skins. The substantive ownership normally rested with *nyineeka*. If a domestic animal died during *nyineeka*'s absence, members of the household would preserve the delicacies (*enyama enkuru*) for him till his return. Violation of such codes of behaviour could lead to adverse consequences including fines, separation, curses, and so on. The same applied to any woman found eating cooked meat, eggs, locusts, and so on. These taboos were taught and re-emphasised, and sanctions to their violation constituted part of the societal knowledge.

Omuryango (sub-clan) had external control over land of families at lineage level. At a higher broader level, *oruganda* had external control. Both would intervene during times of conflict arising from violation of the established property rights, external threats, and so on.

We find that production was based on various factors like nature of the job, the skills and the specialisation involved, and division of labour based on age, gender, location, and so on. The BCR noted gender and generational disparities in Kigezi including household labour provision. It stated that most cultivation was done by women and children.

Polygamy was a common practice in this region and there was no limit to the number of wives a man could have. The average number of wives was three to four depending on the wealth to pay dowry. However, some had more wives. For example, Mutambuka, Head of the Baheesi Clan at the time of colonial invasion, had 27 wives. He refused to join the anti-colonial Nyabingi Movement led by Muhumuza and this forced Muhumuza to fight him before attacking the colonialists. Mutambuka sought safety with the invading British forces and his forces combined with the British forces to defeat the anti-colonial Nyabingi Movement.

Women were desired for economic reasons. They were required for production of wealth and reproduction of children. So women were referred to as *abazaana* or *abairukazi*, which literally means female slaves or women-slaves. The word *abakazi* (women) like *abakozi* literary means working people. The same report noted that 'polygamy is common ... children are desired, irrespective of sex...' A lot of children were required as sources of labour for households' social reproduction and investment or insurance against external threats, hunger and old age. Child labour was important in production of wealth, future defence and expansion of *oruganda*. There was a higher preference for male children owing to the people's production and security concerns.

The question arises whether it was possible for an average male to have three to four wives unless the population was predominantly female or whether possession of wives depended on wealth. In this region, various factors determined the mode of marriage. The whole issue revolved around the capacity to pay bride price. The bride price was commonly paid for in cattle. This was one source of increasing a family's livestock. The people had a saying which they developed into a folksong. It means he who did not have a sister would never marry (*Otaine munyaanya tashwera!*). It demonstrated the socio-economic significance of girls in society and the importance of courting them. The second source of bride price was from cattle belonging to the household. This was one of the reasons why nearly every household strove to own cattle and other livestock. These two sources of livestock aided men to marry many wives.

What comes out clearly is that the more wealth one had, the more wives one could take. In addition, there was no age limit. An old man could marry a young girl. Yet, young men could not easily marry due to lack of bride price. Another explanation is that their parents would have to arrange their marriages with families that they chose after putting into consideration different factors regarding those families.

In arranging marriage for their son, the boy's family had to ensure that the girl belonged to another *oruganda*, came from a wealth family, was social, well behaved, generous, hospitable; the medical/morbidity characteristics of her family – especially madness, whether she came from *oruganda* which was associated with ill luck/misfortunes, whether she was loose, check the historical and contemporary relationship between the two *enganda* (clans), and so on. It would be after all these considerations that they would identify a man of respect to entrust with the responsibilities of a go-between or a link between the two families and conduct the marriage negotiations. This was known as *okushaba* by *mafuka* or *kateera rume*.

The young man and the young woman to marry would know nothing and, therefore, would not be party to the whole process - selection, negotiations and arrangements. This is contrary to contemporary practice where marriage is, in most cases, concluded by the intending couples. Other sources of wives included areas outside the region or picking abandoned or excommunicated women, or women slaves, or labouring for wives. This was locally known as *okutendera*.

Other sources of livestock for paying bride price included buying and exchanging, looting, donation or gifts from friends, begging, stealing and rustling and borrowing cattle on long-term basis, and so on. The saying that a man can neither be ugly, nor old has its origin in the bride price issue. As long as there was bride price, a man could marry any girl. It was not uncommon to find old men paying bride price for the yet unborn. This would be on the understanding that if the child came out as a baby girl, such a man would marry her. On the other hand, boys would marry at a much later age than girls, being restrained by anatomical and physiological differences and lack of bride price. At the same time, custom demanded that men had to take over the responsibilities of their dead brothers or their late fathers, and so on. These responsibilities involved looking after the widows, their families and property. All these reinforced polygamy in the region. Another alternative solution was for the young men to go and provide labour for men who had daughters. They had to labour for such families for a long period before they could be paid with wives. The head of the household would then give such a poor man the oldest of his daughters or the one with deformities. The man would have to oblige. In most cases, the new fathers-in-law would give them land to construct homes and produce food for their social existence.

Besides *okushaba* and *okutendera* there was another practice called *okujuumba* which means paying the bride price for a girl taken as a wife in ambush. This happened when people from one lineage identified a girl from another lineage that one of them desired to marry. This would normally be done by daughters from that lineage who married into the other lineage. This would still have to be reflected on and sanctioned by the elders of the lineage before its execution. In other words, it was not done haphazardly. If the man's family and elders accepted her, then, a conspiracy would be hatched to marry her through *okujuumba* mode. Energetic young men would be entrusted with that social responsibility. That group would have to plan how to waylay her on her return from her chores.

That conspiracy would involve one of the daughters of their *oruganda* currently married in *oruganda* where the identified girl hailed from. After all, they were such daughters of *oruganda* who normally identified girls to be married by young men from *enganda* of their nascence. Their interest would be to have such girls become part of *enganda*. At the same time, it would be considered as paying back or revenge. Her main role would be to lure the girl into an ambush being laid by the young men from her *oruganda*. On the planned day, they would have arranged so that the cattle for the bride price would be grazed near that girl's place. As one party would be struggling to take the new bride to the new bridegroom, another section headed by old men would be driving the cattle to the home of the bride.

It was advanced that women did not belong to any particular *oruganda* as they would gradually get married off to other *enganda*. They would not, therefore, expand their paternal *enganda* through procreation and be able to defend them. This led to the bias of referring to male children as arrow bearers (*enkwata-mata)* and to girls as sorghum stalks (*ebikonko*). Sons participated in defence and other military demands of their *enganda*. They took over the roles of *nyineeka* when the father grew old or passed away. However, in addition to production of food, crafts for home use and other services, daughters were crucial for bringing in wealth as bride price.

Women did not belong to the lineage in which they were born. Their ability to belong to any lineage was transitional and temporary. Before marriage, they belonged to the father's lineage. After marriage, they became members of their matrimonial *oruganda*. However, in the event of separation, the woman lost her identity and rights in that *oruganda*. She could return to her original lineage and if she remarried, she would assume membership of the new *oruganda*. The only important thing was that women could not get married in *enganda* of their nascence or those with which their *enganda* had enmity. The argument against marrying in one's *oruganda* of nascence was to avoid problems of inbreeding (*amatembane*). If we look at this more broadly, we find that this was also meant to prevent promiscuity and premature marriages. On the other hand, men belonged to the lineages of their fathers. They did not belong to the *enganda* of their wives after getting married.

This mobility of women became a basis for denying them property rights by some of their unscrupulous male siblings. However, unmarried women or those whose marriages failed did enjoy the proceeds from it. Interestingly, the role of distributing these proceeds lay mainly on the wives. In a situation of death of the mother, or divorce, then, her children would retain the property attached to the household. The older daughters would take over the mother's duties in production, utilisation and distribution.

On being married, the brides would have to work for their parents-in-law. When the time came for them to start an independent life, the husband's parents would give the new couple some property to start their married life independently. This came in the form of land, livestock, house ware, and so on. This was known as *okutekyesa amahega*. Though these were given to the couple, it was the wife to whom they would be addressed. She had reference and user rights but could not take them to another *oruganda,* either of nascence or through re-marriage. However, the husband retained the ownership and control rights. So, he would retain that property and not surrender it to her parents in case of failure of the marriage. In case the woman got married to a polygamous man, then, it would be the duty of the husband to give her property instead of his parents. This did not preclude her parents-in-laws from gifting her fixed and even mobile property. In case of separation, this property stayed with the *oruganda*.

In polygamous marriages, men had a roster for staying in every wife's house. They would ensure that they divided the days equally amongst all the wives. The political object was to avoid creating bases for conjugal grievances and feuds.

As earlier shown, stability in marriage was a source of women's respectability and guarantee of rightful ownership of property. This meant that such property would be distributed among their children. It should be noted that unmarried daughters - whether spinsters or those who returned to their parents' homes after their marriages had failed would be entitled to share or inherit the property attached to their mother's household. This property would be for their sustenance or reproduction.

Land ownership belonged to the *oruganda*, under direct control of *nyineeka*. However, its products belonged to the household which worked on it. The same applied to livestock. Actual ownership of the livestock would be proved when *nyineeka* wanted to take another wife, give it away, and so on.

There were cases where women headed households. Such cases included women who had established their hegemony in the *oruganda* and beyond. Such women included *abagirwa* like Muhumuza, medicine women, and so on. The main determinants included age in marriage, number of issues produced, grandchildren and in-laws, status in society (because of skills and other contributions to the society) or even widowhood. This refers to widows who were not taken on by men after their husbands' deaths because of age, status in society, and so on. They would have to assume responsibility, take direct control of their households and their actions would not be questioned or contested. Another situation could rise out of wars. If there were crises that could lead to death of men or if men went in search of food during famine (*okushaka*), then the women would take over control of the households.

Exploitation based on age was prevalent. Children were initiated and integrated into production at a very early age. They were instrumental in food production and preparation. They fetched firewood and water, scared away birds from cereals, grazed and shepherded livestock, looked after younger ones and ran errands. Drawing from this exploitation of child labour, a saying developed that the child is for *oruganda*. Everyone was expected to feed all children. Another proverb for this exploitation of child labour was that a child who accepts to run errands defecates a big mound. That means he would have so much to eat for going to various places.

The distribution of cooked food in a family was illustrative of the power relations at household level. Given their dominant position, men were expected to play the politics of benevolence. This was an important mechanism of power which ensured the longevity of the hegemony of the heads of households. It would be well demonstrated during meal times. Before eating, *nyineeka* would have to partition the food served to him and send part of it back to the women who had prepared the meal. This was known as *okubegyera* or *okuha enjeru*. It should be noted that women slaves were never treated that way. This was because they occupied a different social position in society. If children were around, *nyineeka* would then hand some food to everyone of them before eating. This was known as *okubegyera abaana*.

The order of eating was also particular. *Nyineeka* was not expected to start eating before all those below him had started eating. At the same time, he was expected to end eating before all of them finished. He was expected to leave some food in the container for the children and those who prepared it. This was known as *okusigira* – reserving some food for the children and women. It was an abomination for a man to eat everything served him or even to finish eating at the same time with the young ones and women. This had three major significances.

The first one was to ensure that the women and the young ones did not starve. The man had to ascertain that they fed well. The second one was to demonstrate through this benevolence that the giver was powerful and had to be respected and obeyed. The source of food signified socio-political and economic power. Although the food was cooked in the kitchen, it was the man who had the powers to distribute it, and even give part of it to those who cooked it. It reflected the various forms of exploitative relations within the region - a person who never participated in the production process having the power to distribute it to those who produced, cooked and served it. The third one was the inculcation and preservation of a culture of benevolence, generosity, sharing and responsibility in all members of *oruganda*. It also inculcated a strong spirit of love and attachment within the household and *oruganda*. Through these arrangements, households ensured self-sufficiency in use-values and defence, and they maintained internal cohesion.

Mothers trained their daughters in the social roles prescribed for women. These included food production and preparation, processing milk products, making utensils, and so on. Boys were integrated into roles performed by men like bush-clearing, construction, animal husbandry, defence, tool and weapon-making and usage. The gist of this training was home control.

Seen broadly, females were initiated into roles of direct food production, and minor roles in animal husbandry like processing of animal products and cleaning the kraals. Their education emphasised subordination, faithfulness, managing polygamous life and hardships, and so on. On the other hand, male initiation was into actual ownership and management. The main tool of production - the hoe - was in the hands of women and children While the tools of defence, ownership and discipline were in the hands of men. They included the machete, spear, bow and arrows, and clubs (*obuhiri*).

This exempted *Abatwa* and *Abanyabutumbi* who were at band level and whose main mode of production was hunting, gathering and fishing. Every member of the band must have his/her instruments of production and defence. Their conception was above religions. The fact of the matter is that they despised religions and they used it in a joking way to threaten the peasants and exact resources in form of food and drink from them.

The exploitative relations that characterised this formation revolved around *nyineeka*. Differentiation took place based on homesteads and skills. Exploitation involved women, children, apprentices, dependants, and scattered slaves – *abahuuku, abashumba* and *abazaana*. Desperate people from poor families or without any help would go to big families to work for food. In other cases, during wars between *enganda*, women and children would be captured and taken as slaves and wives while the men and boys would be killed for fear of revenge. Payment or remuneration in this formation was mainly in kind, in form of food, clothing, livestock, accommodation and individual protection, and so on.

It should not be misconstrued that men did not participate in the production process. They occasionally participated in cultivation, animal husbandry including herding and breeding, undertook bush-clearing and scaring away animals, hunting, trapping, fishing, and so on. What needs to be noted is that most of these duties were non-repetitive and labour intensive.

A household was not a totally sealed off, isolated production and consumption unit. Performance of certain activities of collective or social nature demanded more labour and more skills than one household could provide. Heavy duties like construction, roofing, hunting, defence, and so on required combined labour. This was possible at the level of *umuryango, oruganda* or beyond. Although communal labour rotated among them, ownership was mainly at household level. These demonstrated forms of property relations. Co-operation extended to animal husbandry. Grazing of livestock rotated among households. This was known as *okutaana*. In other cases, livestock would be put under another household's care on mutually agreed terms. This was known as *okuhereka*. Co-operation was also important in hunting wild animals for self-protection, crop-protection and animal products. They jointly planned hunts and executed them, combined their dogs and nets, divided roles, and shared the meat and skins; based on the established rules. However, with the exception of *Abatwa* and *Abanyabutumbi* peoples, hunting was a complementary occupation. Co-operation was also used in cultivation, especially based on gender and age.

Jobs which required skilled labour were also based on gender and age division. Examples of men's jobs included smithing, carpentry, leather tanning and cloth-making. Acquiring such skills required a long period of apprenticeship, dedication and care. Other vital jobs included medicine and midwifery, prophesying, religious leadership and rain-making. These were shared by both genders.

In spite of their main role in production of wealth, women and children were prohibited from eating certain delicacies which were exclusively reserved for men. These included the kidney, the heart, the sternum, the tongue, and so on. Men created myths, superstitions and other ideologies around these foods. They also put heavy penalties around them to bar the women and children from challenging these privileges. They invoked their religions, gods and spirits to watch the behaviour of members of their households in all these and to punish all contraveners. Surprisingly, the established women – especially mothers-in-laws and sisters-in-laws – were the custodians of these impositions and deprivations.

These practices created and multiplied social injustice and grievances within families and society. This created a basis for various struggles, both militant and silent, divorces and separations, poisoning, and so on. This dissent became the basis for *Nyabingi* to come in on the side of the oppressed and be accepted by a big majority for both spiritual aspirations and social liberation.

Industry and Trade

There was a vibrant thriving iron industry in this area. This was an exclusive monopoly of men *(abaheesi)*. This was partly because it took long to acquire skills for smithing while girls spent most of the time in food production and had to be married off at an early age. It was argued that they did not want these daughters to take these skills to the families they would marry into. This would have the effect of undermining their trade and social status in society while arming the side where the woman would be married. It is probable that the men did not want women to learn smithing as that would enable them to produce weapons which could be used for emancipation from men's oppression and domination.

Abaheesi (smiths) and their apprentices prospected in iron-ore, produced charcoal for the smelting and produced items for local use. Their products included tools like hoes, machetes and knives of all sorts, axes, weapons and ornaments like *enyerere, emiringa, entayomba, enjogyera, amajugo,* and so on.

This region is greatly endowed with pure iron ore. Their main product, the hoe, also acted as a measure of exchange. It was an important item in food production, marriage negotiations, transactions and ceremonies.

By the colonial invasion of this area, a locally manufactured hoe had been become a dominant tool of production and a factor in trade. It was not only a commodity but it is also a medium of exchange. As such, four to six locally smithed hoes were exchanged for one big goat while thirty to fifty hoes were exchanged for a cow, and so on.

Provincial authorities in the early 1920s reported that great iron-smelting was going on in Kigezi which was capable of development and was serving local needs... According to them, '...a large local trade in iron articles made by local blacksmiths and natives from Belgian Rwanda bring over food and livestock to barter for these articles...' (WPARs 1920-24; 1911 BCR; Blue Books, 1917-1925; Turyahikayo-Rugyema, 1974; Tiberindwa, 1973).

Abaheesi enjoyed a very high social status in society. Their products were highly demanded and durable. They were able to accumulate wealth through their sale. They used their higher bargaining position to get advance payment from their clients when the latter put in their initial order for the commodity. Through this mechanism, *abaheesi* were able to acquire wealth without providing the commodity at the agreed time. Accumulation of wealth would be reflected in livestock, the size of families - number of wives, children and dependents the size of agricultural output, the form of clothing, and so on.

The trade was associated with many taboos. Anybody with a history of bedwetting was never allowed in *ebirubi* (forges). The same applied to men whose male organs were suspected to be deformed as if they were circumcised.

Abaheesi played other significant social roles. Girls who feared the sexual act would be taken to the *ekirubi* and left under the care of *abaheesi*. *Abaheesi* had methods of initiating such spinsters and making them ready for marriage. Muscular bachelors would hold them down and make them watch the smiths as these fanned their furnace with their bellows. It was believed that after a while the spinsters would get carried away mentally by these activities and, in the process, overcome her fear of the forge and, by implication, men. In other words, they used hypnosis to help the girls overcome their men phobia.

Their skills were also sought for beautifying girls by creating gaps between their front teeth by reshaping them. This was known as *okubanga.*

Pottery and weaving were carried out mainly by women. Carving, leather tanning, cloth-making and craft-making, salt manufacturing and the honey industry were men's preserves (File District Book, KDA). In 1936/37, the district colonial officials recorded the existence of 161,961 beehives in Kigezi. As all these trades required skill and specialisation. Families which monopolised them guarded them from other sections of society.

The people produced their own food, implements of production, weapons for defence and hunting, and they provided their own shelter, and so on. In peasantry settings, some form of specialisation and division of labour had emerged. Traders dealt in iron products, grains, livestock, salt, handicrafts, household appliances and utensils, *engozi* and drums. These people were in the process of accumulating surplus labour. Cattle owners exchanged animal products for grains and labour from peasants (Turyahikayo-Rugyema, 1974). Commerce and trade was facilitated by money in form of cowries, bundles of salt, cows, goats, sheep, iron products and/or barter form plus exchange of gifts characterised by a mode of commercial and social interaction.

The BCR reported that no trade existed in this area. This then would have meant an absence of the consciousness of exchange relations. Interestingly the same colonialists reported that these people sold food to the mission.

Although merchant capital had not yet developed, trade was in existence. This was attested to by the Kivu Mission, which in 1909 reported the presence of Greek, Asian and Arab merchants trading in European products. In June 1909, Ireland recorded that he 'established friendly relations en route by prompt payment for all food unlike the Belgians who never paid for anything'. He recounted that when peasants realised that they were being cheated, they withdrew the food supply. He was forced to exercise a rigid discipline with regards to peasants and their property by, 'just treatment of them and prompt payment of their supplies'. This underlines peasants' experience in exchange relations. By 1911, a market at Ikumba Colonial Administration Headquarters had become famous for food, honey, fowls, livestock, and so on. Colonial officials and their train paid in beads, wire, *Americani* cloth, and so on. According to Reid, other markets included Nyakishenyi, Kinkizi, Nyarushanje, Kigezi and Rujumbura (Intelligence Reports of March and April, 1910).

The BCR acknowledged that Belgians were circulating money in lieu of barter and confirmed abundant food sales (*op. cit.*) Maj. Jack recounted that 'food came pouring in as soon as the natives found it could be exchanged for the much-desired beads or cloth, and in the short time I was able to stop all supplies from Ankole and feed the porters much more economically and conveniently on the spot'. Roger found them, 'very friendly, but terrible Jews who cavilled at the quality of the cloth and beads given in payment for food' (Roger, *op. cit.*). This demonstrated their experience in choosing manufactured imports.

In the account of her experiences at Bufundi-Kabale, Mandelbaum (1957) noted that some direct barter and sale as well as some rudimentary markets existed in pre-colonial days but they were more of resorts for emergencies than part of the regular order of everyday life. She said the markets consisted of designated places and a customary time with no middlemen; everyone was either a buyer or a seller. They all went to the market because of a special need.

The most famous trade in pre-colonial Kigezi was the salt trade. Men took grain or livestock to Katwe to exchange for salt which was sold there. This process was known as *okuhonera omwonyo*. The colonial officials reported that goats, flour and other produce were brought from great distances to be bartered for salt with the caravan route through the Ruchuru Valley. Jack reported that there was a constant movement of large herds of sheep and goats for bartering in Ruchuru Valley. A packet of salt was exchanged for a goat. In Rwanda, it was exchanged for two goats.

Industrial products from Western Europe had infiltrated this area long before the British colonial invasion. These were in form of cloth and iron products. Jack noted that cloth was replacing skins, and peasants arranged their hair in long strings or festoons, and ornamented it with beads, shells, or cent pieces. The photographs of the different indigenous inhabitants of Kigezi which were appended to the 1911 BCR show all these succinctly.

Mode of Politics

At the household level, men dominated the socio-economic and political life of the household. At the macro level, male elders dominated the political, social and military affairs of their lineages. This, however, did not exclude notable women and those with special skills like medicine women, prophetesses, and so on. Areas where states had emerged experienced hierarchical forms of power, which were patriarchal.

The state did not develop organically in the whole area but was imposed from above by the colonialists. In some areas, state formation was still in its infancy. Such areas included Kinkizi, Kayonza and Bufumbira. The Mpororo Kingdom, however, had a very highly developed state structure stretching from the territory of eastern DRC to the districts of Rukungiri, Rubabo, Bushenyi, Ntungamo, Kabale, Kamwezi and Northern Rwanda. This kingdom was headed by Omukama – the king. Makobore was the last king the colonialists disempowered.

This kingdom, like all other kingdoms and empires prior to the modern capitalist hegemonic regimes of power, did not have any fixed borders. Its size in terms of territory and population depended on the capacity of the individual rulers of the time, their military, political and organisational prowess, courage and leadership skills. It should be noted that the whole of the GLR was covered with strong kingdoms. These included Rwanda, Buganda, Bunyoro, Mpororo, Nkore, Buhweju, Koki, Igara, and principalities in Burundi, and so on.

The narratives, folktales and stories, songs, self-praises, poems and other oral compositions are full of kings and queens, princes and princesses as the main characters, and they revolve around kingdoms, palaces, property, power distribution, and so on. These testify to the earlier existence of organised states. Karugire (1980) and Aseka (2005) deal with this subject in detail.

Politics and Gender Relations in Pre-colonial Kigezi

Taking politics as the expression of contradictions and their resolution at the superstructural level and the relations at the economic level, it is clear the *nyineeka* was the dominant figure at the household level. Internal struggles within that social formation were mainly between husbands and wives, youths and parents, daughters and parents, co-wives, and so on, and they tended to revolve around land, the developments on it and movable property, especially livestock. In cases of fights, elders were called to arbitrate, and so on

Virginity was concrete evidence of a mother's good training of the daughter. In fact, girls who lost their virginity before marriage would in most cases be returned and the bride price would be refunded. The female culprits of pre-marital pregnancies were punishable by death. They were thrown over the cliffs. In rare cases some girls escaped before detection. They would render themselves into slavery to some wealthy men.

As mothers were expected to train and police the daughters, pre-marital pregnancies also caused controversies between husbands and wives. This could lead to fights, or even separation, and so on. In addition, it was the responsibility of mothers to teach their daughters how to behave in polygamous marriages and in face of possible sexual harassment by fathers-in-law.

A mother's respect would increase after her daughter was married off 'properly' and brought in livestock. This accorded her a higher social status both in that family and in the family the daughter married into. The proceeds derived from bride price would be attached to the mother's household. This entitled the household to the products of the livestock. Even in the process of negotiating the pride price, part of the payment would be specifically for grandmothers, aunts and maternal uncles. The in-laws were supposed to take great care not to confront the mother of the bride or visit her without prior warning. Violation of this code of conduct would lead to serious consequences against the son-in-law. He would be fined (*okutanzya ekiiru*).

Brides were expected to respect their parents-in-law and all those that custom accorded such entitlements. When a woman gave birth to children, this uplifted her position in society. A woman who gave birth to boys was accorded more honour and privileges. Special care was given to a woman who bore children. Children were a basis for giving women more land, livestock and clothing. A dutiful, responsible woman was expected to rear children, feed all people living in the compound and the guests. She was expected to remain faithful to her husband and loyal to the new family. Women were warned against engaging in witchcraft which could hurt people in that family, and so on.

In their new homes, brides were expected to be hard-working, well-behaved, responsible and faithful. The time of their stay with the mothers-in-law was for mentoring and integration into married life and into the secrets of the new family. They had to do most of the work in the household. This included cooking, making containers, and so on. This period was known as *okwarama*. During *okwarama* – which was more or less a time of probation in marriage – the couple would pass through an initiation into independent marriage life. The couple would be given land, instruments of production, pots and other household wares and utensils, including part of the containers that the bride would have woven during *okwarama*.

After undergoing this initiation ceremony, the couple would go to live in their separate house. However, the wife was expected to continue feeding the people in the whole compound, working for the mother-in-law at the beginning of the planting season and thereafter. At harvest time, daughters-in-law had to take the first meal of the new harvest and uncooked food to the mother-in-law.

In case the wife's relatives brought provisions and presents to her, locally known as *ebitenga,* they would be delivered into the house of the mother-in-law. The mother-in-law would choose what she wanted before the remaining things would be taken by the couple. They also had a claim to the labour and protection of children and grandchildren.

Mothers-in-laws had a big say in the management of the households, and the distribution of resources like land and livestock to the sons and their wives. The older a woman grew the more legitimacy she acquired and the more assertive she became both in the home and society. Many mothers-in-law tended to be very oppressive and demanding on their daughters-in-law. It was enshrined in their custom for the daughters-in-law and sons-in-law never to pronounce the names of their mothers-in-law. This was known as *okusinda.* On their part, mothers-in-law were expected to love their daughters-in-law, counsel them, provide them with initial property to assist and facilitate them in marriage. In short, they would be taking over the duties of the brides' mothers, and so on.

However, mothers-in-law and their daughters became self-appointed overseers and informers about the wives to their sons. They counselled the latter on how to tame their wives. Thus, mothers-in-law occupied an oppressive and exploitative position, which was sanctioned by tradition.

Aunts were also accorded a high social status. They were instrumental in the marriage of the girl and teaching her some of the secrets of married life. So, they were given a share of the bride price.

There were also struggles between co-wives in big families. Some wives dealt with these contradictions using witchcraft, magic or poison. In anticipation of such destabilising, deadly solutions, husbands threatened them with *emandwa, esiriba, Nyabingi*, powerful witchcraft, and so on.

There were controversies between some women and their fathers-in-law over sexual harassment. This was not a monopoly of men. Some mothers-in-law slept with their sons-in-law. This act was called the proverbial chasing away of red ants – *okutamba empazi.*

Controversies arose between barren women and other members of the family, and between women who bore only girls and members of *oruganda.* This was proverbially labelled the destruction of *oruganda* – *okucwa oruganda.* In households with slaves, men slept with the female slaves and they bore children. This caused controversies between household members and the offspring of such unions as they too would be entitled to property, including livestock for bride price.

There were also contradictions revolving around exploitation of labour. These included contradictions between slaves and their masters, specialists and apprentices, and prospective fathers-in-law and *abatendezi* - those who laboured to be rewarded with wives.

The *Nyineeka*'s superstructural loci enabled them to create ideologies, myths and proverbs to justify and protect their exploitative position. They initiated all brides into this relationship on the first day of marriage. The bride would then be surrounded by religions of which *nyineeka* was the religious head. Obedience was enforced through invoking gods and ancestors (*okuhindiza*) and ostracising the dissenting members (*okucwa*).

Okuhindiza was a religious act of invoking the supernatural forces to punish the culprits while *okucwa* was materialistic. *Okucwa* entailed depriving him/her of the right to inherit property, or to enjoy anything in the household and family. It also included denial of protection and belonging. While *okucwa* was an exclusive monopoly of *nyineeka* and other elderly people, it was assumed that the supernatural forces would be on the side of *nyineeka* to enforce this pronouncement. *Okucwa* was assumed to bring miseries, infertility, disasters and untimely death. These were major weapons that *nyineeka* could use any time to control their adult progenies. This created fear among the children and shaped and controlled their behaviour indirectly, and so on

Men resolved contradictions between them and their wives through fights, separation, rejection of the wives' food and/or refusal to enter the wives' huts. This kind of practice was known as *okuzira*. In case it was proved that the woman was wrong, she was required to appease the husband by preparing special meals and brewing alcohol, and so on, for the husband before he returned to her. This appeasement was known as *okuhonga*. On the other hand, if the husband was proved wrong, he would be asked to return to her. *Okuzira* was a major weapon that many polygamous husbands applied to control their wives. Resolutions like separation and refund of the bride price (*okuzimuura*) depended on the nature of the disagreement, judgment and the attitude of husband, the wife and her people. All these formed a strong base of discontent and tension which Nyabingi exploited to penetrate and gain popularity in this society.

The Clan as a Political Unit

Clans or *emiryango* were responsible for handling larger and more important matters that transcended households. These included defence, celebrations, deaths, crises, marriage cases, property, divorce, justice, murder and revenge. They required the attention of clan elders (*bakuru b'emiryango*). These were expected to be men of integrity, who were fair, upright, courageous, articulate and unwavering in decision-making and good at defence. They had to have property and big families. Like *nyineeka*, they were not elected by all members of the lineage. They emerged through personal exploits.[13] They met as a body known as *karuubanda* or *enteeko* to attend to different cases and issues. Other issues included rights, migration and going in search of food, during famines. These practices demanded broader attention and reflections than those of singular heads of households.

Various lineages constituted *oruganda*. As earlier noted in Chapter One, the concept *oruganda* is broadly used by different societies to mean people of the same blood, common ancestry and destiny. Its usage denotes unity. The Alur in the Democratic Republic of Congo call it *jouganda*. The Jaluo in Kenya call it *oganda*. The different bantu-speaking groups in Uganda call it *oluganda* or *oruganda*. These constructions informed the British definition and naming of the country, Uganda.

While the family would be in the same geographical location, *oruganda* was not confined to one geographical location. What united lineages belonging to the same *oruganda* were their common ancestry, totem and taboos, and common interests like production, defence and military campaigns. *Oruganda* attended to, *inter alia,* contradictions between its various lineages, organised defence for its people, and determined diplomatic relations and co-operation with other *enganda*. In practical terms, everyone was responsible for *oruganda*. In the councils of elders, even women, youths, and children were heard although they could not participate in the hearing of the cases, and judgment or in political, economic, military and social matters. Their parameters were prescribed. However, old women with skills and reputation attended. Through such processes these lineages and *enganda* were able to maintain internal cohesion.

---

13   Refer to songs, stories and oral literature, Nyakeirima-Ka-Muzoora's great prophecies on imperialism and Ngorogoza, *op.cit.*

3

Colonial Invasion of Kigezi

*I would like to remind His Majesty's Government that if our object
in acquiring the Mfumbiro District is to obtain a route for the Cape
to Cairo railway, it will be necessary to include within, a strip of the
Rutshuru Valley, since the hills to the SE present an impassable barrier
to the passage of a railway. The Belgian Post at Rutshuru will be
untenable once the Mfumbiro District comes under us since all food
supplies for their troops and employees are drawn from here (Officer
Coote to Ag CS on 21 January 1910).*

The question of why Africa became the target and victim of European capitalism
in the last centuries has been addressed by a lot of scholars. The reasons lie in
the desperate need for cheap and permanent sources of raw materials produced
by cheap labour for the ever expanding European industries, markets for the
European industrial products, places for re-investment of capital and re-expor-
tation, and places for resettling its ever-increasing unemployed population. Cecil
Rhodes succinctly explained to his journalist friend the European socio-economic
crisis and its possibilities of transforming into a political crisis like the 1789
French revolution and the 1871 Paris Commune if the political class did not
acquire colonies to provide material solutions for it.

The workers' consciousness had been raised through the study groups at
their workplaces with the committed guidance of Marx and Engels. Through
their historical-materialist understanding of human history from primitiveness

through slavery mode of production to feudalism and capitalism, they were able to understand the historical/revolutionary role of labour in European history. Their detailed discussion of the Manifesto of the Communist Party by Marx and Engels right from 1848 had enabled them to understand their historical *loci* and mission, and how they, as a class, were to quicken the demise of capitalism – whose mode of production was full of inherent contradictions. Their threats to capture power and control the means of production, make production decisions and begin production processes based on those decisions became a real threat to the politicians, the industrialists, the bankers, and so on (Marx and Engels 1969). Thus, Rhodes' prognosis and prescription:

> I was in the East End of London yesterday and attended a meeting of the unemployed. I listened to the wild speeches, which were just a cry for 'bread,' 'bread,' 'bread,' and on my way home I pondered over the scene and I became more than ever convinced of the importance of imperialism. … My cherished idea is a solution for the social problem, *i.e.,* in order to save the 40,000,000 inhabitants of the United Kingdom from a bloody civil war, we colonial statesmen must acquire new lands to settle the surplus population, to provide new markets for the goods produced by them in the factories and mines. The Empire, as I have always said, is the bread and butter question. If you want to avoid civil war, you must become imperialists - Lenin, 1986.

Ireland, - the I/C 4th Kings African Rifles (KAR) Commanding Kivu Mission Escort - reported from Ihanga to the Officer Commanding Troops, Uganda Protectorate on 26 November 1909 just as they were beginning to occupy the area - how they were reorganising the area administratively and taking over land to serve colonial interests and facilitate British capital penetration:

> ...some seven or eight villages have sprung up within the last six weeks near the British depot at Kumba. The villagers want land, and are natives from German territory. The political officer is most anxious to encourage these people. ...I am taking several of these natives to Lake Ingezi, at the political officer's request, to show them land north of the lake. They will cultivate and sow what the political officer tells them and sell their produce to passing convoys.

As full control of any market entails political control, the colonialists had to take political control of Africa - hence the inevitability of colonialism. The proponents of the dependency paradigm made a substantive contribution to this aspect (Rodney, 1976; Amin, 1974 a,b, 1975, 1977; Lenin, 1986; Mamdani, 1996; Mukherjee, 1984; Davidson, 1992).

The political officer to the Chief Secretary explained in January 1910, why the three colonial powers struggled viciously amongst themselves and against the peasants for Kigezi (see quotation at the beginning of the current chapter).

The 1911 BCR noted that each collection of huts had its headman, although there was very slight social distinction between these and the common head. Baxter, Roscoe and Reid found that there were no local men of importance whose social horizon was larger than that of their own neighbourhood. To Reid, 'Rukiga is essentially a country of small independent clans acknowledging no paramount chief... no cohesion from a military point of view... most of the heads of clans are cattle owners on a small scale... essentially an unwarlike people and owing to the very local habits of the natives and the absolute lack of cohesion among the different clans, it is very difficult to conceive of any cause which would make the *Abakiga* combine.'

They viewed the inhabitants as a peaceful or politically docile people, posing no political threat to the advancing colonial mission; as lacking causes for going to war or for uniting them for war purposes. This reveals the underlying secret character of the Nyabingi Movement as a unifier. Yet, the colonialists in the subsequent records presented themselves as the victims of the Nyabingi Movement.

Indeed, in preparation for this war, the colonial authorities estimated in 1912 (*op. cit.*) that Rujumbura under Makobore could raise 5,000 fighters and Bufumbira under Nyindo could raise 1,000-2,000 fighters at short notice. What was to follow was a real surprise to them as the local people organised to defend and fight the colonial onslaught under the Nyabingi Movement.

Given that the GLR was not empty and the inhabitants were not objects of history, it is vital to understand the process through which it came under colonial rule, people's reactions to the invasion and the consequent imposition of political control over them from outside. While European missionaries were an important forward force in the colonisation of Africa, this was not the case in this region. What unfolded in the colonisation process was that this area was transformed into a theatre of vicious inter-imperialist struggles which nearly led to a grievous imperialist war on the one hand. On the other hand were anti-imperialist struggles which were to thrive in various forms until the end of the formal colonialism.

The first European parties to settle in the Kivu-Mulera region were Catholic Missionaries. While commenting on the journey with the White Catholic

Missionaries to Rwanda, Mukasa (1912) shows how Catholic Missionaries had penetrated this area, set up nine mission stations which were manned by many Catholic priests and brothers, had many Catholic converts, and had built very good churches of fired bricks and tiles.

The priests were resisted in various ways. Mulera peasants, led by Chiefs Lukarra, Mujaruhara and Manuka killed Fr. Loupias, the Father Superior of the French Catholic Mission on 1 April 1910. They fled the area. Chief Lukarra was given sanctuary by Chief Birahira while the others crossed to the British territory near Mt. Muhabura. The German authorities, headed by the Imperial Resident of Rwanda hunted Chief Lukarra down, captured him and imprisoned him. They, however, could not capture the other two who had left the German territory (The Political Officer, Kivu Mission writing to the Ag CS dated 9 April 1910; KD Report of 3 May 1912).

From Mukasa's account, the new church was already sowing seeds of hatred and enmity among the peasants. He explained that there was great hostility between the Catholic converts and the unconverted Africans whom he labelled 'pagans'. From his account, the unconverted had hated the Catholic priests right from the beginning and wanted to kill them. And the whole area was impenetrable and full of enemies of the European missionaries. By then, the indigenes had killed two White Catholic priests, one boy, three Catholic converts and had lost two pagans in one hour. Mukasa recounted how they crossed Bukamba from Rwaza with loaded guns. Failing to appreciate the importance of the resistance led him to condemn the resisters. His objective weakness stemmed from his conversion to Catholicism.

Modes of Defence

Although the whole region had not yet developed into state structures as it is today, still, the peoples had developed strong defence systems. The colonial officer, in planning reprisals on people in Kigezi, confessed how the colonial military forces could not risk attacking them head-on:

> Military operations in this district would be extremely difficult, owing to the nature of the country and the natives could lay ambushes and escape to the hills where pursuit is useless. The seizure of the cattle and the occupation of the cultivated valleys would probably bring any particular clan to reason. Night operations, though attended by great difficulties, would be the only means of attaining the capture of any considerable body, as during the day time sentries are posted on all the hills and outflanking movements are doomed to failure (*op. cit.*)

However, the area was still at low levels of socio-political development. Defence was a collective responsibility of all members of the *enganda*. This was well captured by the 1911 BCR:

> All able-bodied men are called upon to fight, and in such a case will wear charms, consisting small bucks horns, or small pieces of wood, round their necks. Such charms protect the wearer from death or wounds. Dances take place before the warriors set out for the scene of action and after their victorious return. Their arms are two spears, used either for throwing or stabbing, and bows and arrows. All the male prisoners are killed, and the dead have their hands and feet cut off; but women, and children who can march, are made captives... show great courage and do not hesitate to charge home in the face of rifle fire ...

The above narrative demonstrates a destructive form of war that led to the massacres of men. The decimated men would have given valuable labour as slaves. This reveals the low level of development of these people. Only men without disabilities had to go to war. The physical fitness becomes questionable when it came to being invaded. Secondly, such a luxury could be afforded only if the enemy was weak. The battle against *Ruyooka-Rwa-Maganya-ga-Nkunda-ya-Rukamba*, which is dealt with at length in the following paragraphs, brings out a contrary reality. Arming themselves with protective *engisha* reflected their strong religious beliefs. It also revealed their capacities to harness and synergize religious practices with their practical earthly and material needs and aspirations. In other words, they were able to invoke supernatural powers for their earthly requirements.

While the colonial record showed two spears as their main weapons, it was a cultural requirement for all men and male youth to have *engabo* for self-defence. Men would give endearing names to their *engabo* like *Rutangamyambi*, *Rutatiinamireego*, *Rugutaunga*, and so on. The object was to exhibit the owner's bravery and instil bravery in the young ones. Describing the people as so courageous that they did not hesitate to attack rifle fire, the report revealed how the colonialists massacred them.

The report failed to explain that all the weapons, social constructions and military tactics were produced locally. Secondly, it left out the role of women, children, the disabled and the aged in actual combat. Women and children also participated in actual fighting. They equipped men with stones and in some cases, threw stones. They would shield themselves with *entara* (winnowing trays). In other cases, they would use pestles or the men's weapons, lure enemies into traps, poison them, and so on. They also gathered information about enemies, and so on.

The Anglo-German-Belgian Struggles over the Great Lakes Region

There is need to review the sequence of earlier developments in the region before examining the final conflict, acrimonies and politics of manoeuvrability over the heart of the GLR. Belgium had the first stakes in this region and it communicated this to Bismarck of Germany on 8th August, 1884. Then, other agreements were concluded between Britain, Belgium and Germany over the demarcations of this region. These include the Berlin border of 1885, the Anglo-German Agreement of 1st July 1890 and an arrangement between Uganda Protectorate and the Belgian Congo on 12th May 1894. Then, an accord between England and the Independent State of Congo was concluded in April 1904 and it was followed by the convention of 1906. The Anglo-Congolese Commission followed in 1907-08. It was after those diplomatic and legal undertakings that Britain made territorial claims over Mount Mufumbiro territory in February 1907. Belgium used the former agreements to expose it and force it to retract its territorial ambitions for some time. England resurrected it on 10 October 1908 by writing a letter to Chevalier de Cuvelier expressing its intentions to annex the Mount Mufumbiro[14] territory to its area of influence. It is on this background that the following developments were based. From Coote's letter of 21 November 1910 to CS, Britain's search for a route for the Cape to Cairo railway made it repudiate all earlier claims and agreements by Belgium and Germany over the territory.

Struggles over the GLR

The brutal exploitation and maltreatment coupled with the appalling working conditions gave rise to the mutiny of Baron Dhanis' Congolese army. This mutiny forced the Belgian officer, Captain Hecq and his 'loyal troops' to flee Uvira and seek refuge in the German territory - Rwanda. This created a power vacuum in the Kivu district, Congo. The Germans took advantage of this vacuum and occupied the area (sic!). This was explained in Ebermayer's presentation at 'the Conference Respecting the Anglo-German claims on the Eastern Frontiers of the Congo' which commenced on 8 February 1910; 'Boundaries: Uganda-Congo' and it was dated Brussels, 11 February 1910.

14   Bufumbiro was variably spelt as Mufumbiro, Mfumbiro and Ufumbiro.

The mutiny was defeated and the Belgian Captain Hecq managed to return. This resulted in the concluding of the Hecq-Bethe Treaty by Commandant Hecq and the German resident Herr Bethe. The Germans evacuated the area in 1898. This saga had also led to the Ebermayer-Beernaert Berlin Mission on the Ruzizi-Kivu district. This led to the concluding of the protocol of 10 April 1900, in which the Germans claimed as a right the frontier which it had earlier merely asked the Congo State to substitute for the old astronomical line of the declaration of 1885. This gradually led to the Dersch-Kant Agreement. This Protocol was signed at Brussels on 10 April 1900 by Auguste Beernaert on behalf of Belgium and Comte Frédéric Jean d'Alvensleben on behalf of Germany.

The report was that the Belgian government was actively re-enlisting men in *Boma*, and other centres where such men were working, and were forming a contingent of retired non-commissioned officers. These were to be armed with the efficient Mauser Rifles. The Belgians were also putting together several batteries of quick firing guns. The men were to leave shortly for Mfumbiro.

The British, on their arrival at the beginning of June 1909, found that the Belgians and Germans had already established their territorial imperial claims in the region. Cecil Rhodes' Cape-Cairo railway line dream was, therefore, bound to spark off serious protests.

In his communiqué to the District Officer, Kigezi, Olsen, the Commandant Supérieur of the territory of Ruzizi, Kivu protested vehemently against the British violation of the Belgian territory of Mfumbiro, and demanded for their immediate evacuation in conformity with the arrangement of 12 May 1894 between the Uganda Protectorate and the Belgian Congo on that region. He reminded the British that the arrangement had been determined by the Anglo-Congolese Commission in 1907-08 in line with the April 1904 Accord between England and the Independent State of Congo. Olsen on 2 July 1909 wrote to the Political Officer, Kigezi, on 'Violation de territoire par troupes anglaises'. This was in reply to Coote's letter of 26 June 1909 in which he claimed British ownership of Bufumbira.

Britain protested formally against the Belgian occupation of the Rubona post, following the withdrawal of British troops under Coote on 29 June 1909. Its defence was that its troops had merely withdrawn on the understanding that Captain Wangermée, le chef de Secteur de Rutshuru would not advance beyond the post he was occupying. Britain, therefore, pressed for the withdrawal of the Belgian troops from Rubona back to the posts which they had occupied at the time of the meeting between Cap. Wangermée and Coote.

Captaine Wangermée on 29 June 1909 replied from Rutshuru also complaining that the British violation of the Belgian frontiers and sovereignty had been sanctioned by the British Government.

He underlined how this was the first time since the Belgian occupation and control of this area that the British were making pretensions of claiming ownership of this territory. He, therefore, premised on this to dismiss the British claims of ownership of this territory contained in Coote's letter of 26 June 1909 as false and baseless.

Coote then wrote to Olsen on 2 July 1909 complaining and the latter replied on 12 July 1909 expressing great surprise at the British troops' violation of Belgian territory. He accused the British forces of violating with impunity the earlier concluded agreements by occupying the neutral strip, penetrating the Belgian territory and establishing camps at Mount Rubona and at Burunga. He argued against clearly manifested British intentions to occupy the Belgian territory of Mfumbiro:

> You clearly penetrate into Belgian territory which you claim to administer in the name of the British government. ...the British government demonstrated its intention to occupy Ufumbira, a territory clearly Belgian (Sic) and administered by us since 10 years ago, it has been more loyal, in conformity with its use by addressing itself directly to the Belgian government in Brussels.[T1] [See original text in French on page 97]

He turned down the British invitation for territorial discussions on the grounds that he did not have those powers. He underlined how his most imperial duty was to defend militarily to the end Belgian territorial rights and interests:

> I personally have no mandate to conclude new arrangements with the British government. My mission is only limited to the defence of the rights acquired and the interests of my government, namely the maintenance of the respect for our boundary. This mission, of which I take full responsibility towards my government, constitutes for me the most imperial task and I will fulfil it to the end (*idem*).[T2]

He also accused the British forces of menacing, killing, battering, bruising and imprisoning the natives in the Belgian territory. He accused them of beating and wounding 30 natives in Mushakamba's area, causing instability in the Belgian territory, killing an elephant in the Belgian territory and exporting its ivory. He accused the British authorities of sending armed soldiers to the areas of Lubona to force the indigenous people - Belgian subjects - to supply free food and of threatening the Belgian soldiers by charging their arms on his arrival. He then based himself on this premise to explain how the Belgians had acted within their legitimate rights to arrest, disarm and detain two British soldiers because of their unbecoming activities and indiscipline.

He warned that if the British remained deaf to the ceaseless warnings, Britain would have to take responsibility for the actions which the Belgians regrettably would have to employ to force it to respect the Belgian territory:

> I consider your movement in Belgian territory as a hostile action and I cannot, therefore, have no dealings with you as long as you find yourselves west of the neutral zone. If, despite the warnings which I am giving you, you maintain your occupation in a territory clearly Belgian, the British government will have to take full responsibility for the means which regrettably I will have to use to lead to respect the territory of the Belgian colony (*idem*).[T3]

He expressed hope that the British would not cause regrettable incidents which would trouble the peace of the indigenous people (Sic!); '... *mais j 'ose espérer ... que vous ne vous ferez pas l 'ouvrier d 'incidents regrettables et de nature à troubler la paix des populations indigenès* (Sic!).

He argued that the British violation of the border constituted the most serious affair which had ever happened at their border, and that it was a considerable attack on the rights of 'sovereignty' which Belgium exerted on the territories which the British forces under Coote had covered on orders from Britain.

He then thanked the British for evacuating the Belgian territory as the maintenance of their occupation would have inevitably led to very regrettable incidents and for which the British would have borne the heavy responsibility. He declared that he had severed all communication with the British authorities.

True to Olsen's accusations, Coote succinctly confirmed this in his letter to the CS that he had been ordered 'to occupy and administer the Mfumbiro District.' (Coote to the CS, *op. cit.*) The British justified their primitive accumulation of wealth by arguing that the elephant was spoiling their water. They adamantly refused to refund the ivory. What needs to be clarified here is that neither the British nor the Belgians owned the elephant or its ivory. The reality was that this elephant, like all the other resources in the GLR, belonged to the indigenous inhabitants.

Olsen replied to Coote's letter of 2 July 1909 defending the Belgian action of disarming and arresting the British *askaris* thus:

> ...the Belgian officer was acting out his absolute right by disarming
> and detaining, until receipt of the orders from his bosses, the two
> English soldiers and I would like to believe... that if I told you that
> these two English soldiers violated Belgian subjects by forcing them
> to bring to them aliments, and that in addition, they threatened a
> Belgian soldier by charging their weapons as he approached them,
> so that you agree with me that the Belgian officer was acting out a
> legitimate right.[T4]

Earl Granville wrote to Davignon, Ministère des Affaires Étrangères, Bruxelles on 8 November 1909 against the arrest of the two soldiers, one Muganda headman and five porters whom he claimed had gone to purchase food from the area before rejoining the forces after the above-cited misunderstanding between the Belgian and British commanders. He argued that they were surprised by the Congolese troops under the command of a white officer, for they were all captured with the exception of one porter who escaped. The two soldiers were disarmed; the whole party was bound with ropes and imprisoned for a month. During that time, they were interrogated several times by the Congolese forces about the numbers of the British force.

Davignon, wrote to Granville, on 13 November 1909 explaining that neither Goffoel, the Commandant Supérieur, nor Olsen had any powers to enter into and/ or conclude any agreement on behalf of Belgium as Coote had proposed.

He argued that the British authorities had punished these men for refusing to cooperate and show them where the Belgians were keeping cattle. He spiced this with the rhetoric that this property legitimately belonged to the peaceful inhabitants of the Bufumbira region, the Independent State, for whom the indemnities would have been claimed in favour of. He, therefore, demanded for the reciprocation of protestations or an impartial arbitration according to the existing rules in case other measures failed. He stated that the Belgian colonial administration had set up a commission of enquiry to investigate the accusations of Belgian brutalities, murders, injuries, imprisonment, and so on, on the peasants in Lukyéba village.

Davignon, officially accused Britain of its troops' acts of violence and looting which they committed during their first crossing in Mfumbiro. He argued that their commanding officer threatened the local population with corporal punishment if they remained loyal to the Belgian Government. He accused the British officer of handcuffing and imprisoning in his camp the subjects of Bende and Kibanza, and of tying to the gun the subjects of Chief Burunga. He also accused them of raiding animals within the area of Chief Mushakamba, where the British authorities looted not less than thirty head of cattle as expressed in the following quote:

> …demands and compensations for violence and pillage commited by British troops during their raid of Ufumbiro. The commanding officer then threatened the indigenes about the severe punishment they would endure should they remain loyal to the Belgian government.

> He went so far as to put the sub-chiefs Bendee and Kibanza in irons inside his farm and gave order to tie some of chief Burunga's subjects to a canon. I'm not talking about the simple cattle raids. At chief Mushakamba's place alone, the English officials took away thirty cows.[T5]

Belgium repudiated all the British claims over Bufumbira. Davignon wrote to the Baron Greindl on 19 July 1909 condemning the British violation of the Belgian territory, their establishing a camp on River Kigezi, in violation of the Clause of the General Berlin Act, which prescribed the use of mediation before arms. He reiterated that the Anglo-German arrangements of 1 July 1890 and 19 May 1909 did not attribute this territory to Britain.[15]

Von Schoen wrote to Baron Greindl on 30 July 1909 protesting against the Anglo-German Agreement of 19 May 1909 which divided its territory amongst Germany and Britain (see the map below). This 'Agreement Respecting the Boundary Between the North-Western Portion of German East Africa and Uganda' claimed to derive from the Agreements of 8 November 1884 and 1 July 1890 in which Germany ceded to Britain parts of Mfumbiro region which it held and Britain promised to make no further claims on Germany.

Belgium argued that one would severely judge the procedure which consisted in placing the great power brusquely face to face with the *fait accompli* of a treaty which was stripping Belgium of its property. Worse still, the two signatories had intentionally omitted Belgium's name and replaced it with that of the no-longer existent 'Independent State'. The British Foreign Office replied to these charges on 17 August 1909.

---

15   'Boundaries: Uganda - Congo'. Also see Olsen's letter to the Political Officer, Kigezi of 12 July 1909; and the Political Officer's communication to the Ag CS of 3 September 1909.

In his reply to the Count de Lalaing's letter of 8 July 1909 about the British occupation of Mfumbiro, Davignon pointed out that these developments indicated that the British occupation of Mfumbiro and the adjacent territories had been decided long before the British Government received the response from the Belgian Government and obviously, the Belgian rejection of the British claims on Mfumbiro did not have any influence on the negotiations which had already been finished weeks before. He accused the two contracting states of illegally and conspiratorially dispossessing Belgium of a territory which legally belonged to it (Sic!).

This issue was pursued further by the Count de Lalaing. He wrote to Sir E. Grey and gave historical details to show how the agreements of 1890 and 1894 did not grant Britain the sovereignty over Mfumbiro. He dismissed any pretensions that the recognition of the British sphere of influence in East Africa by the Independent State of the Congo in 1894 as described in the Anglo-German Agreement of 1 July 1890 could become a basis for British claims over Mfumbiro. He then exposed the British conspiracy in which it had solicited and obtained German recognition that Mfumbiro was a British territory. He argued that Germany had willingly consented to this because it did not occupy Mount Mfumbiro and also because it was granted a big compensation in Mount Kilimanjaro. When the Congolese Government had immediately exposed the British claims over Mfumbiro of February 1907, Britain had been forced to back off until 10 August 1908 when it resurrected the same demands through a letter to Chevalier de Cuvelier. This letter expressed England's intentions to annex to its area of influence the Mount Mfumbiro territory.

The Dispute Resolution Strategies

In dismissing the British ownership claims, Belgium insisted on arbitration for a peaceful resolution of this conflict as laid down in the Berlin Act and in the 1906 Convention. Aware of its limited military capacity, it emphasised how its neutrality, which was acquired from all the big powers, could not permit it to reduce the surface of its territory. Its position was that any change from this position would have to be according to the ruling for settling territorial disputes, which would have to proceed by means of exchanges. It spiced this with the colonial rhetoric of the white man's burden: that it had spent a lot of resources and human sacrifice struggling against the local barbarians (sic!). This in simple terms meant that the Belgian colonialists were facing serious anti-colonial resistances in the region.

The Belgian authorities explained how the British move since 1906 was aimed at guaranteeing the British interests for the construction of the railway line on the Nile, a promise which was still awaiting fulfilment. Belgium insisted that Britain had broken all the earlier accords because of its imperialist drive to construct the Cairo-Cape Railway line. '...*une promesse de garantie d'intérêt pour la construction d'un chemin de fer au Nil - promesse qui attend encore sa réalisation.*' Belgium complained that Britain was pretending that the principal objective of the treaty of 1894 was to make the Independent State recognise the French zone in the Nile Basin, that the treaty questioned the border of 1885 while on the contrary it was consecrating them. It underlined the objectives of the Berlin Act as being to ensure peace between the whites within the Convention of the Basin, and to prohibit differential treatment of working towards civilisation. In the hope that the disagreements between whites would undermine their prestige in face of the blacks, it had been imposed within the Berlin Act that in case of serious disagreements, there should be recourse to mediation; and arbitration by advice:

> The solution to the border difficulties resides in the Berlin Act whose triple objectives were to secure peace within among the whites in the conventional Basin, to prohibit favouritism, to open it up to civilisation (sic!). Knowing that disputes between the whites would compromise their prestige against the blacks, he imposed, in case of a grave disagreement, to resort to mediation and to advice the arbitration. It is from this council that the convention of 1906 was inspired, making arbitration an official matter.[T6]

As if zealously imbued to civilise the Africans, Belgium argued that for the whites to succeed in this difficult task of civilising the blacks (sic!), their governments had to undertake the obligation themselves, to make the blacks respect the treaties. This, therefore, demanded that the example of equity had to be more absolute. As such, one of their first responsibilities to make the blacks understand the good works of civilisation was to show to them this reality, this truth that was the basis of civilisation as it was practised by the whites and which was to be found in the respect of the rights for the weaker people or parties (sic!):

> In order to succeed in the difficult task of civilizing the blacks, (sic!) the whites have the duty towards themselves and towards the blacks to respect the treaties, namely the Berlin Act, and display absolute equity. One of our first duties is to make the blacks understand the benefits of civilisation, and to bring in broad day light the truth according to

which respect to the rights of the weak (sic!) resides in this civilisation as practiced by the whites.[77]

It demanded that they had to respect the Belgian Constitution which stipulated that the limits of the states of its provinces and communes could not be changed or rectified unless it was based on the law. It emphasised that Article 68 forbade any cession, exchange, or adjudication of Belgian territory unless this was based on the Belgian law.

Belgium maintained its protest against the British occupation of Belgian territory on the River Kigezi, and against its establishing camps on River Kigezi, at 10 kms from the Belgian post of Muhavura,[16] which was in gross violation of the clause of the General Act of Berlin, which prescribed the recourse to mediation before fighting. It dismissed the Anglo-German Agreements of 1 July 1890 and the 19 May 1909 as incompetent in depriving Belgium of its old territory and granting it to Britain. Belgium emphasised that it had not yet ceased to exercise police and administrative powers over its Mfumbiro territory for thirteen years (Davignon's communication of 13 November 1909).

Britain protested to Belgium against the brutality which the Belgian forces had meted on the indigenes. '…all natives who had helped the British force with food, supplies, information, & c., were being punished by Congolese officials, some having their cattle taken and others being imprisoned... 3rd July a party of Congolese soldiers visited the village of Lukyéba in the early morning; ... Buzukira and Yinanzizi, were wounded, ... Ninakazi was killed; a young girl of about 14 named Yingabiro, was captured and carried off with several men, women, and children; the others were all released after the men had been beaten, ... Yingabiro was taken to Rutshuru for immoral purposes (read 'rape').'

The Belgian version of this subject matter was that Yingabiro had gone to Rutshuru voluntarily and that the others had been wounded by arrows. Granville reported that the investigation by Coote and Captain Couche had revealed circumstantial evidence incriminating the Belgian soldiers. These included bullets and empty Albini cartridge cases at the scene of the crime. He concluded that this circumstantial evidence, coupled with the natives' massive evidence incriminated the Congolese soldiers. He, on behalf of the British Government, demanded for compensation from Congolese authorities to the natives who had been maltreated.

---

16   Muhavura is currently Mountain Muhabura.

Retribution Tools and Strategies Versus Rival Imperialist Powers and Local Agents

The foregoing incidents are a mere eye-opener to how the indigenous Africans suffered under colonialism - beating, imprisoning and/or killing; deprivation of means of livelihood including land, livestock and other movable property. In this particular case, both the Belgians and the British were culprits. At the same time, in the background was emerging a social group of collaborators, like Mushakamba, whose expectations for material rewards from the newly established colonial system were on the increase. The colonialists merely used them as pawns in the imperialist 'colony-chase-and-grab' game. They had invaded this area by force and in the process made the indigenous inhabitants the victims. They then used such cases to articulate their imperialist interests - on the diplomatic front to claim the territories, appearing to be articulating these indigenes interests; and on the local ground, posing as if they were very humanitarian and concerned about the indigenes' interests and well-being.

In his letter to the CS on 10 October 1909, Coote had reported once again how the '... natives of the Mfumbiro District were being forced to provide the Congolese troops with free food ... about one month ago the Belgian officer commenced making payments in beads for all food supplied, as also for porterage, the food however being as formerly levied forcibly.'

From this communication, Britain was claiming to be earning some acceptability by the inhabitants; 'The natives put this change down to our influence, it being opposed to the usual custom of the Congolese officials and to the principle which in the past has actuated their administration.'

He also reported that the peasants attributed the existence of order to the presence of the British troops in the Mfumbiro Valley. He argued that since the return of the British forces, the Congolese troops had been under far stricter supervision; the Congolese officers had displayed a more humane spirit of dealing with the natives as a result of which the property of the natives had been comparatively immune from spoliation. From his reporting, this was a major shift since the Congolese methods of administration and the behaviour of the Congolese troops in this area had formerly been very brutal and uncouth (Political Officer, Kigezi to the CS on 10 October 1909).

The Germans were not doing any better than the Belgians. This was revealed by both Coote and Ireland as they individually reported the counter-insurgency by the German forces. Germany had deployed a heavy force to punish the Bagesera tribe occupying Bukonya district in the east of Lake Bulera. The Bagesera had resisted the German authorities. In this expedition, the German colonial forces had killed many peasants and looted over four hundred heads of cattle. Meanwhile, they were monitoring the movement of the Belgian forces in the *neighbourhood of Churuzi on L. Kivu along the strip in which the British were interested* (emphasis mine). (Ireland's Weekly Report to the Officer Commanding Troops of Uganda Protectorate, dated November 26, 1909).

The locals were not passive observers in this scramble for their territory. Some of the inhabitants of Ankore and Kigezi destroyed the British mail. The whole administration in the Western Province became greatly scared by the constant loss of all their mail. In October 1909 all the mail to Mbarara on the 9, 12, 15 and 16 of October 1909 were lost. While they feared that the resisters had destroyed all the contents of the mail bags, they were more scared that these resisters had understood the inter-imperialist contradictions and were trying to exacerbate it.

The locals had intercepted an urgent telegraph from the CS to Coote and maliciously rerouted it to the Belgian authorities at Kasindi Camp. Though Olsen had sent it to Coote unopened, Coote expressed his great fears that it was 'possible for urgent and confidential despatches from his Majesty's Government to fall into the hands of the Belgians...' (Coote to the Ag CS on 3 September 1909).

Coote's communication to the Acting Governor disclosed important developments in this inter-imperialist rivalry. The Belgians had brought specialists to construct the road connecting the Belgian ferry on L. Kivu with Rutshuru. It was to pass between the Namulagira and Niragongo Mountains, so as to obviate passing through the German territory (Coote to the Ag Governor Boyle on 19 November 1909). Coote's subsequent letter to the Ag Governor of 26 November 1909, reported that 'the Belgians, as a result of the German pressure, have retired to the south shore of Lake Kivu, evacuating the post at Churuzi, and withdrawing their working parties from that end of the road under construction from Lake Kivu to Rutshuru.'

He further reported great progress on the work of connecting the Belgian ferry on Lake Kivu with Rutshuru; and that the road, in view of German action, was to be diverted to avoid Churuzi by passing round the north end of Lake Kivu (Coote to the Ag Governor Boyle on 26 November 1909). He emphasised various important issues on the military activities in the region and revealed ways in which the local inhabitants were instrumental in the colonising process of Africa. The war was on.

Renewed Imperialist Rivalry and Clashes

Captain de C. Ireland's weekly report of late November 1909 to the Officer Commanding Troops of Uganda Protectorate Kivu Mission Escort reported new serious developments and activities within the Belgian Camp. He disclosed on 26 November 1909 that his local informant had faked illness and managed to accomplish his mission by pretending to sell fowls in the Belgian Camps. He however had been uncovered in the process and he had had to flee for his life. He further reported that the Germans had forced the Belgians to evacuate Churuzi Camp and that they would have to change the course of their road-making operations, wide of and west of the north-west corner of Lake Kivu (Report by Captain de C. Ireland at Ihunga, Kigezi to the Officer Commanding Troops of Uganda Protectorate, Kivu Mission Escort).

The Belgian Government had been unable to remunerate their askaris. To compensate them, the Belgian authorities had allowed them to loot villages of cattle and women, unrestrained. The indiscriminate looting and stealing helped to alienate the Belgians and their allies from the local population. In this respect de C. Ireland cited a case in which 15 Belgian *askaris* had deserted the Muhavura Camp on the same night, with their rifles and ammunition. They had moved eastwards towards L. Mulera, and then northeast, unpursued. He also reported that 31 *askaris* had died of dysentery in the previous few days.

The British took advantage of those weaknesses and overtook this territory from the Belgians. So, Belgian imperialism was weakened and undermined in the region.

The Belgians had a camp on Ngoma Hill on Lake Kivu Shore, near Kisenyi, which was occupied by one European and 24 men. These were prevented by the Germans from moving off their post. The Germans had withdrawn a large portion of their expeditionary force, leaving there nine German officers and 200 *askaris* at Kigombi. They had 50 German *askaris* at Kissenyi, and every *askari* kept his rifle all the time. The Belgians in Mfumbiro also let each *askari* keep his own rifle and 40 rounds of ammunition. This was a defensive measure against any surprise attacks.

The gravity of the Mfumbiro crisis caused the British Officer Commanding Troops, Uganda Protectorate to visit Bufumbira incognito. The purpose of his visit was mainly to study the situation and the terrain, and then make the necessary war preparations against the Belgians. The Acting Governor had to intervene to cancel the visit. He explained to the Colonial Office in England that he had stopped it as it was 'an inadvisable action, which was most likely to excite the Belgian mind if by any chance they should hear that the senior military officer in Uganda was present in the Mfumbiro district'. He wrote to the Earl of Crewe on 28 December 1909 and enclosed Ireland's two letters of 15 November 1909 and of 26 December 1909.

It is not surprising that the British Consulate at *Boma*, Congo Independent State, communicated the following day alerting the British to prepare for the impending war. From his account, the Belgians were mobilising all their forces in the Lake Kivu District, in addition to some 2,000 troops already on the spot under Olsen's command while Britain had 800 men. Instead of judging the situation squarely, critiquing the British role in the Mfumbiro, the British Consulate tried to absolve Britain of its crimes by transferring all the blame onto the Belgian Général Lantonnois, 'whose prejudice is said to have conquered his better judgment'. He was overjoyed to report that the Belgian Government had rejected Général Lantonnois's request to launch a war against the British forces in Mfumbiro.

Clearly, the Belgian Government adopted this position after judging that the obtaining situation was in their favour. The Belgian forces out-numbered the British forces by two and half to one. Belgium erroneously feared that a military action might prejudice its interests in the event of the anticipated arbitration. Obviously, Belgium knew its overall military and economic weaknesses vis-à-vis Britain and feared that such a war could be much more costly for it.

He reported a great excitement amongst the native troops about the imminent war between Belgians and the British. In his assessment, this conflict would be most unpopular with the natives and the troops. He argued that the Belgians were misinforming their troops that they were going to fight the Germans; and that 'it was under this pretext that they had been persuaded to proceed to the Lake Kivu district' (The British Consulate, Boma, Congo Independent State on the 27 November 1909). He further argued that the discovery of the truth by the Congolese had raised great discontent, which resulted into a plot among the soldiers in *Boma* to revolt against the Belgians. The Belgian authorities, however, discovered the plot and immediately suppressed it. While they had planned resistance against Belgian imperialism, their grievances arose from their relations with the Belgians; part of which had been highlighted by Coote and Ireland.

The British Consulate also castigated Commandant Olsen for stopping all communication with the officer in command of the British forces up to when all the British troops would have evacuated the Congo state towns. He revealed the speculation that the three towns occupied by the British in Mfumbiro were endowed with gold. He hoped that Lantonnois' in-coming successor, '...would realise the danger of the opposing forces being encamped so near one another' and order Olsen to move the Belgian forces under his command back from the British forces. He also hoped that the new officer would be a little more conciliatory and cordial in his dealing with the British officer-in-command.

Coote informed the Ag CS on 9 April 1910 that the Belgian substitute had returned to the Muhavura and that he was expecting to hear from him in a few days time. Yet, the truth about the British plans had been revealed by Coote's letter to the CS in which he accepted Olsen's accusation; 'The orders I received authorised me to occupy and administer the Mfumbiro District.'

According to the consulate, the Belgians were afraid of attacking the British since they were aware that such a conflict would be the signal for a general local uprising in the Congo against them. To him, the Belgians could not rely on the loyalty of their troops; the existing situation of the Belgian troops where they were facing British troops was highly dangerous for the Belgians in particular; and for all Europeans in the Congo in general. (See the speech of British Consulate in Congo in 1909, already cited in Chapter One.)

The British Consulate's simplistic attribution of these soldiers' struggles to the mere affection of the British was aimed at glorifying the British authorities theoretically. This psychological selection of facts has the effect of hiding reality. It was erroneous. He aimed to project the British as the indigenes' saviour as if it was a logical consequence of Britain's historical mission.

Prelude to the Bifurcation of Kigezi

The British knew that the Belgians were weak militarily; their soldiers' morale low, and their notoriety and untold crimes and atrocities in the region had undermined and discredited them among the population. The British Consulate in Congo communicated all these and underscored the need for Britain to take advantage of the situation. He reported on 22 November 1909 how the discontent of Belgian *askaris* had led to an abortive plot.

While the Congolese nationals had excessive hatred for the Belgian colonialists, it did not follow logically that they had to consider Britain as the alternative or as their saviour. Other than Britain's intelligence claims, there is no evidence to authenticate its credibility. The British self-glorification was shattered, as the Congolese nationals resisted the Belgians and the British in various forms.

The Belgians and the British were edging towards war. They intensified their spying on each other and reported back home on their antagonists' troop movements, military capacities, the possibilities of war and the likely alliances in case of such an event.

According to a memorandum by the Director of Military operations of the British War Office to the Secretary of State for the Colonies on the 9 December 1909 on 'Congo troops and the Mfumbiro Boundary Question' military capacity and operations of the Belgians in this area, the Belgian garrison of the Rusisi-Kivu district had about 1,000 soldiers, of whom 550 were assembled in front of the British post at Kigezi, in Bufumbira District. Belgium had about 3,000 troops in that district. Although he was not sure of the exact figure, still he knew that '... in any case the Belgians could hardly denude of troops this long stretch of country which is inhabited by several wild tribes'. He reported Belgian reinforcements of 1,500 from Lisala and Irebu instructional camps. He submitted that despite the logistical and transport problems, the Belgians were in position to send a considerable force of up about 6,000 troops to Mfumbiro since the Congolese forces were about 15,000 troops with an equal number of reserves.

After describing the weapons owned by the Belgian forces and their efficacy in case of war, he then went on to describe the soldiering qualities of the Belgian troops. The description of the Belgian weaponry gave a clear picture of Belgium's preparedness and also Britain's spying efficiency. From the report, the natives were armed with the Albini rifle, date 1867, and calibre .433. The European officers and the non-commissioned officers (N.C.Os) numbering about 700 men were armed with Mausers, 1899 pattern. Their artillery and machine guns consisted of: the Italian field and Krupp mountain guns, of calibre varying from 70 to 90 mm. It dismissed these as not suitable for combat due to transport problems. This also applied to the Bronze S.B. guns of British origin. Their Light Hotchkiss (37 mm) and Nordenfeldt (47 mm) guns were valued as the relevant weapons; the latter being the standard practical gun for field service in the Congo, as it could follow the infantry practically everywhere, mounted or dismounted. It had a calibre of 1.85 inches, with a total weight of 514 lbs, while the canon shell weighed 3.3 lbs and shot 4.4 lbs. The Belgians' other important practical gun was the Albini Maxim gun. This gun with tripod and shield weighed about 130 lbs.

After assessing the quality and effectiveness of the Belgian weapons and its military capacity in the region, the British Director of military operations then gave a detailed report on Belgium's military deployments and installations in the region from where the Belgian forces could easily procure reinforcements. As an ardent British colonialist, he was scared of the Belgian forces whose fighting qualities he assumed to be good as they were recruited from the local warlike tribes (sic!). His consolation stemmed from the uncertainty of the loyalty of the colonised to the Belgian colonial service. From his submission, '...the Belgians are not loved by the natives and, therefore, they must retain considerable garrisons at their various posts. This fact and the difficulty of supplies... render it impossible to forestall what further reinforcements they are likely to send to the Mfumbiro district.'

To this memorandum was appended the hot news that he had just received a telegraph informing him of the arrival of more reinforcements of 2,000 Belgian troops at Kivu, while 100 more troops were on the way to join them.

Tension mounted as fears, rumours and speculations flew around. In mid-December 1909, Captain Ireland abandoned everything and concentrating on a rumour which had emerged from the Congo Boma to the British Secretary of State that Belgium had sent in reinforcements of 15,000 troops in Mfumbiro, he despatched immediate instructions to the Political Officer to send special scouts out to Ruzizi, on Lake Kivu. He also requested the officer commanding the Uganda Protectorate Troops to send scouts from Mbarara to Kasindi.

'I have before reported the fear the Belgians had of collusion between the Germans and ourselves.' He was of the view that these troops may have been sent to check on both the British and the German troops' movements in the area.[17]

This region became a scene of great activity. The gravity of the situation was revealed in Coote's detailed report about the Belgian military preparations for war. In addition to the four Belgian camps opposite the British post, they had built three other camps and posts at different points in the rear of their lines.

Olsen was clear enough in his last warning in his telegraph of 29 January 1910:

> Last warning to Commander of British troops. By numerous letters I have informed you that I consider any forward movement of your troops tantamount to an attack on our position. My force, being then in the position of lawful defence, will open fire from now, and you will take on yourself alone and entirely the heavy responsibility of the armed conflict which you are provoking.[18]

---

17   Captain Ireland, commanding Kivu Mission Escort to the Officer Commanding Uganda Protectorate Troops, dated Lake Ruakatange 15 December 1909.

18   Telegraph from Olsen to Coote on 29th January 1910. It was forwarded to Ag Governor of the Uganda Protectorate, Boyle who also sent it to the Earl of Crewe.

Confronted by Olsen's telegraph on the imminent war, Britain tried various methods to avert it or at least to try to project Belgium as the aggressor. In pursuit of this objective, the Earl of Crewe ordered the British Colonial Office on 12 February 1910 to despatch all the correspondences on Mfumbiro to the Secretary, Sir E. Grey. Grey was then to inform the Belgian government immediately that the British forces in Mfumbiro had been ordered not to make any forward movement without instructions directly from London, and that Britain was interested in a peaceful settlement of this dispute from the on-going conference at Brussels.

On the practical side, Britain was busy preparing for the war. The Earl of Crewe clarified in his communication that Sir Grey could disclose to Belgium how Britain was very ready for war. It had 800 troops of the King's African Rifles at standby, had troops in the East Africa Protectorate. All these would be available for use in the Mfumbiro district should the Belgian officer provoke hostilities. Britain had also ordered a new 200-strong Indian contingent. This was proceeding from Bombay to Uganda in a few days. They would also retain in Uganda the Indian contingent already in Uganda, and would obtain further troops from Nyasaland. In his words, 'His Majesty's Government are, therefore, in a position to make prompt reprisals should the British force be attacked'.

It was with this bizarre and explosive background that a conference on the Uganda-Congo Boundary was convened on 8 February 1910. This was a conference which Britain manipulated and stage-managed to dispossess Belgium of its territorial claims in the Mfumbiro region. Might was proved right, which was contrary to Belgium's expectations of a rational and just arbitration. The first move to trap and bind Belgium to the proceedings of this conference was the election of Van den Heuvel as its Chairman.

The Belgian delegation was headed by M. Van den Heuvel, the German delegation by Herr Ebermayer, while Sir A. Hardinge headed the British delegation.[19] At the conference, Belgium maintained its old claims since its communication to Bismarck on 8 August 1884 and denounced the May 1909 Anglo-Germany agreement. On its part, the German delegation castigated Belgium for failing to honour the Dersch-Kant Agreement. They then advanced that Germany had been confronted since March 1901 with the British claim to Mfumbiro, arising out of the Anglo-Congolese Agreement of the 12 May 1894; and the Anglo-German Agreement of 1 July 1894. They argued that the claim

---

19   Refer to communication from Sir A. Hardinge to Sir Edward Grey on 11 February
      1910, on the Proceedings of 'the Conference Respecting the Anglo-German claims on
      the Eastern Frontiers of the Congo' which commenced on 8 February 1910.

had eventually been adjusted in the Anglo-German Agreement of the 19 May 1909, which Belgium had later on contested.

While the Belgian delegation stuck to its territorial claims based on the Declaration of Neutrality of 1885, the German delegation counteracted it by arguing that the declaration of neutrality could interpret, but not alter, the provisions of the earlier treaties respecting the frontier. They dismissed Belgium's claim of this territory as merely theoretical since it lacked effective occupation and administration there.

The Belgian delegation dismissed Germany's claims in the area prior to 1884-5 since she was not then a neighbour of the Congo State. They then showed how a German Captain Ramsay had nearly caused a war when he crossed into the Belgian colony and gave a German flag to a native chief, Kakali. The Congo Government's subsequent bitter protests had forced Germany to apologise to Belgium and withdraw their flag in March 1897.

Hardinge's disclosure of that day's proceedings revealed the character and magnitude of the British conspiracy and manoeuvrability in this inter-imperialist conflict. He had the German delegation that Britain was coming to their assistance, and went on to detail the tricks which they were to apply against Belgium. The British delegation met the German delegation secretly and charted out a strategy.

As Hardinge had underlined, Britain was the main beneficiary, since the German claims, as set forth in the Protocol of 10 April 1900, did not extend beyond a line drawn from the north of Lake Kivu to the intersection of the 30th meridian with parallel 1° 20' of south latitude, 'thus leaving a large part of the region ceded to us [the English] by Germany under the agreement of May last to the west of the frontier so far claimed by her as against the Congo state.'

The situation had to be resolved diplomatically or militarily. Events seemed to be leading to the war option. The British had deliberately created the trouble and continued to fuel it.

On their part, the British concealed their military strength and sophisticated weapons. Ireland explained the deception thus:

> ... I have sent specially selected and drilled escorts of Nubis with Magazine Lee-Enfield Rifles borrowed from Sikhs... By simple stratagems the Belgians are completely deceived as to our arms and numbers. On many occasions since June last armed collision with the Belgians has been imminent. On the 1st Mission I was twice waiting an attack with Magazines charged. On the 2nd Mission here

at KIGEZI, on several occasions both the British and Belgians have slept in their trenches. KIGEZI MUTESI, and MUHAVURA are all within a circle of 5 miles diameter.

He explained the objective weakness which Britain had studied and exploited. According to him, the commandant Supérieur of RUSISI[20]-KIVU District, M. Olsen, was too weak a man to deal with. This was contrary to General Latennois, who had urged forcible measures. The Officer returned to Europe and was replaced by M. Fuchs. Ireland expressed ignorance of any knowledge about the new officer. He argued that:

> In the event of the European Conference now being held ordering the British to retire I am of the opinion that an attack is very probable. All local natives and chiefs round Kigezi have notified their intention of retiring to British Territory with the Kivu Mission. They rightly consider their lives and property without British protection would not be worth a minute's purchase.

He requested for 300 rifles to guarantee the defence of Kigezi position, and requested for one Company, exclusive of the Mbarara garrison to be at standby ready to support the Mission. Thus, Britain was ready for war over the GLR.

The British interests were well defined in the secret Agreement between Britain and Germany. The border was fixed west of Lake Victoria, in accordance with the Treaty of 1 July 1890. They agreed that the territory formerly belonging to Ruanda Kingdom be given to German East Africa and any land that Britain lost in the process would be compensated by Germany with the same equal amount of land after the border had been demarcated. Secondly, the territory which was claimed as German territory under that agreement was transferred from Belgium to Germany. In return, Germany would cede to Britain the territory to the north and west of the border which they elaborately indicated on their maps. In exchange, Britain would cease its claims against Germany under Article 1 of the Treaty of 1 July 1890 between Britain and Germany.

The signatories to this agreement were: A.H. Hardinge, C.F. Close and John A.C. Tilley on behalf of Britain; Herr Ebermaier; Von Danckelman, and Kurt Freiherr V. Lersner on behalf of Germany.[21] Thus, the Boundary Agreement

---

20   Rusisi is currently spelt as Ruzizi.

21   Agreement Between the British and German Governments of the 1/7/1890. Also see Extract from 'Minute 5 - Confidential S. M. P. 84/09 on 'Agreement Respecting the Boundary Between the Western Portion of East Africa and Uganda, Signed on 19/5/1909'.

of 19 May 1909 was nullified and a new team was constituted to demarcate a new international boundary, which would accommodate the new changes. It is noteworthy that the British interests were overriding in this transaction. This was because it was the most advanced imperialist power, with a long history of colonialism in Asia and America. It understood the tactics of luring other parties into its diplomatic traps and in the process, brings them into its services. In this particular case, it wanted to realise its Cairo-Cape railway dream.

On the other hand, the capitalisms in Germany and Belgium were still in their infancy and their imperialistic interests were not yet well defined, their wits were not yet well-sharpened. This disadvantaged them in their outlook, demands, negotiations and threats.

The Uganda-Congo Boundary Agreement Convention Between Belgium and Britain of 14 May 1910 was signed in Brussels by Arthur Hardinge, C. Close, John A.C. Tilley, on behalf of Britain; J. Van den Henvel, A. Van Maldeghen and Chev. Van der Elset on behalf of Belgium; Ebermaier, von Dankelman and Kurt Freiherr V. Lersner on behalf of Germany. Another Agreement was concluded on 26 August 1910 in Berlin between Britain and Germany. These culminated into the Anglo-German-Belgian Boundary Commission of 1911; Boundaries: Uganda - Congo; 'Instructions for the Fixed German - British - Boundary Commission', agreed to in Berlin on 26 August 1910.[22] DC Mbarara wrote to the PCWP on 9 January 1912 on 'German - Boundary: New Territory, Ceremonial Transfers'. It showed that, he, with the Resident of Ruanda, Gudowius, and Captain Reid had completed constructing the boundary pillars. In his communication to the Director of Public Works, Entebbe dated 23 July 1912, replying the Director's letter of 23 May 1912 he detailed the boundary demarcation process and the fixing of the boundary pillars of both the Anglo-Belgian side, and the Anglo-Geman side.

The Fragmentation of Rukiga

Evidently, out of these political, military and diplomatic efforts emerged various agreements which in the end largely benefited Britain and Germany while also averting and postponing a war for three years. Britain signed a convention with Belgium and Germany on 14 May 1910 which differed from the earlier

---

22   See Kigezi Monthly Reports of 30 April 1911 and 9 June 1911 on the Border Settlement and the signing between the British and the Belgians; and the: 'Anglo-German-Belgian Boundary Commission. Anglo-German Boundary Sabinio to S.W. Source of Chizinga' - 'The Protocol in English' was signed on 30/10/1911 & the 'Anglo-German Boundary, Protocol' signed on 11/12/1911 (Kigezi Monthly Report of 30/1/1912).

astronomical-boundary line of the 30th meridian as it was based on the natural features. In a bid to foster their separate imperialist interests while also averting the war, another team assembled in Berlin from 23-26 August 1910 to discuss the details of the border demarcation in the Mfumbiro region of the Uganda, Congo and German East Africa frontiers.

The British delegation was composed of Colonel Close, Captain E. M. Jack and Count J. de Salis; the German delegation was composed of Baron von Danckelman, Captain von Marquardsen, Major Schlobach and Captain Fonck; while the Belgian delegation was composed of M. Ortis and Captaine-Commandant Bastien. The air remained charged and the Belgians' suspicion of the other parties was most evident. The Belgian delegation rejected the proposal for the British Commissioner to visit Goma to examine the suitability of that port for the establishment of a commercial depot, on the ground that the selection of this depot lay with a commercial company and not with the British officials.

Finally, they agreed on the 'instructions for the mixed German-British-Belgian commission' on 26 August 1910. The English delegation was to comprise of Captain Jack, Captain Prittie, an officer in command of the escorts, a doctor and three non-commissioned officers. The German delegation was to comprise of Major Schlobach, Hauptmann Fonck and three non-commissioned officers while the Belgian delegation was to be composed of Captaine-Commandant Bastien, and Captaine J. G. Maury. The number of escorts was limited to 60 regular soldiers, while the natives employed could be armed with muzzle-loaders. All these were preparations against resistance from the indigenes. They established the terms and reference of this boundary commission, and guaranteed safe passage for the boundary-demarcating team within their spheres of jurisdiction. They also defined and harmonised the relationship between the commission's work and the earlier agreements.

It was further agreed that in case the Sultan (King) of Rwanda claimed the whole of the area which they clearly indicated on the map, then, the British-German frontier would follow another course, whereby Germany would have to cede to Britain some territory, which they also indicated on the map. The border was finally fixed based on the natural features - from the highest summit of Mount Sabinio (Sabinyo) to the summit of Nkabwe. The major work was concluded and signed on 4 May 1911. Captain Jack wrote to Fox on 5 May 1911 'En Route for Kiduha', notifying him that they had signed the Boundary Demarcation protocol the day before; described the boundary pillars marking their borders with the Germans and the Belgians.

This was a 'brotherly' way of settling imperialist disputes. There was a harmonious evacuation of stations and posts, and the removal of the flags and other emblems of sovereignty '... in such a way as to make clear to the natives the continuance of friendly relations between the two Governments'. This meant that they wanted to hide from the inhabitants the inter-imperialist contradictions which they were trying to resolve amicably.

Consequences of the Border Demarcation

In consonance with the colonial mission and tactics, the process of border demarcation (fragmentation) was unilaterally done by the imperialist powers without consulting the indigenous peoples. As the boundary demarcating process did not take into consideration the interests and rights of the indigenous peasants, it had far-reaching consequences for them. What should be noted is that all the boundaries were fixed based on the existing natural features and not on the pre-colonial political, social and cultural considerations - whether from the Sabinyo summit to the Lake Victoria or from the same summit to the Lake Albert. All that was said and enforced was that 'the native inhabitants of the territories assigned to either party who have hitherto been under the administration of the other party shall, for 6 months from the date of which this Agreement is executed on the spot, have the right of migrating with their movable property and flocks to the territory of the state to which they previously belonged. Those availing themselves to this right will be allowed liberty to harvest the crops standing at the time of their removal... with liberty to move with their portable property to the other side of the frontier for six months from the completion of the demarcation of the frontier on the spot and to harvest, even after the expiration of the six months, the crops standing at the time of their removal.

The agreement prohibited the local British authorities and the Boundary Commissioners from encouraging or forcing Chief Katareiha and his people to move into the British territory (Uganda). Obviously, the arbitrary and artificial demarcation and imposition of borders in the Kivu-Mulera-Ndorwa-Mpororo region was a milestone not only for the imperialists but also for the indigenous inhabitants.

At the height of the inter-imperialist struggle, the Belgian Soldiers had arrested the British forces at Rubona, and detained them for about a month before they escaped to Mbarara. The peasants paid the price for British invasion. The political officer complained to the Ag CS on 3 September 1909 of the invasion by Congolese forces in Mfumbiro. They had looted peasants' property, murdered;

wounded, abducted and raped six women, including Ginagabiro, whom they had taken to Rutshuru for over a month. They had also arrested and detained without any charge 8 men and subjected them to heavy punishment by flogging.

He pleaded that '...all sufferers are entitled to compensation and since all the above mentioned crimes were perpetrated as a direct result of our withdrawal from the country and were intended as petty acts of revenge on the part of the Belgian authorities...' (Sic!) He also appealed to him to sanction '... the immediate compensation of these unfortunate natives; pending the result of official representations at home - since I despair of obtaining any satisfaction locally - it would not only have a most excellent effect in the district but would be a retributive act calculated to clear us of the moral responsibility which at present rests on us.'

He estimated the amount of compensation as nine head of cattle and some 150 sheep and goats. Political Officer Coote wrote to Ag Chief Secretary on 3 September 1909. The Ag Governor Alexander Boyle then communicated this case to the Earl of Crewe, K. G. on 4 October 1909, requesting for the sanction of a compensation of £60 to these inhabitants. He put across Coote's suggestion of recovering this money from the Belgian Government. That was a long-term political investment in the local population. The charge was presented officially by Britain to Belgium in November, 1909. Granville wrote to Davignon on 8 November 1909 (*op. cit.*)

The defence for British colonialism was that the area was not civilly administered until 1912. The implication of that statement is that the area was pre-political, with a vacuum of leadership. That negated the existence of the inhabitants' history and deprived them of any form of politics.

All the mistakes by the Belgians created a fertile ground for the experienced British to edge in and occupy the region, singing the rhetoric of liberation. Drawing from its past colonial experience and mistakes elsewhere, it adopted cunning tactics. This was in contrast to the crude, naked brutality and exploitative practices by Belgian and German colonialists. To this end, the Political Officer urged the British state to do justice by compensating the peasants. He underlined the urgency of appeasing the peasants by compensating them.

On 10 May 1910, Coote reported to the Ag C.S. that they had compensated the victims under their administration the sum of £34.17.8 of the original £60. He then appealed for more compensation of £25 for '... the natives around Rubona also suffered at the hands of Congolese officials though to a lesser degree, the reprisals in their case taking the form of fines inflicted on their chiefs and headmen, who rendered us assistance...'[23] Although these did not affect its imperialist objectives, this approach made the British colonialists appear less dangerous than the others.

The Mpororo Kingdom of King Makobore[24] had been divided and sub-divided between the Belgians and the English. The part taken by the English was then sub-divided between Kigezi and Ankore Districts. This process was to later wipe out the ancient kingdom. Given its relationship with the British colonialists, the kingdom of Nkore was given more territory and peoples. The King of Nkore made claims to Mpororo Kingdom.[25] But this could not be done without any internal reactions.

As the border demarcation process unfolded, Makobore remained under the illusion that he was in control of his whole kingdom. So, his forces, under the command of his son crossed to the Mpororo part of Katana village, in Birua on the Congo side of the border. They injured people there, abducted twelve women, pillaged and looted property, and so on.

This act infuriated the Belgians and prompted L'Adjoint Supérieur to protest to the English Political officer in Kigezi in May 1911. He demanded for the arrest, trial and condemnation of these murderers under the English justice. He also demanded for the immediate return of the twelve abducted women to their husbands and parents. He appealed for rapid and just action as there could be among them some who were breastfeeding or nursing young children and whose prolonged absence could cause the death of the young ones. He also demanded for the return of the looted animals, and for the indemnity of six head of cattle for the murder of one of the inhabitants of that village.[26]

The British authorities were not ignorant of the problem. In his reply, the British officer disclosed part of the problem; 'Birua, until cut off by the settlement of the Uganda-Congo frontier on the 10th May, was in Makoborri's country and nominally subject to him and Makoborri has not during the boundary dispute been subject to any control ....' (*idem*).

---

23   The Political Officer, Kigezi writing to Ag CS on 3 September 1909.

24   This name Makobore was variably written as Makaburri.

25   File: No. C 1040: The Omugabe of Ankole Claims Ruzumbura.

26   Ag Crown Advocate to the Political Officer, Kigezi on 7 July 1911. For details, see communications of 3 June 1911 and 20 June 1911; and File: 'Kigezi: Fighting by Natives: Sentences Passed on Natives of Makuburri's Country.'

The case was solved by punishing some of the culprits. The state charged the suspects with murder; convicted and sentenced Lutobera to six months imprisonment and Miwanda, Kiyikuru and Basomoka to three months' imprisonment each, at Mbarara. The colonial state embarked on a crusade of publicly depoliticising the peasants and threatening the local population, before finally crushing Makobore's powers.

There were also border clashes on the Uganda-Congo border. The peasants from Bufumbira, in the British colony, invaded and attacked the peasants on the Belgian side, near Bunagana. They destroyed and looted property and injured some people.[27]

The colonial authorities from both sides were forced to meet and resolve the issue on 25 November 1922 and the ADC wrote to DC Kigezi about the 'Frontier Fighting near Bunagana'. The meeting was attended by the British authorities in Kigezi and the Belgian officials in the Congo, namely: Van de Ghinster, DC Kivu; Mr. Piquard, Administrateur Territorial, Rutshuru Territory and Rev. Father P. Van Hoef of White Fathers' Mission.

This intra-peasant struggle amongst the oppressed, colonised masses originated from a *shamba* - a piece of land on the Belgian side of the border. This piece of land was formerly owned by peasants that were thrown on the Ugandan side of the border through the border demarcation process. Their struggle for retention of both the ownership and user rights of this land developed into a 'sore point', which gradually developed into actual armed conflict The fighting lasted three consecutive days, from 9 to 11 November, 1922. The peasants from the Ugandan side warned the Catholic priest, Father Piquard, that they would soon come and kill the Europeans. In this battle, they looted the peasants' property and the White Fathers' Chapel. In the process, the peasants from the Ugandan side sustained nine casualties, including two women. The casualties on the Congo side were also high.

The colonial state moved in to arrest the situation. While the peasants were getting out of control, the conflict was harming the Anglo-Belgian relations. The Kigezi district administration went on the offensive to depoliticise and threaten them against the use of force. In this bid, the D.C. went to Bufumbira and addressed two *baraazas* - public rallies at Mabungo and Kisolo. He warned the peasants against any further fighting and fined Nyarusiza Shs. 50/= which he used to compensate the White Fathers and the two *shamba* owners for their lost

---

27   DC to PCWP on 22 January 1923 and C.S. to PCWP on 16 April 1923.

property. The fine was to be paid before mid-December. Mutaganya's property had been assessed at Shs. 10/= but he received Shs. 5/=; and Ndeileme's property, which had been assessed at Shs. 12/= was compensated Shs. 6/=. Worse still, their *shambas* were taken over by the Belgian Congo. Interestingly, the British colonial authorities compensated the White Fathers Shs. 39/= (117 francs) for the damage (*idem*).

Imperial Victory over Local Patriotism

There was no broad, visible, organised political structure in the area, which British colonialism could manipulate to introduce, promote and protect British interests through its demagogy of protectionism called 'Indirect Rule'. As such, it was forced to import wholesale a state apparatus and a train of administrators, soldiers, traders, and so on from Britain, Buganda, Ankore, Tanganyika and India. The dominance of agents from Buganda in the administration led to the establishment of a hybrid of a Kiganda-British form of administration, articulating British interests. The key sensitive jobs were combined and controlled by British personnel. This was due to lack of trained manpower, fear of administrative costs and mistrust of the colonised. Therefore, duties of conviction were fused with prosecution and execution under the same officers. This complicated the issue of impartiality, justice, mercy in the colonial system.

British colonialism used agents mainly from Buganda to invade, conquer, reorganise and administer the region. Buganda region had reached a higher level of state formation with a complex administrative system. Baganda had accepted to co-operate with British colonialism. This was in harmony with the colonial interests to preserve resources. Clearly, the choice of alien agents was quite appropriate. In addition to being of the same colour with the peasants in the region, Luganda language was nearer to the local ones and so was the culture, and so on. This made it easy for them to communicate the colonialists' wishes to the people. Baganda agents were used to implement unpopular, anti-people colonial policies. This helped to hide the real enemy. The oppressed saw Baganda, not British colonialism as the enemy.

Captain Brooks, in his Feb. 1912 report on 'Mahagi Military Garrison', drew some lessons from the military recruitment of Belgian troops from all sorts of tribes as the best method of obtaining efficiency and avoiding resistance. However, this was no sure guarantee against mutinies and desertions although it had the effect of minimising them. Notably, the administration of Kigezi District remained in the hands of British colonialism until independence.

The first people to resist colonial rule were peasants under Makobore. Colonialism saw these resisters as 'a mere curb on the advancement and progress of the district'. It resorted to its ploy of sympathising with one section of the peasants. It isolated the other section so as to lay the ground to attack it. It, therefore, took a pro-peasants stance, 'The peasants in this district appear to be greatly oppressed by the Bahima'. It is no wonder, therefore, that the ADC Mbarara led 30 policemen and crushed the resistance the following year.[28]

One of the administrative solutions of 1913 was to divide the thickly populated area into Sazas and Gombololas with *Baganda* agents in charge and sub-gombololas with *Abakiga* in charge. It would divide the people and also train local people into manning the system. To colonialism, the crisis was that these people were '... addicted to excessive beer drinking and while under its influence, ... were very liable to be quarrelsome and use their spears instead of their fists'. It was confronted with Makobore whom it described as 'the most shifty and unreliable chief in Kigezi', because of his outright resistance to colonialism.

Another peasant resistance took place in Ankore, the neighbouring district with Rujumbura. The issue was over state exploitation through taxation and forced labour (*Ruharo*). A total of 132 peasants crossed into Kigezi. Seventy-seven of these crossed to Makobore's county while 55 crossed to Nyarushanje. The DC of Ankore complained about these matters to the DC Kigezi. The DC Kigezi, therefore, notified both Makobore and Agent Yowana Sebalijja that this promiscuous immigration was not allowed. He ordered them to make the necessary steps to return the people to their districts and also to warn them that they would not succeed in avoiding payment of their taxes (KDR of 8 April 1912).

As such, British colonialism depended on the skills, loyalty and initiative of Baganda agents. However, this led to abuse of office. The colonial state was forced to step in:

> The powers of the Agents have been defined, and restricted, and only one case of anything in the shape of persistent extortion has been brought to my notice. As this was met by instant dismissal, there is an unlikelihood of any recrudescence (KDAR 1913-14).

The Colonial State had acknowledged the role of Baganda agents in the colony the previous year, thus:

---

28   WPAR 1913-14 and 1914-15.

The undoubted administrative gifts of the Baganda have been utilised in these districts by their employment as Government Agents to educate and supervise the local chiefs, a system which is open to obvious objections, but which in its ultimate results has been incontrovertibly successful. This method of administration is ... only tolerable under the closest supervision by District Officers.

The Uganda Protectorate Annual Report of 1912-13 noted how Kigezi had been ceded to the British under the Anglo-Belgian-German Boundary Convention of 1910.

However, when the differences between the colonised and the colonisers became antagonistic, the British officers came in as arbiters between the people and Baganda agents, laid the blame on Baganda agents and replaced them unceremoniously with local agents. The latter had learned from Baganda agents how to man this state machinery. On their part, Baganda agents had been under the illusion that they were expanding *Kiganda* political system and culture. This was subsequently shattered by the colonialists in response to armed struggles in the region. Others, like Sebalijja (1912), also believed that they were only spreading Christianity and civilisation to the 'primitive pagans and barbarians'.

Pursuance of the Military Option

Being still stateless, peasants had developed a complex defence system with codes. This was necessary for their defence against their surrounding enemies who included other *enganda*, the organised *Abatwa* bands and states like Rwanda and Mpororo.

In his report of March, 1912, Cap. Reid had identified two military problems of this area. One was of peasant resistance and the other of European hostilities. He argued that in dealing with the native problem, the population was 'practically entirely pagan and would therefore be unmoved by any wave of religious feeling which might affect Baganda or Ankole'. He showed the objective weakness of these peasants as lack of unity between Makobore's land – Mpororo Kingdom, Rukiga and British Rwanda which formed 'three entirely separate and distinct districts and it is difficult to conceive any cause which could unite the three'. Furthermore, they were unwarlike with no military organisation.

In Reid's account, the only anti-European tendencies had been due to the preaching of local witch-doctors and witches who practised the Nyabingi cult. To him, prompt police measures would suffice to nip this in the bud. He devised two major strategies in case of any insurgency. The first was to localise the disturbance and if it was necessary to employ local levies; to use Makobore's people against the *Abakiga*, the *Abakiga* against the *Abanyarwanda*, and so on. The second one was to seize all cattle and stock (Cap. Reid's Report of 14 March 1912).

Resistance was imminent right from the start. The District Report of February 1911 warned of the need for a strong military force to suppress peasant resisters, who had made their country unsafe for unarmed persons (Kigezi Monthly Report of 4 February 1911). It was already clear to the colonialists that it was going to have a hard time of resistance in the region. The only way open for them was to seize the cattle and occupy the cultivated valleys.

This became the *modus operandi* of colonialism throughout the struggles that followed. One of the first cases in which they implemented this plan was with Lwantali and Bukola's cattle. The Political Officer led surprise attacks at dawn for two successive days; 'In both cases the natives endeavoured to drive the stock into the main Rukiga swamp on the edge of which the kraals were situated... some spears were thrown and it was necessary to fire a few rounds before natives retired... the swamp was entered and the cattle and goats collected...'

Under the Nyabingi Movement, the people waged armed resistance for over two and half decades. Peasant resistance took overt and covert forms. Some were militant, others passive; some took individual courses, others communal, and so on. Despite their differences, the three imperialist powers were forced to co-operate to fight the anti-imperialist Nyabingi Movement.

Original Texts in French

T1
... vous pénétrez en territoire incontestablement Belge que vous prétendez administrer au nom du gouvernement Britannique.

... le gouvernement Britannique manifestait son intention d'occuper l'Ufumbira, territoire nettement Belge (Sic!) et administré par nous depuis plus de 10 ans, il a été plus loyal, plus conforme aux usages, de s'addresser directement au gouvernement Belge à Brusselles.

T2
Je n'ai personnellement aucune qualité, pour conclure de nouveaux arrangements avec la gouvernement Britannique. Ma mission se borne à la défense des droits acquis et des intérêts des mon gouvernement et notamment de maintenir le respect de notre

frontière. Cette mission dont j'assume l'entière responsabilité envers mon gouvernement, constitue pour moi la devoir le plus impérieux et je le remplirai jusqu'au bout (*idem.*)

T3

Je considère votre mouvement en terrritoire Belge comme une action hostile et je ne puis donc avoir aucune entreuve avec vous, aussi longtemps que vous vous trouverez à l'Ouest de la bande neutre. Si malgré les avis que je vous donne vous maintenez votre occupation en territoire nettement Belge le gouvernement Britannique devra supporter le grande responsabilité des moyens qui bien à regret je devrai employer pour vous lamener au respect du territoire ressortissant à la colonie Belge (*idem.*)

T4

... l'officier Belge est resté dans son plein droit, en désarmant et en détenant, jusqu'à réception d'ordres de ses chefs, les deux soldats anglais et j'aime à croire... que lorsque je vous aurai dit que ces deux soldats anglais ont violenté des sujets Belges en territoire Belge en forçant ceux à a leur apporter des vivres, que de plus, ils ont menacé une troupe Belge en chargeant leurs armes à l'approche de cette troupe, pour que vous reconnaissiez avec moi que l'officier Belge a usé d'un droit bien légitime.

T5

...des réclamations à faire valoir et des indemnités à demander pour les actes de violence et de pillage commis par les troupes britanniques dans leur premier passage par l'Ufumbiro. C'est ainsi que l'officier qui les commandait a menacé les indigènes de cettes région des châtiments les plus sévères s'ils restaient fidèles au Gouvernement belge.

Il a été jusq'à faire enchaîner dan son camp les souschefs Bendee et Kibanza, et il a donné l'order de lier à un canon des indigènes du chef Burunga. Je ne parle pas des rafles fu bétail. Chez le seul chef Mushakamba... les fonctionnaires anglais en ont enlevé trente têtes.

T6

C'est dans l'Acte de Berlin qu'est la solution des difficultés de frontière, dans cet Acte dont le triple but était d'assurer la paix entre les blancs dans le Bassin conventionnel, d'y interdire traitement différentiel, de l'ouvrir à la civilisation (Sic!) Dans la pensée que les discordes entre les blancs compromettent gravement leur prestige vis-à-vis des noirs, il a imposé, en cas de dissentiment grave, le recours à la médiation, et a conseillé l'arbitrage. C'est de ce conseil que s'est inspirée la convention de 1906 en donnant à l'arbitrage un caractère obligatoire.

T7   Pour réussi dans cette tâche difficile de civiliser les noirs, (Sic!) les gouvernements se doivent à eux-mêmes et doivent aux noirs le respect des traités, tels que l'Acte de Berlin, et l'exemple de l'équité la plus absolue. L'un de nos premiers devoirs pour faire comprendre aux noirs les bienfaits de la civilisation est de faire éclater à leurs yeux cette vérité, qu'à la base de cette civilisation telle qu'elle est pratiquée par les blancs se trouve le respect des droits des faibles (Sic!)

4

The Dynamics of the Nyabingi Religion

'Nyabingi' is indestructible: thus the break up of the agitation and the arrest of its adherents would not convince anyone of the futility of the adherents' claims but would only point to the ill-luck of the chosen media and to the fact that the Nyabingi had left them to settle elsewhere. It does, however, have a salutary effect in causing others to be more modest before claiming to be possessed by Nyabingi.

Long before the European invasion, Nyakairima-Ka-Muzoora, a *Mukiga* from Kigezi, who was endowed with prognosticative powers and enormous experience, prophesied of the impending colonial invasion. He foretold that people with wings like butterflies and the skin of babies were going to invade and conquer the whole land. He said further that these people would come in granaries which run on ropes. These were motorcars which travel on roads. He warned that these people would alienate children from their parents and societies (colonial education and elitist modes of life). He also said that these people 'ate' land (deprived people of their land); would bring a new religion which would replace *Emandwa*, Nyabingi, and so on, and that this new religion would be worshipped by all people. He said the new rule would last forever, and so on (Ngorogoza 1969, Aseka 2005).

In his discussion of the locus, rise, importance and functions of the African traditional seers, Aseka brings out their contributions especially on the foretelling of the impending colonial invasion. He explains how they provided functionally useful leadership in times of complex social conjunctures by telescoping into the future and foretelling impending social scenarios and possibilities. He makes a cursory generalised reference to the functions of their religions and prognostications. He explains that these traditional religious forecasts into the future were instrumental in characterising community to explorers, European visitors in the interior and establishment of missionary work, and subsequently, the imposition of the colonial state.

Nyakairima-Ka-Muzoora's prognostications had thus prepared the people psychologically for the impending colonial invasion. However, he did not tell the people the day and time when these events would take place and what people needed to do to avert them. However, it should not be taken that the people in this region were totally ignorant of the invasion, but neither were they ready nor well equipped to resist it.

Ideological Underpinnings

This chapter deals with the forms of religions in the area. It studies factors that gave dominance to Nyabingi religion in social, religious and political affairs of the area; the forces that it represented, its character, objects and the developments. Among other things, it questions the materiality and historicity of the Nyabingi Movement, the character and functions of Nyabingi and how it related to people's lives in this area that was largely undifferentiated at the time of colonial invasion. It explores how this religion was transformed into a material political force at the moment of colonial invasion, and the historical circumstances that dictated its transformation into a social movement and a popular ideology for liberation. It seeks explanations why and how Nyabingi religion among the competing religions developed and took the initiative to resist colonialism, the socio-political and cultural circumstances that gave rise to the Nyabingi Movement and how it cut across the whole society. It studies why these peasants chose the identity of religion amidst other various identities.

Marx noted in *Contribution to the Critique of Hegel's Philosophy of Law* that 'religious distress is at the same time the oppression of real distress and also the protest against real distress. Religion is the sigh of the oppressed creature, the heart of the heartless world, just as it is the spirit of spiritless conditions. It is the opium of the people' (Adas, 1979; see also Marx and Engels, 1958).

Can the Nyabingi Movement be dismissed as merely 'religious fanaticism' of illiterate, superstitious peasants led by religious sentiments and fears? Can the peasant resistances be dismissed as reactionary 'savagery', 'anti-European', 'anti-civilisation' and 'anti-progress' - that is, against virtues which colonialism purported to represent? Is it correct that Kigezi was a difficult country which had been a refuge of outlaws and bad characters, with a resulting mixing of type? (1911 BCR). What explains British colonialists' hostility towards Nyabingi religion while at the same time using European religions to penetrate the region? Given that this region was still at a low level of production, undifferentiated, with no developed state structures or army, what explains its inhabitants' choice of upholding militant armed resistance? Can it be dismissed simply, as some scholars have done, that violence was endemic in pre-colonial African societies; a Hobbesian situation which one commentator explains thus: '...in indigenous African experience, life was cheap and full of fear. Only often one's own life was only saved by violence....' (Carothers 1954).

This was similar to Roscoe's representation of the inhabitants of Kigezi. He projected them as the most unruly people he had met in all his journeys. To him, everyone was still in a state of nature, without respect for humanity. Everyone lived in a state of fear of being murdered by neighbours. In this anarchical situation, everyone had to depend on individual protection all the time. To him, they were still driven by emotions, instinct and the love for self-preservation rather than being guided by reason, which he considered as the explanation why these people were easily aroused to anger against each other, and why they used their spears freely, wounding or killing anyone upon the slightest provocation (Roscoe, *op. cit.*).

This was the Western presentation of the colonised people of Kigezi as 'the primitives'. Gallagher and Robinson's (1953) vehement defence and glorification of imperialism is demonstrative enough. In their Eurocentric approach, they used the nationalist movements in Egypt to quickly condemn and dismiss anti-colonial movements as a 'pseudo-nationalist reaction against foreign influence.' In the same vein, Hardwick (1904) castigated the Africans for imprisoning Africa, the largest continent in perpetual barbarism and darkness. He praised the European colonial powers, which, in their march to irresistible civilization were dividing Africa amongst themselves.

At the time of colonial invasion, the area was characterised by polytheism. Whereas some schools including Judaism advance the movement from polytheism to monotheism, other schools base on the proliferation of new religions to advance the monotheism to polytheism thesis while others advance duotheism, from polytheism or monotheism or no religion, and so on. These demonstrate that there was no fixed order, no fixed formula. Among their religions were Emandwa, Ryangombe, Mugasya, Kahukeiguru, Kazooba Bitindangyezi, Esiriba and Biheeko Nyabingi.

From its doctrine of action, militancy and courage, Nyabingi came to be known as Rutatiina-Mireego - one who never fears bows and arrows. Its other names included Omukama and Nyinekyaro, meaning ruler. It took yet another name in 1928, namely, Muzeire-Kasente, that is a parent who accepted money.

Being at a low level of production, with backward productive forces, many peasants were still subjected to the mercy of nature. They still attributed most of what they could not understand and their problems to the supernatural. That is why they had so many religions, still at individual and household levels. They had not reached a level of monotheism. While it looked as an ideology of liberation and resistance, Nyabingi religion was an ideology of domination and exploitation by *abagirwa*. They used it to extract surplus value from peasants, and used it to threaten them. On the other hand, heads of households, who were the spiritual heads and mediums of the other religions, also used these religions to dominate those below them. It was in these circumstances that Nyabingi gradually gained dominance over others.

Nyabingi religion depended on coercion, intimidation, curses, threats and mysterious deaths. These were plotted and executed secretly by *abagirwa*. However, it also gained popularity because of its spiritual and temporal ideals. In social conflicts, it was Nyabingi religion which identified with the oppressed peoples, preached emancipation from oppression and exploitation. It provided a foundation for solidarity, courage and action against the oppressors. (Philipps Report of 31 July 1919; Lacger, 1959; Turyahikayo-Rugyema, *op. cit.*).

Nyabingi extended to Rwanda, Burundi, Tanganyika, Congo, Mpororo, Nkore, and so on. With colonialism, peasants mobilised under Nyabingi religion into armed resistance for over two decades. Despite increased state repression, massacres, imprisonment and deportations, Nyabingi resistances continued flaring up between 1910 and the mid-1930s. Colonialism had to concede how 'purely military measures have been proved useless'.

Regionalisation of the Nyabingi Movement Strategies: The Rwanda Factor

By the time of the colonial invasion, Nyabingi was fast developing. The historicity of the Nyabingi Movement has to be located in pre-colonial feudal Rwanda. The Rwanda feudal state had been founded by *Abatutsi* ethnic group. In their state-formation project, they conquered and incorporated under their rule different groups of people. These peoples' differences ranged from linguistic and cultural, to geographical, physiological, to levels of development and modes of production. This dominant group gradually learnt of the inevitability of holding all these groups under state control at minimum costs while exploiting them. It had to advance beyond the exclusive dependence on force by consolidating its rule. This was done by creating and spreading oppressive ideologies over the dominated subjects; and according favours, privileges, rewards and political appointments to some individuals under their control. *Emandwa* religious institution, which the ruling *Abatutsi* group could either have created or appropriated from the subjects for their ideological ends, was gradually transformed into the dominant ideology. This was accomplished by institutionalising it into a state religion, with the king as its head. This was crucial for ideological and political reasons - to sanction and legitimise their rule and oppression, while keeping their subjects in fear.

The Creation of Local Official Language Strategy

Language plays a multiplicity of functions. It is an indispensable tool of communication between peoples, in establishing and maintaining unity, in cognition, mobilisation, leadership, war propaganda, dissemination and preservation of knowledge and ideas. In a class society, language expresses power relations. It is the ruling class that controls and defines the ruling language. The colonised have to adopt and follow the produced language and ideas. This, however, does not imply that they are devoid of their own languages. The issue is that their socio-economic and political powerlessness precludes their linguistic constructions from the dominant discourses and praxes.

In Rwanda, the deliberate application of the language of the ruling group - state language 'Kinyarwanda' - resulted into two major political and social developments. The first one was the gradual loss of the identities of the different groups that had been merged into this political arrangement. This loss of identity was reflected in the subordination of their cultures and modes of existence and the gradual declining and petering out of their original cultures and languages, through their adoption of the language of the state.

The second major happening was the state's deliberate ideological political categorisation of peoples under its fold into three groups - *Abatutsi, Abahutu* and *Abatwa*. It was based mainly on their locus within the power structure, the production process in this set-up, property relations and the physique of the peoples. This gradually became the basis for economic and political privileging and marginalisation. The colonialists skilfully harnessed and accentuated them for their own interests. This ordering of things underlay the pogroms that rocked the GLR from 1959 to the genocide of 1994. Some find it methodologically important for scholarship, politics, analyses, conflicts and conflict resolution.

It would be ahistorical and dangerous to assume that all the peoples in the surrounding areas were conquered and incorporated into the Rwanda Kingdom. Many fought off these invasions. Others fled such invasions and settled in distant areas they considered safe from harassment of the Rwandese forces; (Turyahikayo - Rugyema 1975).

In the process of conquering, incorporation and subordination, the subjects of the state were faced with its persistent crude subordination, oppression and exploitation, without chance of airing out grievances. It should be noted that the ruling class controlled and manipulated the three groups of people through politics, patronage, ideology, force, military, *inter alia*. This political arrangement generated continuous tensions and conflicts.

However, as their struggles failed to yield independence from the strong Rwandese state, they devised other forms of resistance. The oppressive and exploitative feudal relations became fertile ground for the rise and development of the Nyabingi Movement. This militant movement emerged making popular promises of emancipating the subalterns. This became an important mobilising and recruiting device for the movement.

Confronted with the insurgent Nyabingi Movement, the Rwanda State had to wage a vicious war against it. In this contest for space, the state succeeded in hunting down and killing most of Nyabingi social actors. The survivors had to flee to remote areas, where they continued broadening the movement. Thus, while the Rwanda state had the initial victory, it grasped the reality that the struggle had just begun. The movement was increasing very fast, in membership and geographical space, in its activities and ideological work.

The Rwanda state found itself in a fix when the movement opposed its alliance with the newly arrived German imperialists. The Rwanda state's compliance with imperialist interests provided Nyabingi Movement with the nationalist stance.

The movement was totally opposed to the notion of allowing foreigners in Rwanda, and their subsequent interference with the Rwandese affairs. Even those subjects who had enjoyed some preferential treatment and state patronage found themselves joining the movement against this invasion. The political stand of the movement against this new threat gave it more strength, popularity, credibility and legitimacy. That was its materiality.

The Tanganyika Connection

The Rwanda state joined with German forces to wage war against the Nyabingi Movement. However, instead of wiping it out as expected, it had the unexpected consequence of spreading the movement. This was because the social actors who escaped the wanton killings, or were arrested and banished fled to other places where they continued organising the movement. Muhumuza and her son Ndungusi,[29] both from the royal palace, were among the latter group.

Muhumuza, daughter of Nkanza, was the wife of Rwabugiri, then King of Rwanda. When Muhumuza was defeated, she was arrested and exiled to Bukoba, in Tanganyika, then a German colony.

Being a revolutionary who was knowledgeable about the mechanics of power, politics and diplomacy, and about the geography of the region, she managed to escape from exile and went to Rutobo, which later became part of Kigezi. Instead of making this area a sanctuary, she began to establish power over it. Given her negative experience with the Germans, she clearly knew the virulence and manipulations of imperialism and that the whole region was coming under serious threat.

Then, having lived in the place, she had political ideas and knew the invaders would come. Thirdly, she could not lower herself to live like the commoners. She, therefore, transformed the area into her base for organisation and mobilisation, recruitment and initiation into the Nyabingi Movement. So, the area became the base for inaugurating the anti-colonial Nyabingi Movement in Uganda.

---

29   The name Ndungusi in this book is variably spelt as Ndugusi, Ndungutsi, Ndugusse, Ndugutzi and Ndunungutzi.

Pre-colonial State Formations in Kigezi

At the eve of colonialism in Kigezi, there were two major differences. The first category was areas which were highly differentiated, with some classes living off the surplus labour of others. These were areas where states had formed or where chiefdoms existed. These included Bufumbira, Kayonza, Kinkizi and Mpororo. As such, Nyabingi's *abagirwa* had to use intimidation, coercion and threats to convince the rest to accept the religion. It is noteworthy that whenever there was social conflict, Nyabingi automatically became a religion of the oppressed and exploited majority.

In the rest of the region, where classes were in their nascent formation or where they had not come into formation, *abagirwa* were able to identify some privileged sections, groups and individuals there and the social grievances prevailing. They, then, identified with the majority. In such societies, the dominant lineages and family heads became the object. If the lineage accepted Nyabingi religion, then new objects of its struggle would be found among other lineages.

It is of interest that at time, *Abatwa* used Nyabingi religion to raid peasants. However, the same peasants gradually adopted the same religion to defend themselves against *Abatwa*. With Abatwa and the peasants, Nyabingi had begun as an ideology of domination and then had transformed into an ideology of resistance. To understand the acceptance of Nyabingi religion amidst all these competing religions one must go beyond its intimidating and coercive character to the social grievances and problems that it addressed. Without this, it may be hard to understand the issues, since peasants had the capacity to resist this religion as they did others.

The Nature and Ideological Underpinnings of Nyabingi

Nyabingi was created in the form of a woman - a female spirit. This spirit was assumed to be living under the earth. They assumed that this spirit often appeared to people, with rapid transformative powers into feminine personalities. It was assumed that it could transform into different forms of destitution, like that of a desperate, poor old woman. Their interpretation of this was that Nyabingi would do so to punish whoever mistreated it or scorned it or refused to welcome it or denied it hospitality. People feared that Nyabingi would punish them with diseases, deny them marriage, cause them death, and so on. The moral lessons from this included discipline and reforms, enforced humanity, generosity and humility amongst the oppressed. All these feminine imaginations about Nyabingi and the dominance of selecting females into its service suggest strongly that Nyabingi could have been created by the dominated, oppressed women.

The practical approach of Nyabingi religion to people's problems and its spiritual aspirations increased its acceptance and popularity among the oppressed of the society. Despite its intimidation and coercion, more women came into its fold. These worked hard to spread its fame. This arose mainly from women's resistance to male domination and oppression.

The pronouncements and promises drew more people into Nyabingi's fold. They were also drawn into this institution for their spiritual beliefs and partly in fear of its powers and malice. *Abagirwa* were responsible for defending it theoretically and militarily. They promoted it, spread it and recruited new membership to its fold.

Its increasing dominance can also be traced to the fact that women were more united through production, polygamy and extended families. As women went on the same routes to work or met more often than men, and worked together in fields, it became easy for them to give out freely their individual expressions about Nyabingi, the latest rumours, miracles, teachings, and so on. *Abagirwa* would command men to build its shrines, feed those in its service, offer it sacrifices and dedicate young daughters to its service. This was known as *okutweija*.

The situation was different with other religions. These were mild and were headed by oppressors like *nyineeka*, who interceded for the rest of the household. The various conflicts between him and the other members of the family made him more of a petty tyrant protected by supernatural powers than a mere arbitrator. Worse still, men tended to exploit such situations by enforcing obedience through religious threats.

The invoking of gods and spirits of the dead by old people to punish the big-headed or insolent was a common practice to enforce obedience, exact labour, and so on. Whoever challenged the established order or refused to carry out their wishes became a target. From this religious role, household heads derived political powers. Thus, the position of women and other minorities was that of subordination.

To side-step men's oppression, the minorities found refuge in Nyabingi. *Abagirwa* made it clear that nyabingi did not approve of quarrels amongst its membership. Of course, this was another way of maintaining control over the membership. Abagirwa were mostly women. It emphasised moral discipline, love, generosity, and so on; and gave rewards to good people in form of children, livestock, and so on.

As the privileged sections of society were the foundation of its expansion and the object of its struggles, both its membership and leadership were dominated by women and youths. It should be noted, however, that *abagirwa* lived off the surplus of labour of peasants and enjoyed some privileges. Therefore, the so-called 'liberation' of these sections of society was a basis for the expansion of these privileges.

Furthermore, Nyabingi's demands on *nyineeka* undermined men's status and infallibility at home and in society. This was worsened by women's positions as *abagirwa*, who would order men to carry out Nyabingi's wishes. This attracted more marginalised peoples into its fold.

The Material Base of Nyabingi Movement

When people fell ill, they would attribute it to Nyabingi or any other spirit. They would consult *omugirwa, omufumu* (traditional doctor) or *abaraguza* (seers) on what was to be done. These would apply their skills and cunning to diagnose the problem and prescribe the required sacrifices. These professionals did not offer free services. The clients had to pay *omukiimbo*. The same applied to the rain makers – *abajubi* or *abahaniki*.

Abagirwa were supposed to intercede for people in times of crises, treat some sicknesses, and so on. It should be noted that their initiation involved learning medicine and the treatment of different diseases; learning how to expand the imagination in cases of new, unique crises, and so on. In the same vein, they were taught how to create fears, curse offenders, fight and lead people in defence of Nyabingi. People believed that Nyabingi cured both physiological and psychological diseases, and those caused by supernatural forces.

There were two forms of surplus extraction by abagirwa through tribute in form of sacrifices to Nyabingi. These were *okuterekyerera* and *okutweija*. These involved sacrificing cattle, food, meat, beer, young girls, and so on. Whoever asked Nyabingi for a favour had to give some offering or gift. Such requests included children, husband, cattle, good harvests, healing for the sick and so on. Nyabingi was assumed to be the source of all things. Pledges to Nyabingi included young girls, cows and so on. Those who did not have the means would pledge to bring them later. People were taught that if Nyabingi asked for something and the concerned person failed to bring it, then Nyabingi would take offence and refuse the requests. In other words, Nyabingi was not necessarily for the very poor, without the wherewithal. Whoever promised something would have to fulfil the promise. So, requests to Nyabingi and sacrifices were mainly in material form and the latter was compulsory. This was the surplus value that maintained *abagirwa* and their source of wealth.

Nyabingi gained its popularity from the interests it appeared to project and fight for. Its *abagirwa* preached resistance by the down-trodden and articulated their interests. Peasants found this very acceptable. What convinced them most was that those in its service could not abandon the membership in times of hardships. Instead, new leadership came up when the old one got separated from membership.

People who believed in Nyabingi consulted *abagirwa* for its consent before going to war. Then, those in its service would exercise their imagination and judge the situation. If peasants learnt that it had sanctioned the war, then they would go to it knowing that Nyabingi was leading them. Its followers believed that Nyabingi would not lead them to war if it did not sanction it. It was assumed that Nyabingi would punish them if they fought badly and lost the war that it had sanctioned. This forced them to fight courageously. Nyabingi religion preached action, courage, and encouraged struggles against oppression and exploitation. In these circumstances, where the enemy was an already established strong institution, secrecy was a *sine qua non*. Therefore, *abagirwa* stressed the importance of secrecy, and punished all traitors under the cover of Nyabingi.

In the absence of any organised force to protect the people from internal and external threats, the oppressed found a vent in Nyabingi. New developments led women to the fore in some of these military ventures. This was greatly achieved with the emergence of colonialism. People prayed to Nyabingi and dedicated their lives, relatives and property to its care. Colonial repression and witch-hunt forced the membership of Nyabingi to become very secretive and change the methods and time of worship.

Mobilisation Strategies Encompassing the Populations' Majority, Gender and Political Leadership Dynamics

The selection of young females into the ranks of Nyabingi religion was highly secretive, mysterious and frightening. This process always took place at night. The sign for the selected girl was a metallic rod, which would be placed in between the thighs of the chosen girl. From that morning, it would be clearly known how Nyabingi had selected so-and-so into its service. No-one would object or contradict this choice. The people would begin to respect and fear such girls.

Abagirwa carried out the secret missions of selection in the night so as to maintain the myth and sacredness of the exercise and institution. A breach of this practice would have undermined the process, the Nyabingi institution and would have forced peasants, especially men, to resist such choices and the legitimacy of *abagirwa*. It was, therefore, imperative for *abagirwa* to make people believe that these were works of supernatural forces. The chosen girl would then go into the service of Nyabingi under a senior *omugirwa*.

Such girls would no longer engage in production, nor would they get married in the customary way to bring in wealth in form of the bride price. The bride price was very important in wealth accumulation and in acquiring wives. In these societies, women felt some pride and enjoyed some rights and prestige, if they brought in wealth in form of bride price. *Okutweija* divorced those girls from the honour of women. They could not live a married life that they might have been dreaming of and rear their own children. Such chosen females could only marry by the high priest giving them freely to a man that Nyabingi wanted to reward.

The chosen girl(s) would be initiated into its secrets and defence. This allowed them the chance to hold instruments of coercion: the spear, the traditional big knife, and so on. Nyabingi institution ruled that everyone in its service had to use these weapons for its defence. While this seemed to extricate these females from the direct oppression and exploitation of *nyineeka*, they had now come under the direct control of the high priests/priestesses and the strict discipline of Nyabingi institution. *Abagirwa* believed in Nyabingi, feared it, and had to obey its commands. As such, this choice deprived them of private lives with personal wishes, actions and programmes.

These expensive economic sacrifices became a source of discontent and fear among men. However, they could not say anything for fear of Nyabingi's reprisals. This worsened when *abagirwa* began accumulating wealth in form of cattle, which they had acquired from men in the name of Nyabingi. Though many men harboured some internal grudges, they could not express them openly. This was another reason why it was essential to initiate all those in the service of Nyabingi into defence of Nyabingi, themselves and their property. *Abagirwa* had, therefore, to be militant and were always armed.

In a context of continuous armed struggles between Nyabingi followers and the established order, privileged groups and persons, Nyabingi religion had to preach more vigorously, ideas of insurgency and the application of instruments of violence by the oppressed. This was a departure from what obtained where weapons were the exclusive monopoly of men.

As Nyabingi was against armed established order, its fold had to be militant for self-preservation. They also had to broaden its social base among the population.

As already seen, this became easy as women would meet other women so easily in the gardens and fields, or as they worked or while going to dig and transmit information about Nyabingi, its exploits, and so on. That way, they were able to learn about Nyabingi and gave free expression of their desires.

Women were also in a better position to pass on the teachings and influence of Nyabingi to the young ones. All these made Nyabingi get rooted into their lives. Therefore, there were many female *abagirwa*, who organised, led and sustained these anti-colonial resistances under Nyabingi for over two and half decades. It also partly explains why it was impossible to defeat Nyabingi militarily despite superior arms, technology and skills.

In total, Nyabingi religion tried to address the socio-political, economic and military issues of the people. So, the anti-colonial struggles were not a continuation of the Hobbesian situation where 'human life has no value amongst them'. ADC Sullivan to PCWP on 30/9/1913; PCWP to CS 10 October 1913. They were a response to a social crisis and had specific objectives of self-emancipation and preservation. Nyabingi religion gave resistance ideological guidance, leadership and strength. The military option, under Nyabingi, was the feasible option for them against the invading armed forces. In this contest, Nyabingi sided with peasant resisters.

Being a new dynamic religion, it had developed a mechanism of providing new leadership and theories in times of crises. This shows that in a desperate situation, with no organisation, minorities usually resort to any forum, which allows them a platform for articulating their interests. In such circumstances, it gives them a chance for realising or defending their rights. It gives them some form of promise and sense of direction.

Religion, at this stage, increases in relating to the people's material existence. It is only in religion that they find some solution.

In Nyabingi's context, there was marked development in the role of women both in its service and defence right from pre-colonial to colonial Kigezi. As society changed, the Nyabingi institution also underwent changes. It developed very fast at the advent of colonialism.

Colonialism gave Nyabingi a broader platform for mobilisation and action. Anyone who mobilised peasants into armed struggles against the colonialists had to use Nyabingi. So, the first armed struggles were characterised by spontaneity, and were short-lived because of poor planning against the well-armed, sophisticated enemy forces. The colonial forces had continuous victory over the Nyabingi Movement. However, the objective factor stems from the different levels of development of these contending forces.

In the war against the colonial powers Nyabingi became very vibrant. There were serious, long and bloody resistances emerging under the leadership of various personalities, with different historical origins, training, experience and knowledge of fighting. Some of the leaders were army deserters from colonial forces, and colonial chiefs. Others had returned from deportation, where they had acquired a lot of knowledge. Also, during their colonial service or detentions, they had made friends and allies in the enemy's forces. Most important was the planning and timing of their struggle when the imperialist war was raging, their capacity to incorporate various sections of society into the movement, their ability to sustain the struggles for years without selling out and their willingness to die struggling.

When the colonialists invaded the area, the charismatic *abagirwa* took the initiative of studying the situation and mobilising people into militant resistance. The group had a long history of resistance to draw from and outstanding guidelines to follow. Colonialism was not the first threat. It only increased the number of adversaries Nyabingi had.

Abagirwa had had to defend their spiritual beliefs, inspiration, ideals and secular interests. Nyabingi was also the source of their social status. As already shown, *abagirwa's* function, for people's temporal and spiritual needs had increased. Tied to their roles was the accumulation process taking place. Their position had become lucrative as they accumulated livestock and other forms of wealth. As Nyabingi expanded to more lineages and areas, this meant broadening both their social and economic bases. The truth was that without Nyabingi, *Abagirwa* institution would be no more and so would be the privileges that accrued to that position.

In their encounter, colonialism had come by force, imposed itself, and had to survive by force. It cannot be forgotten that all states are armed institutions and must depend on coercion - whether they are organically developed from below or imposed from above. The presence and legitimacy of the colonial states were, therefore, contested bitterly. They attacked colonialism and its allies. As the former were hidden away, its local allies, who were the visible representatives of the system, became the immediate target. These lived nearest, were the men on the ground implementing the contested policies, imposing colonial demands, administering, judging cases, assessing and collecting taxes, and so on.

The Nyabingi Movement went through a transformation during the struggles. As the struggles intensified, some *abagirwa* took up Nyabingi's personality. This was mainly for political and military purposes. The need for the transformation sprang from the conflicts between *abagirwa* and some lineage heads who opposed the war or defied being led by women to war.

Abagirwa realised the importance of this transformation in asserting their authority over the membership. It helped them to dictate commands and orders over the membership and maintain control over them. This had the effect of imposing discipline. It allowed them chance to deal with any individual(s) or group(s) with dissenting views in any way that they wished. It encouraged the peasant resisters into courageous struggle as they felt that they were led by Nyabingi's personality. Their fears of Nyabingi increased. This helped to consolidate their resistance, beliefs, unity and secrecy. Its weakness was that the resisters were blinded by this illusion to attack the sophisticated enemy without retreat:

> 'Nyabingi' is indestructible: thus the break up of the agitation and the arrest of the adherents would not convince anyone of the futility of the adherents' claims but would only point to the ill luck of the chosen media and to the fact that the 'Nyabingi' had left them to settle elsewhere. It does, however, have a salutary effect in causing others to be more modest before claiming to be possessed by Nyabingi (DC's Report of 26 June 1919).

Colonialism had learnt that the character of the Nyabingi society '...does not shrink from organising attacks in force on fortified positions held by troops'. By 1930, the colonialists had understood the complex character of Nyabingi; 'Nyabingi is a female spirit which is the god and religion of these people, and, therefore, the difficulty in eradicating the beliefs is extreme and will take years until education gradually helps to stamp it out' (DC to PCWP on 29 May 1930). This was a correct prediction. Colonial education aimed to create an African that would be alienated from both his/her people and the colonisers in comprehension, behaviour, and ways of life, expectations, attitudes, judgment, consumption habits and tastes. It produced intellectuals whose existence would oscillate like pendulums. For example, among their people, they would tell the time based on the African conception of time – from day-break to dusk and from dusk to day-break. Africa has equal days and nights, and which are separated by darkness and daylight. Night time is for sleeping and day time is for active social production. Time in Africa is not handicapped by seasonal changes which interrupt the time system.

The intellectuals would however have to shift their telling of time to the European conception as soon as they joined the Europeans and those in their system.

To the European, time begins at midnight to midday and from midday to midnight. While this made sense to those who lived in areas with erratic seasons, where darkness could start at midday, it could never make sense to the Africans. So, these African intellectuals would shift their time-telling from 'one hour' and say '7 a.m'. The Europeanisation of African intellectuals spread to other areas of their lives: knowledge, understanding, religions, cultures, and so on. What is tragic is that African intellectuals have failed to consider this a problem. They tell different times according to their audience. Unfortunately, most of them have never experienced darkness at midday but equal days and nights.

Precursors to the Nyabingi Movement

Colonial invasion followed a series of crises that had hit the peasants and weakened them. A persistent disastrous drought had caused a great famine which resulted in untold deaths. This was followed by plague and other diseases. At the heels of these disasters followed *Abatwa* bands, who invaded them for food and killed many of the survivors. Those who survived and took refuge elsewhere, lost their cattle, lives or wives to the people they had run to. The survivors and returnees then confronted Belgian forces, followed by Germans.

The encounter between Belgian colonialists and peasants of Bugarama and Kitare concretises this. The peasants hid in rocks. They used ropes to lift their cattle up the rocks. When the adversaries came, peasants rolled rocks down on them. When they tried to shoot up at them, they hit the rocks and finally left defeated. Another case took place at Kavu, in which Belgians killed 35 peasants including 13 men, 16 women and six children and captured 120 cattle which they took to Kakarama on 21 March 1916. Le Général Commandant in Chief admitted this on 22 October 1916 and paid 170 heads of cattle. The colonial report of 6 September 1911 described the situation thus:

> Apart from the recent change in European control which is in itself
> an unsettling factor in the native mind, two principle causes have
> continued to make the settlement of the district... slow and difficult...
> the severe famine which devastated Rukiga and the adjacent countries
> some four years ago - Rukiga was almost depopulated and the few

remaining inhabitants fell an easy prey to marauding bands of Batwa, a hill tribe from the south... The majority of the Abakiga took refuge in the neighbouring countries of Ruanda and of the Chief Makaburri and have only in the last two years commenced returning... in most cases the Abakiga lost the greater part of their stock, either from the famine, the *Abatwa* or from the heavy toll levied by the inhabitants of the countries they took refuge in as the price of their temporary sojourn (Kigezi District Monthly Report of 6 September 1911).

A focus on the subjective factors revealed that while the conditions of oppression were widespread, the peasants' organisation against it was limited. The cause lies at their low level of production. The household was a self-satisfying economic unit in terms of material resources; and in response to crises, organisation at community level was still on ad hoc basis. There was no organised armed force or an in-built systematic defence system.

It was a time of profound crisis. In some cases, especially during the famine, some women had to carry out men's roles like building shelter, when the men were too weak to do anything, or labouring for food to save their households from death, or going to relations or families of their original parents and so on. This had the effect of promoting them to a higher level than ever before.

Then that women began to hold weapons for self-defence in case of attack - when their husbands were very weak, sick, away or dead. Although the crises wiped out thousands of peasants, fragmented societies and forced many to flee, women and youths were released from the former strong male domination. Women became tougher and more resolute. They had more time to worship and practise Nyabingi religion, put their lives under its care and make a lot of requests and promises to it. *Abagirwa* increased in number, and assisted the people in solving their problems and sicknesses. This gave them chance to preach Nyabingi religion and broaden its base among the peasants.

With the advent of colonialism, all sections of society were forced into action. Members recalled the experience they had had with Nyabingi and the role its *abagirwa* had played. In areas which had not been seriously hit by the crises, the same old social relations obtained. There was a situation of struggles at various levels. At one level was the struggle with Belgian, German and British imperialism. At another level was a struggle against men's domination at household level or against inefficient, exploitative chiefs by a cross-section of the society. At another level were struggles between minorities and other dominating sections of society. There was also a level of spiritual struggles. The various religious beliefs struggled for supremacy and converts.

Interestingly, the prophecy of the colonial invasion foretold by Nyakairima-Ka-Muzoora had spread through the region, but the people did not take it seriously. They realised too late, and knew that defeat would be disastrous to them as individuals and as a people. They had no other option but to defend themselves, their lands and property.

It was at this time that *abagirwa* declared war against the invading force, and led the people to war. They promised to turn bullets and guns into water and chase away the Europeans, and so on.

On the other hand, the British lay claim to the area. They assigned themselves the role of liberating peasants from all these problems; and from 'the alien Nyabingi, its *abagirwa* and their demands', Makobore and his Bahima, crises like famine, *Abatwa*, paganism and above all, from anarchy and violence and from the terror of Germans and Belgians.

Categorisation of the Nyabingi Movement

The Nyabingi Movement can be divided into four periods. The first one was in the pre-colonial period. In this period, Nyabingi religion developed at the expense of other religions, mobilising peasants against internal enemies and external aggressors. Various peoples used it. As an instance, *Abatwa* used it to raid the peasants. Turnbull (1961) illustrates how peasants were prisoners of the supernatural and witchcraft, and how the Pygmies took advantage of the peasants' backwardness to frighten them and deprive them of their property. These peasants gradually adopted the same Nyabingi religion to defend themselves against *Abatwa*, and other lineages.

In differentiated societies, the oppressed peasants were informed and guided by Nyabingi to struggle against the ruling class. Peasants' belief in Nyabingi became instrumental for their defence against the wrath and potency of other religions and lineages. Nyabingi gradually permeated deep to household levels. Oppressed sections saw solutions to most of their problems in Nyabingi. Nyabingi gradually became important in being invoked to seal and oversee certain sensitive agreements, social practices and promises.

The second phase of Nyabingi spanned from 1909-1914. Then, peasants were faced with the new invaders. They realised the dangers of the invasion, and the immediate solution was a call to action.

Nyabingi religion was very dynamic, and more *abagirwa* sprang up to replace the separated leadership, and broaden the struggle. This situation, which demanded prompt action, undermined certain rituals and initiations like *okutweija*. Recruitment was mainly based on nationalities, lineages, and groups: *abagirwa*, lineage leaders, elders, and so on, played an important role in the recruitment of membership into the movement. Then, voluntary joining of peasants into the membership was still limited. And a leader joined the movement with all those under him. Even lineages and peoples who had earlier refused to accept Nyabingi religion came to believe in it as all their other religions were silent about the solution to this crisis.

The other religions were limited to a much more individual level, and lacked a united mass of worshippers and a revolutionary programme. Their main weakness stemmed from the absence of spiritual leaders like *abagirwa*. As different sections of society saw the military option as vital, they accepted Nyabingi's leadership and joined the struggle.

It was during this period that women came to the front and played an active role in leadership and combat. Seeing the various challenges and internal opposition, some *abagirwa* transformed into Nyabingi personifications. This phase was marked by spontaneous, sporadic insurgencies. The minimal organisation of peasants was mobilised into a sustained, coherent struggle. The peasants were still rooted into the ground like their crops the leadership had not developed the capacity, skills and focus to create and sustain a struggle for a long time. People still struggled within their environment, in a circumscribed area.

The two major differences between these struggles and the pre-colonial ones lay in the fact that women formed the bulk of the leadership and the principal enemy was from outside, and visible. However, they did not understand concretely the basis of the invading forces, their military strength, and the need to make a more comprehensive military planning, organisation; to forge a broader unity among various *enganda* so as to resist at the same time, and so on. Another objective weakness arose from the divisions between *enganda*. The pre-colonial divisions were based on past antagonisms. This blocked any possibilities for their unity. So, the first struggles were fragmented, spontaneous and short-lived.

The third phase began with the First World War of 1914-1919. Then, the Nyabingi Movement reached its climax. Not only did its membership increase numerically but it also developed qualitatively. There was a marked change in the recruitment process. A new leadership emerged, which was versed with the enemy and his methods of war, knew the enemy's strengths and weaknesses, and so on. Most of this leadership arose from the colonial services or from deportations and detentions. That gave them the opportunity to understand their military weaknesses and the need to acquire, incorporate, master, and use the enemy's methods of war and weaponry. They also acquired firearms and ammunition from the adversary.

The leadership had learnt and appreciated the need for mass organisation, intensive preparations and active involvement of the population into the struggle. Their stay in the enemy's camp also enabled them to appreciate the need for mobility and the importance of preserving the fighting forces from annihilation. They changed tactics, from the former method of direct charge to guerrilla warfare. They created and sustained armed struggle for years with mobile guerrilla forces.

Recruitment of the membership also underwent some qualitative change, especially from its massive, spontaneous forms. In some cases, recruitment was now based on willingness, ability and military skills.

There was intensive conscientisation and preparation. The leadership adopted more secretive methods, introduced important cultural practices that could help to unite the movement. They trained the membership in the mechanics of attack and self-defence, mobility and concealment in the rear-bases, and among the peasants, and so on. This was re-emphasised by colonial attacks, joint-military expeditions and screening. Counter-insurgency helped to sever the resisters' roots from the agricultural rhythm.

The fourth phase was in the 1920-1930s. Then, the Nyabingi Movement was undermined by various factors. These included constant defeats, the deaths of the strong leadership - Ndochibiri,[30] Ruhemba, and so on whom the resisters and the peasants took to be immortal. This was worsened by the adversary's counter-insurgency, reprisals and raids. The various reforms and programmes that the colonialist initiated to undermine and defeat Nyabingi, the continued repression and witch-hunt for Nyabingi supporters and so on, had a great impact on the resisters. Coupled with this was the availability of other alternatives to Nyabingi religion - namely Christianity and Islam. Peasants begin to appeal to the state, and to use the colonial legal machinery against the state and its related institutions.

---

30   This is a variant of the name Ndochibiri. It was spelt differently by colonialists as
     Ndochibiri, Ndochimbiri, Knochibilillis, Ndochi-biri, Ndochi-mbiri, Ndochimbili,
     Ndochi-mbili, Ndochikembiri, Ntochibiri, Ndocki-mbili, N' docki-bili and Bichubirenga
     (the clouds that are disappearing). All these misspellings by colonialists demonstrate
     the formidable resistance that he led and how it made the colonialist reached extreme
     levels of desperation.

New Survival Strategies: The Evolving of Dual Religio-Political Body politics

By the late 1930s, the Nyabingi Movement had been undermined. Through defeats, public addresses, lies, threats, opportunism and/or peasant rationality, and so on, many peasants opted to join the new religions. They began active participation in these new religions and by late 1930s, women led another religious movement: Revivalism (*Ruvaivuro*).

The Revivalist Movement, adopted the new religion instead of Nyabingi or any other old religion. This was a great achievement for colonialism as it became easy to control the peasants. To pre-empt the movement, the colonialists approached the CMS. The latter confirmed that it was 'in full control of the enthusiasts'. It promised the state 'to impress on their followers the necessity for obedience to civil authority on all forms'. It was in this light that Dr. Church promised to take disciplinary action in any case of insubordination.

After an interview with Archdeacon Pitts and Dr. Church, the DC left the CMS with the duty to control the Revivalist Movement. The DC instructed the chiefs that they had tribal powers to ensure the obedience of women to their legal guardians, and to control unruly gatherings (*op. cit.*) This was very instructive. The DC meant that the colonial government had transferred to chiefs legal and political powers over women. Mamdani correctly captured this as decentralised despotism (Mamdani; 1996).

However, Christianity failed to provide solutions to the key socio-economic, health and political issues in the subsequent years. Therefore, a religious movement, known as Mukaaka emerged in 1970s and attracted a cross-section of society. Its origins and development can be traced to the economic, social and political crises of the time and the mounting dictatorship in the 1970s.

In the face of the mounting socio-political and economic crises, Mukaaka gave way to another movement known as *Abarangi*. Its leadership was predominantly composed of females. Obviously, although the Nyabingi Movement was defeated, it was never wiped out.

The new movement incorporated some aspects of Christianity with some traditional and Nyabingi aspects. However, they were paid money. After pretences to commune with the supernatural force, *omurangi* offered medicine and advice to the client. *Abarangi* attended to all types of socio-economic, psychological and supernatural issues.

The established churches were threatened by Abarangi Movement and preached vehemently against it. *Abarangi* attracted more people from the other religions. So, they accumulated wealth much more easily and quicker than the pre-colonial *abagirwa*.

Although the Nyabingi and Abarangi were not linked in any way, there were some similarities between them. This is evident in the problems they addressed, their composition in terms of gender, their extraction of the surplus value from the peasants and the accumulation process. The rise of the new religious movement and its popularity lay in the economic hardships arising partly from exploitation, corruption, inflation, landlessness, diminishing yields, the impact of anti-people programmes and advice of IMF and World Bank, especially SAPs. There was deepening misery. The peasants did not understand scientifically what had gone wrong, and, therefore, resorted to the new, exploitative religious movements. Abarangi institution thrived on people's misery and destitution.

5

Peasants' Resistance to Colonialism

'We have come to pay tax!' shouted over 1,400 peasants who were carrying spears and other weapons instead of money.

The Society does not shrink from organising attacks in force on fortified positions held by troops, as witness the attack upon CHAHAFI fort held by Anglo-Belgian troops (a few days after a strong German attack with guns had been repulsed) in January 1915. Some two thousand fanatical natives were engaged, and were only driven off after over six hours close fighting.

With colonial invasion, members of the society began thinking about the crisis, the prophecies of Nyakairima and the possible solutions. Various solutions emerged, which guided people's different courses of action. The people's grievances revolved around material issues although resistance took a religious tone - politics and religion. The concrete issues that peasants raised revolved around the division of their geographical environment, imposition of borders and the territorial claims by the colonial forces. This resulted into restriction of movement of peasants, and limited their operations and chances of expansion of their production and trade activities.

Other grievances arose because of land and political alienation, forced labour in the form of *Ruharo*, *Kashanju*, head porterage and conscription for military purposes. Some others revolved around the newly imposed institutions, rules and laws, oppressive alien judgment, persistent demands and forced contributions, forced sales and forced production for sale under the label of 'market gardens'.

This chapter analyses the Nyabingi resistance to colonialism. It examines the claims Nyabingi was anti-people, oppressive and enslaving, while colonialism was for liberation (Rwampigi, 1980).

Colonialists had invaded and occupied this area militarily. Their appearance largely determined the peasants' response. Their militaristic character contributed greatly to the continuation of the resistance. The various atrocities committed against peasants by colonial personnel increased social grievances. These included looting, collective fines and the imposition of the 'Collective Fine Ordinance'. They were aimed at punishing peasants and impoverishing them. There were other crimes by colonial personnel like rape, massacres, murders, and so on.

The continued occupation by foreigners was resented by the peasants. This had the effect of raising the level of nationalism in the peasants. What compounded the problem was the imposition of Baganda agents and their superiority complex, languages, corruption and bribery, crude and strange punishments, disruption of the peasants' social set-up, deliberate attempts to destroy peasant religious institutions, and so on. To accomplish this, colonialism outlawed free worship by peasants, which it termed 'witchcraft'. The colonial state instituted the 1912 Witchcraft Ordinance. This was aimed at prosecuting anybody caught practising the local religions. It also designed and instituted a Deportation Ordinance in 1912. These were some of the issues that informed peasants' resistance in the first phase of the struggle.

On their part, *abagirwa* had to try and retain their economic base. As they lived off the surplus from peasants, and some had begun to accumulate property, they had to try and defend it. They were able to combine politics and religion around all these concrete issues. Peasants saw sense in *abagirwa's* teaching and were moved to resistance. Heads of households were also opposed to the *modus operandi* of colonialism and the new religions. These undermined their political power and social status by setting the young against the colonialists and their established order.

Despite these impositions, the British officers heeded the advice of PCWP on the dangers of imposing Poll Tax in cash:

'...until the natives have some means of earning money; which at present they have not... should give them time to realise the advantages of being under the British Government and by degrees they will learn that they must contribute something in return for the benefits they enjoy. Premature taxation without opportunities for earning the wherewithal to pay it would cause discontent and might result in migration to the Congo or GEA (WPAR 1913/14).

Despite the absence of a centralised leadership in the area to defend the people's interests, they did not sit idle as the three imperialist powers were scrambling for their land, dividing and sub-dividing it amongst themselves. They were not ready to surrender their land and autonomy.

The population factor needs to be understood. Though the area had not reached a high level of social differentiation, which was worsened by the crises that had faced the peasants prior to 1910, it had reached a high population level. The population of the new district, Kigezi, was estimated at 206,090 people in 1921 and land per head was 5.4 acres (figures from Kigezi District Resettlement Office, Kabale).

The high population, vis-a-vis the available resources and rudimentary technology contributed to peasants' mistrust of the colonialists and fuelled their militancy. So, the colonial state was very careful not to encourage raw material production in Kigezi. That would have required the upgrade of the technical level of labour due to the land shortage. Yet the British were not willing to plough back the resources that they were siphoning out.

Secondly, the colonial option was shaped by the peasants' continued resistance for decades. The state, therefore, opted for labour migration. The creation of Kigezi into a labour reservoir has its origins in colonialism. However, it should be noted that the state colonialism was not hard-pressed by land for these raw materials. It had nearer places like Buganda and Busoga where it was already growing them very cheaply. So, it was economically rational and politically expedient to transport labour from the highly populated area than taking risks to invest resources there.

The Course of the Nyabingi Movement up to World War One

At the time of colonial invasion, an omugirwa of Nyabingi had organised peasants into resistance and overthrown Chief Ruhayana[31] of Kinkizi. Interestingly, it was in Ruhayana that colonialism found an ally. It took advantage of this situation and reinstated him:

---

31   At the time of colonial invasion, the colonialists spelt Ruhayana as Nduraiane.

> The Chief Nduraiana (read 'Ruhayana') is very old and infirm. I
> found a section of his people in revolt against his authority under
> the leadership of a local witch doctor, whom, I arrested. These witch
> doctors are rather a feature of Rukiga and the neighbouring countries.
> Their influence is great and the mischief they cause considerable, as
> the doctrine they preach is entirely subversive of all authority whether
> local or European.

At the same time, Chief Muginga[32] in the neighbouring Kayonza, refused
persistently to subordinate his authority and peoples to the British colonisers.
Instead, he organised them into resistance. So, Cap. Reid deposed him, and
replaced him with his collaborating brother, Duybumba (KD Report of 6
September 1911). However, the CS had warned against the action as '...not
desirable to interfere with the native regime until we are firmly established in
this country'.

The Ag CS wrote to the Political Officer on 2 October 1911 promising that
'the new ordinance on the subject of witchcraft would have to be enforced
(when finally approved) as soon as the country was added to the Protectorate'.
His memo of 3 October 1911 and letter of 6 October 1911 ordered the Political
Officer to transfer Muginga to Mbarara or Masaka pending the Secretary of State's
approval of the ordinance - 'a witch doctor should be temporarily transferred
to another place'.

Muginga was convicted on charges of banding with Ndochibiri against the
state, consorting with the enemy and fighting against the British. He was also
accused of exercising considerable influence in the district and fuelling resistance
even while he was away. It was in the interest of peace and good government
that he was deported to Bunyoro, where he could have no intercourse with any
of the other natives, who had been deported from Kigezi.[33]

Muginga's deportation order to Bunyoro, in accordance with 'The Uganda
Deportation Ordinance, 1906', spelled out that this was aimed at preventing
continuance of his misconduct and intrigue against the British rule. The Acting

---

32   The name Muginga was variably spelt as Mginga.

33   DC writing to PCWP on 9 April 1917. Also see Comments of PCWP on Muginga's
       deportation on 18 April 1917 and the affidavits of 8 June 1917 all opposing his return
       from deportation. File *op. cit.* File: Natives Affairs. Mginga: Deportation of. Also see the
       Attorney General's letter to Ag CS of 28 July 1917 and the Governor's Communication
       517 Minute 1 of 2 August 1917.

Governor signed Muginga's Deportation Order on 29 June 1917 (File: Native Affairs: Mginga's Deportation).

To break him further and consolidate his separation from his people, which also emphasised the lesson that he had to conform when he went back to his land, he was detained internally in Mparo after his term of deportation.

Ndungusi gives an interesting leadership in this movement. There were various Nyabingi insurgencies, whose leadership claimed to be Ndungusi, son of Rwabugiri (King of Rwanda) and his mother, Muhumuza. The claim was made because of the socio-political, military, religious and organisational capacity of both the personality himself and his mother, Muhumuza.

Ndungusi and his mother were forced to flee Rwanda due to the power struggle. Ndungusi failed to replace his father as king of Rwanda. It was during this anti-colonial Nyabingi Movement that Ndungusi became a Nyabingi *omugirwa*, like his mother. He learnt the tricks and importance of Nyabingi personification. He developed military and leadership skills from other *abagirwa* and lineage leaders in the struggle. He participated in the battle at Ihanga in 1911, managed to escape death and capture. He then retreated into the peasantry, where he began mobilising peasants into more armed resistance. From then, various personalities made claims to this name for political purposes, to gain legitimacy and acceptance among the peasants. One of them joined forces with Katuregye against colonialism. He was killed in the forest.

KDAR of 1922 reported Muginga's return from exile at Masindi. KDAR of 1923 noted that Mginga had taken over Kayonza Gombolola. The District Report of 3 May 1913 noted that the Imperial Resident of Rwanda had been engaged in operations against Ndungus and Basebya,[34] Ndungusi was killed and Basebya escaped across Lake Bunyonyi.

Another Ndungusi was caught mobilising peasants into resistance in 1913 and deported to Jinja, where he finally died in 1918. Another claimant to this name organised the broad-based regional resistance of 1928. He escaped capture and disappeared among the peasantry. Another claimant to this name was captured mobilising peasants into resistance in 1930. He was convicted and imprisoned. There were other young men who made similar claims to this name. Ndungusi had become an inspiration to resistance. Gradually, the name Ndungusi declined and receded into legend. However, whoever made claims to this name raised a large following and would be hunted down by the state.

---

34   The name Basebya was variably spelt as Bassebya, Basebia and Bassebja.

Because of the charismatic character of Ndungusi and his role in anti-colonial leadership, the colonial state charged one of the claimants to this name with responsibility for 'riot, rebellion, sedition and bloodshed in Kigezi'. He was deported for being a 'dangerous and undesirable person to be at large in this district'. The ADC argued that Ndungusi had incited numerous chiefs into open revolt against the government and attacked collaborators.

Rwagara, a local collaborator, testified against Muhumuza and Ndungusi two years later. He accused them of being:

> ...bad people and disturbed the Rukiga county. They came to this country about two years ago... went from place to place and took the people's cattle they preached against the English. If a chief refused to obey them they warred on him, they did this to Chief Mutambuko.[35] They killed his people and burnt his houses and took his cattle. Everyone was in fear of them. Cap. Reid with the soldiers arrested Mamusa and killed many of his people but Ndungutzi escaped. Mamusa and Ndungutzi had three stakes. They said they would place me on one. Agt. Sebalija on the other - and Agt Yonozani on the third one... Ndungutzi went into German territory and did many bad things there but the German drove him into English country again and he stopped at Lubungo. He told Lwantali and all the chiefs around there not to obey the English but to follow him; they did so. The people all refused to obey the Government owing to his words. He moved from one place to place inciting the people to rebellion. He accused me of bringing the English into the country and wanted to fight with me (Rwagara's testimony of 25 March 1913.)

Our respondents accused collaborators like Rwagara and Baganda of fighting for Europeans for loot and posts. To attribute all the peasant resistances to individuals as the colonialists did was to negate the people's history. Peasants resisted in various areas of the district at different times without Ndungusi's knowledge or influence. However, he was convicted of being dangerous to peace and good order, 'endeavouring to excite enmity between the people of the Protectorate and His Majesty and... intriguing against His Majesty's power and authority and the Protectorate':

> It would be a great mistake to allow Ndungutzi to return to Kigezi for some considerable time to come as he would be certain to cause trouble again. Experience has taught me that to haste forgiveness or lenience with natives who have misbehaved themselves (especially with fanatical ones) is misplaced kindness and instead of being appreciated is invariably abused (PCWP to CS on 23 December 1913).

---

35   Mutambuka was variably spelt as Mutambuko.

It was reiterated in July 1914 that his return would be most injurious and would lead to a recrudescence of the disturbances, which had led to his deportation.[36]

The ACS wrote to the PCWP on 6 April 1915 on the same decision and on 3 October 1916, the Governor informed the Secretary of State for Colonies that the question of the return of Ndugusi to Kigezi would have to be deferred until normal conditions had been restored and the district brought under closer administration. This objection was reiterated the following year by the Governor to the Secretary of State for Colonies. This Ndungusi died in exile in April 1918 (PCWP to CS on 2 May 1918. Also see DC to PCWP on 30 December 1918).

The Abatwa Resistance

Abatwa ethnic grouping who are pejoratively called 'pygimes' lived in the whole of the Great Lakes Region, including Rwanda, Burundi, Uganda and the DRC. Their mode of existence was principally hunting and gathering, which they supplemented by primitive plunder of wealth characterised by massacres, arson, property destruction and looting. They constituted a military and political threat to the local peasants.

Jack exaggerated that they were 'cannibals'. Colin Turnbull, however, gives a more convincing picture of the *Abatwa* (pygmies) in the Ituri forest, their mode of production, organisation, character, bravery and skilfulness. It is no wonder, therefore, that *abagirwa* mobilised peasants against *Abatwa*:

> ...of a treacherous and thieving disposition, and at certain times of the year band together for the purpose of raiding their more peaceful neighbours... peasants near Mabaremere and other parts, lived in the most lively dread of the *Abatwa* who always attacked by night, killed all their people and stole their food.

Abatwa could not accumulate wealth through this process of hunting and gathering, leading a nomadic life. They were not engaged in settled production of either animal husbandry or crop husbandry. They could not accumulate and concentrate the looted property to make it reproduce itself. As there was no form of accumulation of wealth, no classes existed among them. This made them very vulnerable. The Colonial state capitalised on these weaknesses to isolate and

---

36   See Communications of 10 July 1914 and 21 January 1915 barring him from returning. Also Governor's communication to PCWP of 3 October 1916; the D.C's communication to PCWP of 27 September 1917 and PCWP's communication to the CS of 4 October 1917 all barring Ndungutzi from returning. Governor of Uganda to Secretary of State for Colonies on 21 January 1915 responding to the latter's letter of 13 June 1913 No. 284. File *op. cit.*

defeat them politically and militarily. In their primitive plunder, *Abatwa* would burn whatever remained after acquiring whatever they wanted. They killed all livestock as they could not look after them. The respondents argued that *Abatwa* were so wasteful because they did not participate in production of wealth.

The 1911 BCR presented *Abatwa* as a race of fierce, savage and undersized people, looked upon with suspicion and dislike by the other natives whose land they constantly raided, always independent and truculent, acknowledging none but their own chiefs. Contrary to the colonial view, it should be understood that *Abatwa* were also inhabitants of the area, regardless of the sentiments of other ethnicities. After all, there were conflicts at different levels in other ethnicities, too.

Because of their military expertise, skills and lack of a settled mode of production, it became easy for them to hire themselves out to fight for organised states and peoples. The colonial state anticipated that they were not likely to give any trouble but that if it was found necessary to deal with, then native levies could be raised without difficulty to assist in driving them from their bamboo forests (*op. cit.*).

One of the colonial tactics was to exploit pre-colonial conflicts between the local peoples. In the case of *Abatwa*, the plan was to ally with other ethnicities against them. Though they were still dependent on nature, they were militarily superior to the other inhabitants. Because of this level of organisation they could invade, terrorise, loot and pillage the populous peasantry who were disunited, politically disorganised, and militarily weak.

However, *Abatwa* soon realised the dangers of the new enemy and started attacking it and its allies, disrupted its communication system, and so on. The three colonial powers combined forces, intelligence and military information to fight them. They found it easy to mobilise peasants against *Abatwa*, by exploiting the past hatred against them. So, while wars were waged in Lake Bunyonyi by the British against Katuregye,[37] the Germans and Belgians were also fighting against *Abatwa* in their colonies.

The question arises as to why their resistance was defeated. While colonial powers were ready to smash any local resistance, *Abatwa* received no sympathies, material or military assistance or alliances from the peasants in the neighbourhood. They lacked continuous food supply. At the same time, the area where they could go to for supplies had come under different colonial powers. As

---

37   Katuregye was variably spelt by colonialists as Katuleghi and Katuleggi.

a result, they faced shortages without replenishments. Another explanation is that they never held to any territory as they lived a nomadic life. As such, they were able to move from territory to territory, while being pursued by colonial forces. Studies revealed how Rukara and Muramira led collaborators with Europeans against Katuregye et al.

Their resistance under Katuregye gave colonialism and its local allies considerable trouble. They attacked and killed 'friendly natives on two occasions', and interrupted communications by seizing the canoes on Lake Bunyonyi. They attacked and fired at runners, messengers and natives sent to fetch wood for the troops. The British sent a strong force to dislodge and defeat them. This was led by one British Major and four Lieutenants – Major Lawrence and Lieutenants Turpin, Moore, Sullivan and Wagstaff. The strong, well armed force failed to dislodge and defeat them. This was because of the resisters' excellent knowledge of the terrain, their military skills and the protection that they enjoyed from the population. The inhabitants were not willing to betray them by giving incriminating information to the colonialists.

Basebya combined forces with Ndungutse, and led the resistance against the German colonialists in Ruanda in 1912. While Ndungutsi was reportedly killed, Basebya escaped to Rwanda. The British colonialists could not rest with Bassebya at large, just across the border in German East Africa. They, therefore, communicated to the German colonialists in Rwanda on 22 May 1912, proposing to them the necessity of instituting measures to strengthen their protection 'by a simultaneous closure of the border'. This was concurred to by the Imperial Resident at Kigali as he submitted that '...the natives in not a few cases have escaped punishment by crossing the border or they commit crimes on the other side of the border in the hope that they will not be called to account for them. The many problems of the open country in the border areas favour such behaviour, which is unpalatable to both governments. Without doubt, a common action by the German and British authorities will stop the border population from committing crimes.' It was in this spirit that he announced the summary execution of Bassebya just a week before. From his account, Basebya had been caught, arrested, prosecuted, convicted by the German Court Martial, which in all senses was a kangaroo court, and executed on the same day:

> I succeeded on 13/5/1912 to arrest the *Abatwa* chief, Bassebja (Read 'Bassebya'). Bassebja was condemned to death by the military tribunal on 15th May and the sentence was executed on that very day. Bassebja's raid on English territory has thus been avenged.

The Imperial Resident, Kigali on 22 May 1912: 'Betr. Einfall Bassebja's in Süd - Rukiga' No. 1/433 replying to the Political officer's letter of 21 May 1912 No. 48/12 on a joint military co-operation against *Abatwa* opined that there was no more need to take measures against *Abatwa* living near the border after Bassebya's execution. He informed the British officers that the second Abatwa Chief Grue had been submissive for the past two years, and that he, together with the British Border Commissioner had stayed in Grue's place in December 1911. He had deliberately refrained from calling on him in the recent expedition in fear of arousing Grue's suspicions.

Not ready to take any chances, he planned to monitor and curtail *Abatwa's* activities. He was to ensure constant monitoring of Chief Grue's activities. He would achieve this by imposing a *Omutusi* chief upon *Abatwa*. In his own words, he would employ an energetic *Mtusi Mtwale* (an omututsi chief)to oversee Grue's *Abatwa* at the latter's residence. 'I consider this measure ideal in trying to stop the *Abatwa* from making raids on British territory in the future.' He planned to employ an agent 'chief' from the privileged Abatutsi ethnic group to oversee the Abatwa.

Abatutsi ethnic group had constituted the dominant ruling class in Rwanda since the inception of Rwanda Kingdom in the 15th century. What endeared this group to the colonialists was its long experience in administration as they had been the overlords in this region.

Secondly, they had allied with the German colonialists at the advent of the colonisation of Africa. As such, the Germans found it convenient in all regards to get cheap labour from them and also be able to penetrate the society at the lowest levels without any direct interaction. It also gave them legitimacy and in cases of conflicts between the colonised and the local agents, the Germans came in as just arbiters (*idem*).

The anti-colonial struggles by *Abatwa* were patriotic. They attacked colonialism and its collaborators. However, they got dispersed through the defeats and deaths of their leadership (*idem*). The fault with colonial reports is that they attributed the raids to influences by the Germans. That view presented the resisters as having been prompted from without. Katuleggi (read 'Katuregye') was reported to have died of wounds sustained in a fight with colonial forces under Abdulla (KDAR 1915-16 and KDAR 1916-17).

However, the colonial governments were determined to defeat these resistances at whatever cost. The Political Officer clarified this in his report entitled 'Fighting Among German Natives.' He advanced the need to take advantage of local conflicts:

> 'With regards to our people, there are certain clans such as Musakamba at Kigezi who are bitterly opposed to Bukamba of Mulera, and reprisals for recent raids would cause no surprise... the *Abatwa* and the unruly natives to the South of lake Bunyonyi be punished for their raid on British territory in November last, as soon as the opportunity presents itself. Mugengi, Katuleggi's brother GEA... wants bringing to his senses in a prompt and effective manner'. Report of Lieut. Kigezi of 11 October 1915 to the Political Officer on 'Fighting Among German Natives'.

Given their mode of existence and their professional linkage with the Rwandan state, *Abatwa* were above religions. As such, their resistance to colonialism was consciously organised.

Progress of the Nyabingi Movement with the 1914 War: 'Local Agent Collaboration as State Treason' Treachery

The ceaseless Nyabingi struggles against the imperialist powers were matched with the latter's unyielding recalcitrance. The question is what measures the three rivalling colonial powers employed to defeat it, stop it from expansion and stop others from flaring up. The peasants' reactions to these colonial measures have also to be analysed. What did their success depend on? What was their level of consciousness and their perception of their enemy(ies)? What explains the varied tendencies within this region at that time? Why did some individuals and groups take to collaboration with colonialism?

There was a great advancement in the anti-colonial struggle in 1914. The peasant resisters in the three colonies amalgamated their grievances and articulated them together. They organised peasants around these issues. This enabled them to reach deep into the three colonies in terms of mobilisation, recruitment and fights. This guerrilla force took maximum advantage of the defeat of Imperial Germany and the colonial borders.

The ideology of the movement was still around the colonial occupation, colonial borders, land for the state and the in-coming missions, forced labour and contributions, imposition of alien administration and administrators, laws, cultures, new religions, and so on. The colonial state had also marginalised local chiefs like Nyindo[38] and Muginga and deprived them of the opportunity

---

38   The name Nyindo was variably written by colonialists as Nindo.

to extract surplus labour from their subjects as prior to colonialism. To worsen the situation, new demands were imposed upon the peasants to support the war. Sebalijja and Abdulla were instrumental in resource mobilisation. The World War had forced the colonial state to intensify its methods of extracting resources from peasants. This had forced it to increase labour demands, food and livestock to feed the troops. The ADC had underlined that the colonial state needed 12,000 goats and sheep to feed the troops in the district per year (*op. cit.*).

The latest strategy for resource extraction was taxation, which the PC had warned against in 1913. They had been prompted to introduce taxation due to pressure for resources to meet the administration costs, support the British in the war and meet other expenses. That increased the peasants' discontent. The state used chiefs to collect it, and gave them tax rebates. Even the method of tax collection terrorised those who failed to pay it. Tax collectors unleashed terror in the peasantry through patrols for tax defaulters - *potoro*. In the process, some money paid for tax got embezzled.

Other issues revolved around the new religions and their demands, and the privileges that colonialism was according them. Yet, these privileges were acquired through looting peasants' property. Worse still, a new conflict emerged between the peasants and colonial personnel over promiscuity. This arose partly because those in colonial service did not bring their wives with them. Colonial service had subjected all of them to a bachelor life. So, they began go after the peasant women and girls.

The new development had adverse consequences. Girls became pregnant and ran away. Others were harassed by members of the society for fraternising with colonial personnel. Victims were forced to flee to Kabale Station. A new institution of prostitution began to emerge around administration centres. This was reinforced by women who came from other areas of the country, not in search of men but to eke out a living. However, as the state did not employ women in its service, the only way out became prostitution. Even colonial personnel used their state positions to force some women to sleep with them.

This was detested vehemently by the peasants. Worse still was the introduction and the spread of venereal diseases, not only among prostitutes and government personnel but also among the peasants.

The persistent armed resistance of peasants in Kyogo and its environs against British colonialism showed the peasants' determination to regain their lost independence. This led to the bloody war of March 1915.

The PC had reported in January, the previous year how Kyogo peasants had indulged in some outbreak with spears. He was optimistic that 'as soon as the rains commence, these people will devote themselves to cultivation instead of beer drinking and fighting' (WP Monthly Report of January 1914). Not long after, the ADC accused them of armed resistance. They had murdered a government agent in December, who had gone to ask them to supply their quota of forced labour. They attacked and chased away messengers for the ADC and the agent persistently, denied passage to anyone in colonial service regardless of colour or origin. They attacked the agent's *boma* twice and the colonial forces fought back. There were to heavy casualties on the side of resisters.

The Ag PCWP wrote to the on CS 12 July 1915 regarding the measures taken towards the end of March against certain Natives of Kyogo:[39]

> They have persistently refused to do any work or to bring food for the feeding of the troops, and have endeavoured to get other natives to follow their example. This was followed by the murder of one of the Agents followers, and two attacks in force were made on the Agents Boma... I requested Mr. Turpin ASP... to seize the cattle of these rebels, and thereby bring them to reason as half measures are worse than useless when dealing with savages of this type (*idem.*)

Attributing the peasant struggles to German influence, the British obscured both the reality and the basis of these struggles. They did not resist and later cross the border on the grounds that they had allied with the Germans, but because they considered the whole region as part of their land and were running away from their enemies. The proverbial route of the one being chased which is mapped out by the chaser became clear during that period.

The Meting of Politically Inspired Punishments as a Strategy to Curb Resistance

This military encounter was characterised by courageous resistance despite the peasants' weaknesses in planning, military skills and technology, organisation, and leadership. In his report, Turpin argued that Kyogo peasants had attacked the government forces with spears and arrows; declined to listen to the agent, challenging them to fight if they were men. This portrayed the peasants'

---

39   ADC Sullivan's Communication of 11 April 1915 to PCWP & PCWP to the CS on 3 February 1915 & on 12 July 1915. Vide Report by Turpin, at Ngarama to ADC, Kigezi dated 28 March 1915 on 'Kyogo Counter-Insurgency'. Also see ADC's report of 5 July 1915 and June 1916 & PCWP (vide Min. 16 in SMP 2471 D).

weaknesses as they had failed to realise that the force had come for war. He had, therefore, considered the position so dangerous and opened fire on them. Although the peasants fought bravely, they lost this battle. Even Kahondo peasants, who rushed to their aid, were repelled by the colonial forces.

In the battle, over seventy-one resisters were killed, and 180 cattle, 650 sheep and goats, and 500 loads of millet were seized. These were treated as a collective political fine on the grounds that 'the conduct of these people requires exemplary punishment... must be taught that they cannot treat the government with contempt... 1,000 goats and sheep are required monthly as food for troops in this district, at the cost of Rs. 1500/= per month' (*idem*).

This was a time when Nyindo, Semana and others were mobilising peasants into resistance in the south-western part of the district. It should be recalled that, by the time of colonial invasion, Nyindo was chief of Bufumbira. Bufumbira was highly differentiated. Chiefs extracted surplus through tributes, presents and other forms.

The government feared that Nyindo could raise a thousand spearmen in the field on short notice. So, they took careful steps not to confront him directly.

There is evidence showing that Nyindo was related to Musinga, King of Rwanda and that it was Musinga who had appointed him chief. Despite all the precautions by the colonial state not to draw Nyindo into armed struggles, Nyindo saw the dangers of colonialism and began to organise people into resistance. By then, the state had transformed him and other pre-colonial chiefs like Makobore, Muginga and Ruhayana into nominal figure heads. His first move against colonialism was in 1912/13. This was when he led a group of peasants to Rwanda, kidnapped Kalemarima, a CMS teacher and killed him. The colonial state arrested them and convicted them.[40] Nyindo was fined fifty heads of cattle; Minyana and Badutwarumu were charged twenty-five heads of cattle each and Biteraboga was fined five head of cattle. WPAR 1912/13 commended it thus; 'This I believe has had a good effect, and is expected to result in applications for redress being made to the District Officer, instead of reprisals, when an offence has been committed' (idem. Also see WPAR 1912/13).

Some of the fine was given to the widow, some was paid to eleven small chiefs, who 'rendered valuable assistance but who had not been rewarded for their assistance in dealings with the natives'. The rest was sold and credited to the state.

---

40   File: Murder of a Native Captured in German Territory. Also see PCWP's to CS of 26 March 1913 on 'Fines Imposed'.

Such heavy punishments were a source of resources to run the state. The state also wanted to encourage more people in its service and wanted to inflict pain by impoverishing the culprits. This was aimed at discouraging more resistance. Capturing livestock of resisters was aimed at depriving them of material resources essential for supporting the resistance. The heavy punishment given to Nyindo was meant to pre-empt any further rebellious activities by him. The state also wanted to placate the CMS and encourage them to come to the District to carry out the ideological and educational work. Implicitly, it was aimed at showing its capacity to protect those in its service.

The local leadership timed when the colonialists began war against each other and commenced their resistance. They had also realised that the colonial state was 'not strong enough to take rigorous action on the frontier at the commencement of the war...' Nyindo and others had been aware of their objective weaknesses vis-a-vis the joint British and Belgian forces. They were also aware of the racial differences between Europeans and Africans. Their search for allies went beyond the borders down south to the Germans. They were able to link with them through King Musinga, of Rwanda. It was clear that he had no interest in the Germans and neither did the Germans have any personal interest in him and his group. Neither could they trust any Belgian or English, who formed the object of the struggle. He had faced it earlier on and witnessed other atrocities meted on other peasants - the witch hunt, collective fines and imprisonment etc. He knew the risks involved. The only option remained the peasants and the Germans. It was under those conditions that he and his group struck some agreement with the Germans. Colonial Intelligence Reports show that two German officers visited Nyindo under the disguise of being White Fathers and sealed an agreement for cooperation. These reports showed that Germans had promised Nyindo et al more cattle and expansion of territory (WPAR 1915/16).

The resisters allied with the Germans to take advantage of the inter-imperialist conflicts. They aimed at using them to drive out the British and then break loose from the Germans. In the arrangement, the Germans wanted to use them to defeat both the British and the Belgians and then occupy that area as the new colonial power. This was a situation of manoeuverability. What is evident is that these peasants neither wanted the presence of any of these colonial powers, nor their new rule (*idem*). The reasons for the resistance go beyond the colonial view; it aimed to reinstate Nyindo.

What followed was that with the beginning of the First World War, some peasants crossed with their cattle to Belgian territory, others under Nyindo crossed to GEA. They, then, began attacking 'loyal peasants'. (WP Monthly Report of August 1914.)

Although the peasants were busy cultivating in October, the PCWP was certain that 'the condition of this part of the district must remain unsettled as long as Nyindo is at large across the frontier and from under the wing of the black eagle sending threats to our people...' (WP Monthly Report of October, 1914). It is not surprising that the resisters attacked British forces and their allies near Mulera the following month. Meanwhile, there were also other attacks led by Katuregye. These continued for months. By then, British colonialism had mistaken Katuregye's retreat and change of tactics for surrender or abandonment after his mother's arrest. (WP Reports of November and December, 1914).

The native leaders mobilised peasants into continuous resistance against colonialism. They blocked the colonial resource mobilisation in form of taxes, labour, forced contributions, and so on. To concretise this, they attacked colonial forces under agent Abdulla near Miserero's, where he had gone to collect forced labour. They reorganised and attacked again within a month. In this encounter, they attacked, killed or wounded 'loyal natives'. A section of resisters under Semana 'burnt nearly all Mushakamba's villages' and about twenty other villages of loyal chief Mutesi and Abdulla's *Boma* in October 1914, and looted their livestock:

> The District Political Officer of Kigezi reported to the CS on 9 November 1916 about Nyindo that; 'The natives of these villages were loyal and were attacked without provocation or excuse' (sic!) (File: Kigezi: Nyindo - Deportation of). Nyindo and others led new attacks against colonial forces at Kisoro and defeated them. The latter fled towards Ikumba Headquarters with losses, bruises and humiliation. The resisters then burnt the administration quarters and looted the cattle there. More bloody battles followed under the war cry that they were going to drive the Europeans out of the country (Affidavit by C.E.E. Sullivan on 6 December 1916).

The Political Officer accused them of 'circling round to cut me off from Kigezi Hill, and I was lucky to extricate myself...' He and his forces fired and shot several locals. In this encounter, Nyindo commanded over 1,200 peasant resisters, the following day, against the colonial forces and the local collaborators. Their major weapons were the people, arson, arms, belief in Nyabingi, courage and unity. Their rear base was across the borders. This battle lasted for four hours. The resisters killed many loyal natives and looted most of their livestock.

Evidently, the allies of colonialism were the immediate targets. They were the visible enemies. The real enemy was distant and sometimes not clear. These allies were regarded as an obstacle, which had to be removed before resistance could reach the principle enemy.

The state retaliated viciously. It arrested some of them and confiscated their cattle. Kirongore, Karafa, Mutago and Biunyira were sentenced to one year RI in Kampala gaol with fines of cattle and goats. They were sent to Kampala with the aim of widening their narrow outlook: 'Besides the possibilities of escape from Kabale gaol, detention here would make them realise that Kigezi is not the only district under British rule'. The four resisters lived at Namakumba. The argument was that Ndochibiri had been residing there (ADC to the PCWP on 19 April 1917). He explained how their short-term imprisonment was determined by their low level of consciousness, and mobilisation: 'These men are ignorant and superstitious semi-savages and not on the same plane as intelligent chiefs such as Nyindo.' (idem).

The Introduction and Use of the Court System to Defeat Politically Inspired Resistance

The Attorney General advised the District Magistrate/District Commissioner (DM/DC) not to imprison them under martial law in the existing circumstances of the war but to deport them on an affidavit. This was because he feared that such imprisonment would require the British to accord them some rights as prisoners of war in accordance with International Law. Secondly, it would show, internationally, British acceptance as an army of occupation and its recognition of existence of people's struggle for self-determination. As such, they were convicted under sections 148 and 149 of arson, attempted murder, theft, causing hurt, and so on, and deported after imprisonment.

The Attorney General had advised the DM/DC that under the existing colonial law, mere participation in the unlawful assembly made a person liable for all offences committed by the others in prosecution of the common object of the assembly (Ag Attorney General to CS of 16 May 1917). They were charged with lawless acts and sentenced. Mitobo was sentenced to $2^1/_2$ years RI and Karafa, Mutago, Kilongole, and Biunyira to 1 year RI each. DC informed PCWP on 23 August 1917 that rebel Semana had been sentenced to 5 years RI (*Idem*. Also see communication from PCWP to the CS of 4 May 1917 on the lawless acts and judgment, Ag Governor's letter of 16 May 1917. Ag DC to PCWP on 11 August 1917).

When Nyindo finally surrendered, his property was confiscated as punishment for resistance. His charges included fanning anarchy, attempting to murder the civil officer in charge of the district, inciting people to murder agent Abdulla on many other occasions and burning the agent's house at Kisoro, mobilising peasants to loot the Indian shop and to attack the Boer family. He was also accused of constantly attacking the civil officers and their escorts between Kumba and Rutshuru, organising peasants into resistance on the Congo border and looting the post of Goma, inciting his forces to attack, kill and rob local allies who refused to join the resistance, killing a missionary teacher and allying with Germans and Ndokibiri against the British.

Other charges included aiding Chief Katuregye in raiding and looting loyal natives, instigating numerous petty raids at various times and places, rioting, and commanding peasant resisters to kill Europeans. The police statements by Abdualla Namunye and Sulimani Ntangamalala of 7 January 1918 and 10 January 1918 confirmed these. Other statements include those by Mushakamba's son, Kanyamanza, Luwanya and Police Constable Saidi Bitensi on 8 January 1918. Statements made by six constables confirmed that the resisters overwhelmed them, defeated them, forcing them to flee to Ikumba, and that the resisters burnt their homes and captured all their cattle.

Nyindo was convicted and deported to Masindi. To silence his followers, the state replaced him with his child as their chief. 'The son is a small boy of about 6 or perhaps 7 years of age, who can do no harm for some time to come' (*Op. cit.*) He was deported for '...peace and good order in the Kigezi District ... would be dangerous to peace and good order... if he were ever allowed to return there to; and to prevent effectually his having any evil influence in this said district...' (*op. cit.*) That way, the state was able to separate the leadership from the membership, and deny them direct contact to mobilise them into advanced resistance.

Resistance Under Ndochibiri Bicubirenga

Available evidence shows that Ndochibiri and his comrades got initial military training in scientific warfare, skills and military tactics from the colonialists. They had been employed in colonial forces as *askaris*; they then deserted with arms. This was important for his career as a guerrilla leader. There he had gained military skills, training, command and knowledge of geography. He had also learnt the weaknesses of the Europeans and their weapons. He capitalised on these in the struggles that followed.

His involvement in colonial war also helped him to make more friends, comrades and allies. He was able to recruit more combatants and seal comradeship and brotherhood under the practice of blood brotherhood and other cultural practices. It also gave him opportunity to popularise people's cause and the need for self-emancipation from colonialism in the whole region.

Their other important achievement was that they acquired weapons and ammunition from dead soldiers, the reckless and from stores. Others were got from the defeated Germans on their hurried evacuation. Resisters were to capture some weapons from the enemy. These activities led the colonialists to suspect him. They tried to burn him in his house but he managed to escape with serious burns. It is alleged that his three fingers were lost in the tragedy. Ndochibiri in the local language means two fingers.

It was this event which forced his resistance into the open. He began actual organisation, politicisation and recruitment of peasants into struggle.

Another important method he employed in preparation for the struggle was of creating blood brotherhood wherever he passed. By 1916, the colonial state confessed that, 'witch doctor Ndochimbiri has been the cause of considerable trouble; in April he ravaged the country within a few miles of posts garrisoned by the UPS.B.' It was, therefore, forced to station a post of 10 special constables near the border to try to prevent his rebel activities.

The new leadership had no illusion of returning the society to the pre-colonial one. Their wide travels in the whole region and beyond and their experience with the colonialists had given them enough chance to appreciate the importance of organised administration, with a standing armed force. They aimed to rid the area of the force of occupation, and establish a strong administration aimed at defending people's interests. This was reflected in his strong, broad-based leadership, which included men and women.

Furthermore, the leadership came from various ethnicities in the whole area. This was also reflected in the membership. However, the leadership was divided over Nyabingi. Some of them believed strongly in Nyabingi and were backward-looking in terms of the society's movement, to return to the period when there would be no taxes, no chiefs, and no any other ruler other than Nyabingi. However, other members who had been in colonial service appreciated the inevitability and usefulness of some of the colonial institutions and weapons.

Anti-colonial struggles under Ndochibiri came into the open in January 1915 in the Kivu-Mulera-Kigezi region. He, too, used Nyabingi religion for military, political and ideological purposes. By 1916, the colonial state was highly paralysed by the peasant forces under his command operating in the Kivu-Murera-Kigezi region - Rwanda, Congo and Uganda.

He began by organising peasants into a powerful resistance. Ndochibiri understood clearly the importance of Nyabingi religion in enforcing unity, discipline, determination, secrecy, cultural bondings, and so on, among the fighters and the peasants who formed their sea. His maiden attack was a great blow to the government: 'a crowd of fanatical natives, with a 'Sacred' sheep as an emblem, were with difficulty driven back, with the aid of two *mitrailleuses*, after some hours fighting' (Ag DC Kigezi to Monsieur Le Commissaire de District Ruzizi - Kivu of 7 June 1919).

The two main objectives of the attack were to defeat and dislodge the Belgians and English forces from that fort and to capture arms. The ideological content of this sacred White Sheep was that it would send the Europeans away. Ndochibiri encouraged the peasant resisters that he could turn bullets into water. In January 1916, reported that peasants in Ruanda behaved in 'a disloyal' and defiant manner and, under the leadership of Ndochibiri with his sacred sheep' attacked Chahafi; and that the prophet was severely wounded (PCWP Monthly Report of January 1916). The wounding was later discovered as wishful thinking of the colonialists.

In April that year, Ndochibiri led another attack on colonial forces, looted collaborators' property and livestock and disappeared into Kayonsa forest.[41]

These resisters waged a series of incursions on colonial forces and then retreated into the peasantry, forest or across the border. What increased the colonial fears was that these 'rebels' had overwhelming peasant support, were well armed with lethal weapons and were also capturing both colonial troops and their arms. Worse still, there was a major shift in the methods of struggle from those prior to the war. These resisters employed guerrilla tactics and did not want to engage the enemy into direct combat. The PCWP monthly report of July 1916 noted that before retreat, they had lost 13 combatants; ten were killed and three captured (PCWP Report of June 1916; vide ADC to PCWP on 21 December 1916).

The state was compelled to deploy a strong, well-equipped force against this movement on the enemy's terms. The September Report noted that 'inhabitants of Ruanda are still out of control and likely to remain so until Ndochibiri and

---

41   PCWP Monthly Reports of April and May 1916. *op. cit.* Also see C. 228 II. Intelligence Reports, Lake Detachment. Also see Excerpt from Intelligence Reports, Lake Detachment. Kigezi, Punitive Expedition Against Ndochibiri.

his followers are finally dealt with, and until such time as the Belgians over the border manage to exercise control over their natives' (Telegraph of 4 November 1916 from OS):

> Rebel Chief Ndochibiri causing great trouble around Kabale in Kigezi District... Governor considers it advisable he should be dealt with at once... release one company of the police service battalion with maxims for this purpose... Lawrence suggests Mwanza Company as any punitive measure...[42]

The colonial state arranged a combined military venture with Belgian forces from Rutshuru and Kigali on the Congo and Rwanda frontiers (Telegraph from Major Lawrence, commanding UPS.B. to Commissioner of Police, Kampala on 16 December 1916, Tabora). The Commissioner of Police, Kampala awaited 'final instructions for dealing with Knochibililli's people... I hear they are well armed and this seems a good opportunity to bring them to reason - and disarm them'.[43]

The Belgian authorities were enthusiastic to revenge the murder their mail runners and two of their soldiers. Another strong force came from Mwanza under Major Lawrence.[44]

However, the resisters learnt of the expedition and foiled their plan by dispersal method before the enemy's attack. In retaliation, colonial forces arrested peasants and their leaders for assisting Ndochibiri.[45] There followed series of attacks on the expedition, leading to heavy casualties on both sides. There were

---

42   Telegraph of CS to OC Lake Detachment Ndala of 11/11/16. Vide telegraphs of 6 November 1916 of CS to Major Lawrence and Governor's telegraph of 8 November 1916.

43   Telegraph of Commissioner of Police, Police Headquarters Office, Kampala of 16 December 1916. Vide telegraph of CS to Col. Riddick of 20 December 1916 and to Political Officer, Kabale; and another to the PCWP on 22 December 1916.

44   Commissioner of Police, Mwanza to CS on 21 December 1916. Also see Telegraph from Maj. Lawrence, to Commissioner of Police, Kampala on 16 December 1916. Le Commandant le C.O. Kigali Stereng G. to DC on 28 November 1916: Coups d'occupation Commandement participation eventualle des troupes Belges à capture de N'DOKI-BILI.

45   Maj. Lawrence to the CS on 21 February 1917. *op. cit.* and O.C's report to CS on Expedition dated 17 February 1917. Vide Report on the Expedition Against Ndochibiri and Kanyarwanda on 29 March 1917.

arrests and capture of colonial troops. This increased the strife among peasants and hostilities between them and colonialism.

The state failed to achieve its objective despite all the preparations and superior arms because of the local leadership's level of organisation, intelligence network, knowledge of the terrain, and the methods of struggle; the integration of the population into this struggle and the peasants' participatory role in the struggle. Any victory was the peasants' victory. It was impossible to separate them from it. Even those who would have informed the colonial forces of the resisters' movements were denied access to such vital information.

In frustration, the colonial forces resorted to repression and the scorched earth policy 'destroying *shambas* and property as reprisals for supporting the rebels' increased insecurity (OC Expedition to CS on 17 February 1917). This had disastrous consequences. Worst among these was famine. This was because the peasants were drawn out of production. The state blamed it on the resisters: 'Owing to the former raids of Ndochibiri during the time Ruanda was supposed to be under the protection of the Belgians the people were prevented from planting adequate crops. There is now a considerable scarcity of food, and there is some fear of a famine'.[46]

Lt. Col. Riddick accepted the local leadership's superiority in both organisation and execution of armed struggles. They had used the masses as the sea, despite the colonialists' brutality, cruelty and illusions. He confessed that both Ndochibiri and Kanyarwanda were seasoned guerrilla fighters, who were outsmarting the colonial forces in the forest, in the caves, among the people, knew when and how to engage the enemy and when to retreat, had learnt about their enemies' military capacity, weapons, tactics, allies and movements, and above all won the confidence, support and love of the people. He concluded:

> ...without the power to punish the people who were aiding and abetting his escape, Ndochibiri was master of the situation, there were no roads, very hilly country look out huts and signal fires on every hill and every native as far as lay in his power apparently under Ndochibiri's control - none of whom we could touch.[47]

---

46   WP Report of November, 1916. Vide telegraph from Commissioner of Police, Mwanza to the CS, of 3 January 1917 and of 13 January 1917 and reply of 21 January 1917. Also see Telegraph of Commissioner of Police of 31 January 1917.

47   Report of the Commissioner of Police Lt. Col. Riddick to the CS dated 29 March 1917 on Expedition Against Ndochibiri and Kanyarwanda.

In despair, British forces under Lt. Col. Riddick embarked on massive arrests of peasants, accusing them of being relatives of Ndochibiri. Two women and their children were identified and arrested on the claim that they belonged to Ndochibiri. They also arrested four leaders for being Ndochibiri's confederates. In total, he arrested 37 peasants, of whom some were claimed to be Ndochibiri's wives and children. The Belgian Lieutenant rejected Riddick's proposal 'to capture and keep in custody his (Ndochibiri's) women and so on, and to punish those who helped him with food, and so on. He, therefore, released them (KDAR 1916-1917).

It was Kanyarwanda, who was forced to surrender after colonial forces captured his son and held him as a bait. He was charged with being a member of unlawful assemblies which committed murder, arson, hurt with dangerous weapons, theft and other crimes. He was convicted and sentenced to four years RI in Kampala. His fate for deportation would be decided thereafter. As a rebel, all his cattle were confiscated.[48]

That way, the state was able to separate the leadership from the membership and, deprive them of resources and ability to make war.

The British colonialists invited the Belgian forces to participate in a joint military venture in 1919. The DC notified them that the rebel Ndochibiri had appeared from Buitwa on the frontier of Kigezi at Namikumbwe, Kwa Kabango, slightly south of Chief Itembero and reminded them of 'the double danger of the movements headed by this man in that they are essentially anti-European, and supported by fanatics inculcated by NABINGI worship, which, by terrorism, renders every native his spy and a willing host... was recently joined in BUITWA by Wakiga LUMULI and LUHEMBA and the latter's wife KAIGIRIRWA,[49] a Nyabingi... are organisers of dangerous and fanatical anti-European movements in the KIVU-MLERA-KIGEZI area'.

The colonialists resolved that 'even should no disturbances occur, these rebels should be hunted mercilessly in our respective districts. Their death or capture alone will ensure peace'. The Ag DC wrote to Mon. le Commissaire de District Ruzizi - Kivu of 7 June 1919 outlining the British military plans against the peasant resisters. They had set up a military post on Birahira's in

---

48   PCWP's communication to CS of 5 July 1919. The Ag DC to PCWP on 11 August 1917 on 'Lawless Natives in Kigezi District'. The Ag DC to PCWP on 28 July 1917 & PCWP to CS on 9 August 1917 on Kanyaruanda's conviction. Also refer to File Native Affairs: Kanyaruanda.

49   The name Kaigirirwa was variably spelt by colonialists as Kaigirwa.

British Ruanda, another at Kinkizi[50]-Kayonza opposite ITEMBERO's (Kisalu). (Refer to the Map below.) This course of action was agreed to, although Belgian authorities remained sceptical:

> We shall find it extremely difficult to effect his capture since he is always informed of our slightest movements. He is held in terror by the native population by reason of his supernatural associations, and no one dares to denounce his gatherings from the additional fear of reprisals... he seldom risks remaining in villages and takes the precaution of establishing his camps in places which are far from population and kept secret, these rendezvous even he changes frequently (Communication from DC Ruzizi - Kivu to DC Kigezi, on 18/6/1919).

---

50   The area Kinkizi was also spelt by colonialists as Chinchizi.

Figure 1:   Map Showing the British and Belgian Patrols Against Nyabingi Movement in June 1919

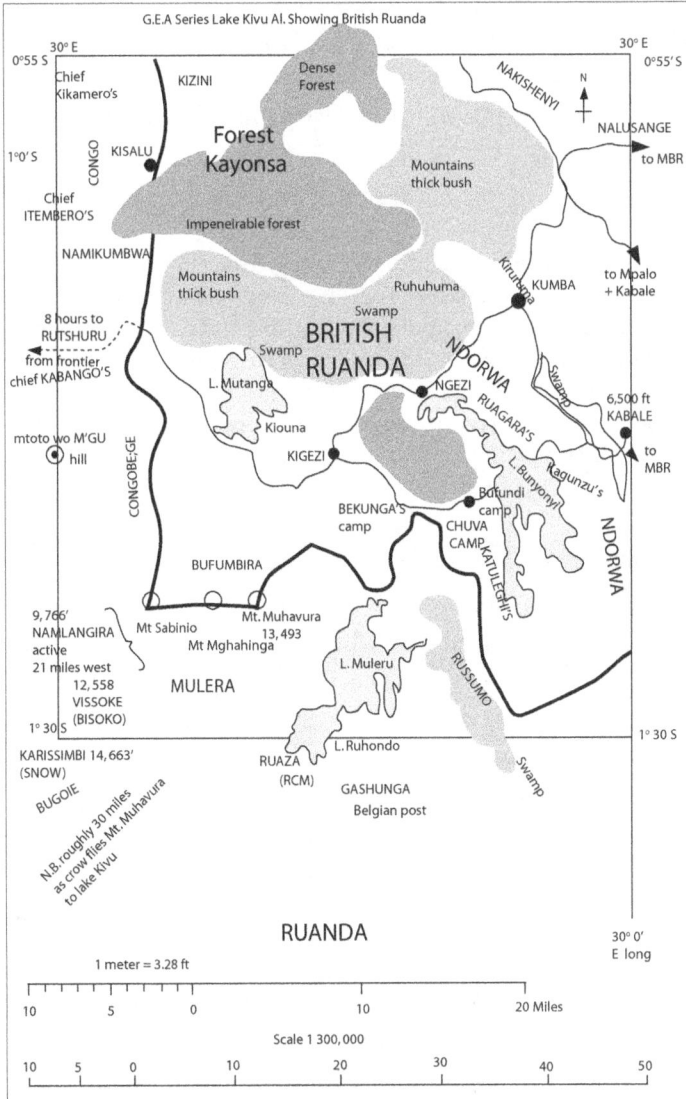

G.E.A Series Lake Kivu Al. Showing British Ruanda

30° E
0°55 S

Chief Kikamero's

KIZINI

Dense Forest

NAKISHENYI

N

30° E
0°55'S

NALUSANGE
to MBR

1°0'S

CONGO

KISALU

Forest Kayonsa

Mountains thick bush

Chief ITEMBERO'S

Impenetrable forest

NAMIKUMBWA

Mountains thick bush

Ruhuhuma

Kirubusha

KUMBA

to Mpalo
+ Kabale

8 hours to RUTSHURU
from frontier chief KABANGO'S

Swamp

BRITISH RUANDA

Swamp

NDORWA

NGEZI

Swamp

6,500 ft
KABALE

L. Mutanga

RUAGARA'S

mtoto wo M'GU hill

CONGOBEGE

Kiouna

KIGEZI

L. Bunyonyi

Ragunzu's

to MBR

BEKUNGA'S camp

Butundi camp

CHUVA CAMP

KATULEGHI's

NDORWA

BUFUMBIRA

9,766'
NAMLANGIRA active
21 miles west

Mt Sabinio

Mt. Muhavura
13,493

Mt Mghahinga

L. Muleru

RUSSUMO

12,558
VISSOKE
(BISOKO)

MULERA

1° 30 S

1° 30 S

KARISSIMBI 14,663'
(SNOW)

RUAZA
(RCM)

L. Ruhondo

GASHUNGA
Belgian post

Swamp

BUGOIE

N.B. roughly 30 miles as crow flies Mt. Muhavura to lake Kivu

RUANDA

30° 0'
E long

1 meter = 3.28 ft

10   5   0   10   20 Miles

Scale 1 300,000

10   5   0   10   20   30   40   50

Source: *Uganda National Archives.*

The PCWP confirmed in November that the peculiar geographical features and the power of blood brotherhood among these wild and backward peoples make it impossible to rely on the local natives at all (WP Report of November 1919). Van de Ghinste informed the DC, Kigezi on 23 June that a Belgian force of

25/30 rifles under a European was going to patrol the frontier so as to cut off the retreat of the Ndochibiri rebels. They were going to patrol the frontier between Rutezo and Mt. Nkabwe (Communication of DC Van de Ghinste to DC Kigezi of 23 June 1919 in reply to DC Kigezi of the previous day 22 June 1919). He communicated to the DC Kigezi that Chiefs Kabango and Itembero had feigned ignorance of the movements of Ndochibiri that morning (Van de Ghinste, DC Ruzizi - Kivu, Rutchuru on 23 June 1919). It was that night that the colonial forces caught up with the top leadership of the resistance and wiped it out:

> ...strong force rebels crossed frontier into KAYONSA nineteenth ... enticed from forest and attacked KUMBA three hours north KABALE ... their retreat cut off and gang entirely dispersed leaving leaders NDOCHIMBIRI and LUHEMBA instigator NAKISHENYI rebellion, with two other rebels dead in our hands ... 'Sacred' Nabingi sheep captured together with two rifles, bayonets, bows, arrows and British and German ammunition ... Our casualties – one wounded (D.C's telegraph of 24 June 1919 and his letter of 25 June 1919).

The death of these resisters was celebrated by the colonialists throughout the GLR - in Entebbe, Kampala, Kigali, Rutshuru – and also in England. The jubilation for this victory was clearly manifested in the various communications as they now hoped for an immediate permanent peace, which was not to be.

It is of interest that Ndochibiri's head was cut off and hurriedly despatched to the British Museum for public display. Incidentally, it has never been returned and no African has ever asked for it. The death of the rebel leaders was seen as a great success for colonialism. In the PCWP's words, had they not been so promptly and successfully dealt with, 'within a month, we should... have had very serious native trouble in Rukiga and perhaps in Ruanda also' (PCWP to CS on 5 July 1919). So, it was celebrated in Kabale where they exposed Ndochibiri and Luhemba's bodies. Ndochibiri's two-fingered hand was cut off and circulated in public 'to assure publicity of the death'. They also burnt to ashes the captured 'sacred' white sheep publicly at Kabale. These were aimed at proving their death to the public, to demystify and discredit Nyabingi, and restrain the peasants from Nyabingi resistances (*op. cit.* Refer to nationalistic songs on these struggles under Ndochibiri).

The DC confessed '... considering the 600 rebels known to have crossed into British territory with the Nabingi this month, and the simultaneous presence of its fighting leaders around Kabale, I can only repeat that I am of the honest conviction that a very serious general rising organised by a powerful anti-

European 'religious' society, has been most narrowly averted.'...it is difficult to realise the immense importance locally of the death of this rebel who has defied two governments for five years and was a leader of an anti-European secret society which has terrorised the RUANDA - RUKIGA County for four generations (sic!) (*op. cit.*)

After the death of Ndochibiri and others, the Kigezi DC on 26 June 1919 replied to the PCWP's letter of 5 June 1919 on 'Defence Scheme'. He expressed real fears in his letter. He argued that on the successful conclusion of operations against the rebel Ndochibiri, it was necessary to study the possibility of further disturbances organised by the Nyabingi society, and, in this connection, the entire indefensibility of the administrative station at Kabale. He argued, 'The Nabingi cult, since at least the end of the 18th century, has been a foreign element throughout Rwanda. It has been opposed to the established native religion. It has been revolutionary in method and anarchic in effect. On the advent of the Protecting Powers (sic!) the European element was included, equally with two other privileged classes of *Watussi* and *Watwa*, within the scope of its virulence. By means of an unusually developed knack for witchcraft, in which hypnotic suggestion plays a leading part, the country within the sphere of its operations is completely terrorised.'[51]

They were aware that this was a temporary set-back on the movement since the leadership had all the reasons to fight on. However, they imputed wrongly the actors' main driving force to revenge and religious fanaticism '...the same dangerous and illogical problem of religious fanaticism the world-over' (*idem*).

Factors Underlying this Movement's Longevity

It is important to understand some of the factors that contributed to the sustenance of the guerrilla movement for so long. Firstly, the resisters used strategic places like forests in the district and at the border as their bases. They had a mastery of the terrain, weaponry and developed sophisticated, mobile guerrilla tactics. As the DC argued, to defeat them demanded luring them from the forest. Secondly, they attacked all in colonial service. That way, they defeated joint Anglo-Belgian forces.

---

51 Memorandum of J. E. Philipps, Ag DC Kigezi to the PCWP on 26 November 1919, in reply to the P.C's letter dated 5 June 1919 on Defence Scheme; & copied to the Commissioner of Police, Kampala, Uganda.

The colonialists got scared of the movement which was '...deeply rooted throughout North Ruanda and Ndorwa. Thus, ideal means and conditions are created for both the fomenting and organisation of rebellion, and (the most serious feature of all) absolute secrecy ensured.' Worse still, it had defeated the successive offensives by the successive Rwandese kings for over a century. They were scared as it did '... not shrink from organising attacks in force on fortified positions held by troops, as witness the attack upon Chahafi fort held by Anglo-Belgian troops (a few days after a strong German attack with guns had been repulsed) in January 1915. Some 2,000 fanatical natives were engaged, and were only driven off after over six hours close fighting.' The colonial government was compelled to admit that 'anything, therefore, in the nature of purely military force appeared futile'. So, the colonialists formed a joint Anglo-Belgian patrol along the impenetrable forest (DC's letter of 25 June 1919). The British government was compelled to broaden its social base among the peasants and deploy many of them to spy for it and monitor all activities of the Nyabingi Movement.

Thirdly, the resisters used the peasants in the three colonies as their sea. These also formed their intelligence network. They used watch-fires, songs, dances and other sounds to communicate information about the enemy. Colonial efforts to render this communication system useless met with limited success. Whenever pursued, they would apply guerrilla tactics of dispersal, leading the enemy to confusion. Therefore, the resistance created real fears in the colonialists.

The resisters exploited all existing social and cultural practices such as blood brotherhood, Nyabingi religion and its rites for making and sealing new alliances, recruiting new fighting forces, other active and supportive purposes, and punishing waverers, sell-outs and betrayers. This is best exemplified by one of those in its top leadership- Ruhungo. His victims included an *askari* he had killed in Rwanda (*op. cit.*) Another interesting example is of two domestic boys who killed their 'master' for betraying the Nyabingi Movement. They burnt him with the house and fled across the border (*op. cit.*)

Again, there was increased cooperation in both membership and leadership. The best instance is of Kaigirirwa, a priestess, who was in high command with men. She commanded a strong peasant armed force of about 600 fighters from Congo into Uganda and stayed with them in the forest awaiting instructions from Ndochibiri and 14 other top leaders already around Kabale. She took over the movement's leadership immediately after their death.

Also, Ndochibiri derived his strength mainly from large numbers of peasants joining the movement. In fact, he was able to convince many people in colonial service to join the struggle. The best examples were peasants of Rwagara hill - former allies of colonialism. He formed a bond with them through blood brotherhood and other cultural bondings, and mobilised them into resistance twice in early 1919 against forced labour, taxation, *inter alia*. He was able to recruit them into the struggle as both supporters and active participants, drawing on their social grievances.

The leadership's capacity of organisation and military strategies were exemplified even in the last encounter. By the time their forces, under Kaigirirwa, crossed into Uganda, Ndochibiri and 14 other leaders were busy doing political work around Kabale. They were making military plans and preparations for the next offensive, preparing arms, carrying out initiations, broadening their cause, carrying out cultural and Nyabingi rites, mobilising and encouraging the peasants. They were cementing their faith and courage, using Nyabingi, patriotism and blood brotherhood and all other relations that could be exploited. Surprisingly, 'not a whisper of their presence reached any alien native, much less any political agents connected with the government'.

In terms of modern weaponry, they had over 25 rifles during that night. They maintained their patriotic stance even in death. They neither surrendered nor allowed the enemy to capture their guns. Instead, they portrayed great heroism and bitter hatred against colonialism as they resisted it until death. The DC acknowledged, 'their rifles they deliberately broke, shouting as they died, "we will not look upon a white man, he shall not have our iron but a curse!"' (*op. cit.*)

One of their main military tactics was arson. Arson as a weapon is easy to apply. One method they used was to tie a bundle of fire on an arrow and then shoot it at the target. This weapon caused great fear among the colonialists. 'In detail, native tactics locally massed attack just before dawn. As at Nakishenyi, houses are burnt to 'bolt' the occupants. All station buildings are mud and thatch. No approach to water can be commanded by rifle fire from any of these, least of all the Office. There is no '*boma*'. Water is a mile away. Any force fighting its way to water would find itself in a swamp with mountains on either side.' The resisters applied this weapon very often either individually or collectively. The colonial authorities also feared that a section of resisters could burn the headquarters and claim that it was Nyabingi which had burnt them and chased away the government (Report of PCWP of 28 October 1920 on the Safety of Kabale Station).

The Commissioner of Police, Kampala on 17 July 1919 suggested the construction of a cemented underground water tank by the PWD and the roofing with corrugated galvanized iron (Ag CS to Director of PWD, Kigezi Station. Ag CS to the Director of PWD of 24 July 1919: Kigezi Station). Given that fire was a cheap but effective weapon, the district colonial authorities also used it widely against the natives (Ag DC to PCWP on 26 June 1919. File: WP Kabale Station, Defence Precautions). This led to loss of property and credibility in the area (*op. cit.* PCWP to Commissioner of Police on 7 July 1919). In this light, the DC wrote to the Commissioner of Police and the PCWP underlining the urgency of choosing a site, a boma and constructing the District Government Headquarters of Kigezi in a defensible position, with a water supply within a reasonable range of fire:

> No natural cover is available. The District Office and Police Store, which would be the first object of the officer in charge to preserve as containing specie and ammunition respectively, are situated on the lowest spur of a steep mountain range rising steadily for some five miles behind it. The two officers' houses are on the mountain slope ½ of a mile above. Early in the proceedings the more isolated buildings would be burnt. There is no receptacle in the station for storing water larger than a bucket. ... There is no natural position or cover affording a field of fire, nor water, upon which to base a reliable defensive scheme except by instantly abandoning all Government buildings and taking up a position in the open.

> It is difficult in normal times to maintain the telephone line intact, permanent guard huts and patrols being necessary to prevent its being cut. In any case, from 12 noon to 8 a.m. the terminal is earthed at Mbarara. The telephone therefore is scarcely a factor for consideration.

> ... I feel it essential to point out in this connection that Kabale Station, as it stands, is wholly indefensible against any kind of attacks which might be expected, i.e. a sudden and fanatical night attack in force. The Nabingi organisation is comparatively well supplied with arms retained by deserters and discarded by the Germans themselves in Ruanda during their hurried evacuation.

DC had noted the guerrilla tactics of these resisters:

> Speaking generally the rebels expressly avoid fighting and retire into the forest or across international frontiers whence they dart out to raid and retire before any news can even reach the station (*op. cit.*)

He therefore recommended alterations of Kabale Station and an increase of the police establishment to seventy.

Some natives sought individual solutions to the social crisis. Some fought on individual basis, committed murders or suicides in utter anger or in despair. Others refused to pay tax or to provide free labour as groups or as individuals. A good example was Kayonza and Kinkizi.

As reported, 'Several villages of criminal fugitives and malcontents are situated just across the Belgian frontier... At the first sign of tax collection or labour demands the greater portion of the people prepare to move across the frontier'. The government instituted an Anglo-Belgian Patrol in 1921 to collect taxes on both sides of the border (WP April 1919 Report. KDAR, 1921). While some migrated across the borders, others opted for opportunistic alternatives - collaborating with the colonialists for material rewards and other benefits.

The colonial states could not accept this. Using references to the Map of German East Africa, Lake Kivu, the DC Kigezi on 30 April 1921 reported about the Anglo-Belgian Patrol on the Frontier of Bufumbira County in January 1921. He reported that there were 'almost continuous series of frontier disturbances by lawless elements' in the area stretching from the South-West of Lake Bunyonyi to the East of Lake Chahafi. He noted that these lawless elements were using this portion of joint frontier separating Bufumbira County and Belgian Rwanda to evade obligations to their lawful chiefs, execution of justice and payment of tax. He, therefore, wrote to the Resident of Belgian Rwanda on 16 December 1920 soliciting his cooperation in a joint patrol of the frontier for purposes of maintaining order and enforcing Poll Tax Regulations.

The Resident of Belgian Rwanda replied in the affirmative on 21 December 1920. He directed M. Douce, Chef de Poste of Ruhengeri to meet the British authorities at Chahafi and work out the details. He met with the ADC of Kigezi, Captain Persse. The two were to head the operations on their sides of the frontier.

As the main salient was on the Belgian territory, the Belgians had to provide more troops and logistics. The British attention was mostly confined to patrolling the outer part of the salient and guard possible bolt-holes. The Belgian administration wanted to effect the arrest of certain criminals (read 'resisters') like the murderer of Fr. Pere Loupias, and so on. It reported that spies had furnished them with some useful information regarding the whereabouts of the wanted persons.

Persse and Douce worked out at the Old Fort of Chahafi on 5 January 1921. A patrol of 8 police under Andrea had been despatched on 3 January 1921 and it arrived on 5 January 1921. Its task was to prevent fugitives from crossing the border. Captain Persse commanded a patrol of 12 Uganda Police while the Belgian force consisted of 24 *askaris* with about 300 followers under their sub-chiefs. It was concluded on 11 January 1921 though the wanted criminals were not captured. They instead dealt with civil matters of settling cases of frontier thefts of cattle.

The DC wanted more of these joint patrols and expressed confidence that the act of Anglo-Belgian uniforms again seen in these parts operating in close cooperation and harmony 'would have an excellent effect among our recalcitrant frontier population' (DC, Kigezi District, 30 April 1921).

The Territorial Spread of the Resistance

Contrary to the wishful anticipation of peace in the District for some months, the Nyabingi resisters did not sit to mourn the dead leaders. They understood the critical demands of the struggle and the need to promote it. As such, they intensified it. To concretise this, there was a strong, armed force of Nyabingi militants (whom the colonial adminisrators termed 'malcontents') that assembled near Lake Bunyonyi on 26 June 1919. The DC appealed for an immediate reinforcement and he received twenty policemen. These policemen had to augment the security patrols in Kigezi till December (See DC's letter to the Commissioner of Police of 26 June 1919; vide his telegraph of July to the PCWP on the same issue).

Seven 'compatriots of the late Ndochibiri', who tried to conscientise the peasants were beaten off at once by British forces. On the same day, 'there was a simultaneous gathering at Itembero's (Congo-Belge frontier) of Nabingi malcontents with 28 rifles'.

Both the Belgian and British authorities responded with scorched earth policy and strategic hamlets. They burnt the villages of Kisalu, Kayonza and Kinkizi, and evacuated peasants from the border areas. They opined that 'while one cannot hope for any permanent result from this section, it has nevertheless had a salutary effect' (*op. cit.*)

The murder of Biramba and the burning of his body by his domestic boys illustrates some of the ways the resisters dealt with those who betrayed the struggle - the so-called 'pragmatists' or, in colonial language, 'progressives'. The PCWP recounted with profound shock and dismay:

On the night of July 31/1 August the Ruanda Chief BIRAMBA of Bunagana was murdered by two servants who were sleeping in the same house adjoining that of Agent Abdulla. They burnt the house over his body and fled to the Congo. BIRAMBA was a useful progressive chief who had accompanied me twice on tour and given under secrecy much valuable information by the Nabingi movement. The latter have announced the act as one of vengeance on an 'informer' (*op.cit.*)

This resistance continued despite the mishaps that the movement was encountering. The DC Kigezi notified the PCWP on 24 September 1919 of the continuous resistance in various forms: passive, military harassment and attacks by the Nyabingi Movement. In chronologising their activities, he revealed that they had carried out border cattle raids by night in the south-west Bunyonyi, then crossed. The following day, Kitumu, the successor of Ndochibiri crossed with other resisters into Bufumbira to Magenge's area. This had been followed by an armed encounter the following day. This caused casualties and the capture of one Nyabingi Movement leader near Kadio's area. The resistance had continued the following day on Kisolo hills. Its membership included Nyabingi resisters from Uganda and the Congo, under the leadership of Nyindo's ex-Katikiro. (Telegraph from the Districter, Kigezi to the PCWP on 24 September 1919).

The colonial government was forced to exempt certain areas like Butare, Bufundi and parts of Bufumbira from taxation for fear of resistance (WP Report of November 1919). It was clear to them that 'the basis of all negative politics is that alien Government is only temporary... is also a basis of NABINGI 'religion' (Sic!) (DC to PCWP of 17 September 1920. Also see his communication to the CS on 1 October 1920).

There was a passive rebellion in Ikumba area. The DC went to investigate it and he attributed its causes to the drinking season and the Nyabingi Movement. It, therefore, intensified political work and organisation of the District. The PCWP telegraphed the DC on 24 September 1920 instructing him to deal with that Nyabingi organisation 'quietly and efficiently on lines similar to previous occasions obtaining co-operation from the Belgians on their side'.

The PCWP to the DC on 29 October 1920 blamed the DC for not using all available means to suppress the disturbances. He told him to plan repression by listing 'all chiefs, headmen and people known to have been implicated and from time to time... effect arrests and mete out punishment on individuals; such action would have a very good effect on untutored people as they would understand that the Government's arm though slow is long... These disturbances are the normal work of your district; as time goes on and our influence extends they will decrease but must be expected for some time.'

He enlisted the military services of an ex–sergeant major and had sent him reinforcements. They had captured two rifles and other weapons.

The PC warned against strong punitive measures against the resisters as this 'would bring temporary success'. The DC's defence was that punitive measures were necessary to quell all international disorders.[52] The resisters employed the weapon of propaganda to explain the phenomena. For examples, new diseases like dysentery and influenza were lumped together with the poll tax and other colonial impositions as plagues introduced maliciously to wipe out people (KD September Report. Vide Communication of the CS to the Principal Medical Officer on 7 November 1919).

The natives were extremely cautious of the colonial motives. They understood the colonial hunger for people's land and other resources. As such, Nyabingi *abagirwa* and resisters refused protected spring water in 1929 and warned peasants against 'a sinister scheme to poison the water and the people, so that the whites in Kenya could seize the land!' (KDAR 1929)

Philipps' allegation that Nyabingi was non-indigenous because of being anti-European was aimed at discrediting it at a theoretical level. It also aimed to deprive the Nyabingi Movement of any legitimacy to mobilise peasants and articulate their interests. Hidden in this argument is the misconception that Nyabingi religion was as foreign as European colonialism in the region and so, neither of them had the right and legitimacy to articulate peasant interests.

Even if their argument was true, the major issue would be its relevance to the lives of the peasants and how it addressed their interests. Furthermore, the natives' choice of Nyabingi and their involvement in the Nyabingi Movement dispels colonial defences. In other words, the natives had the capacity to think, judge, decide and act. They were not sacks of potatoes.

Colonial Methods to Defeat Nyabingi Movement

The state applied various methods to defeat the Nyabingi Movement. These included force, rewards and prices on leaders' heads, persuasion, deportation, plunder and destruction of resources to handicap peasants from making war. The major method was, intensifying military expeditions, using local allies

---

52   D.C's telegraphs to PCWP of 6 October 1920; 9 October 1920 and of 12 October 1920. Also refer to D.C's report of 17 September 1920 about the same issue.

and agents from different ethnicities. The latter were normally rewarded with resources captured from peasants, power and promises.

To this end, the state deemed it 'desirous of adequately rewarding those who have done so well on this occasion 'in nipping the incipient rising in the bud... desire to offer encouragement to others to emulate their good example, if we should have occasion to call for volunteers again, in the event of Kaigirirwa attempting reprisals for the loss of her husband and brother-in-law'. They expected her to attack soon 'in the hope of driving from her native country the hated European'. It, therefore, awarded substantial rewards for Nziraba Muzale, Alibatusede and Bigirwenda and booked Sebalijja for 'some non-pecuniary recognition'.

The Governor sanctioned rewards of sixty pounds to them in recognition of their services for saving the protectorate of the loss of many lives and heavy expenditure by their action. Sebalijja was awarded with the title 'Kago' and a medal (DC Kigezi Philipps to PCWP of 25 June 1919, No. 55. Ag CS to Deputy Governor on 16 July 1919, 18 July 1919. Governors' Authority on 22 July 1919).

The colonial state wanted to smash the resistance before it spread to the whole area. It had everything to lose; and it was its duty to restore and maintain law and order. It also had to prove its capacity to smash any resistance, contain the situation and protect the people. It employed brutal force and repression on both membership and leadership; mounted military expeditions either individually or in cooperation with other colonial forces, massacred peasants, witch-hunted resisters and Nyabingi worshippers, and so on. It had no mercy, carried out operations, arrested en masse, carried out public executions both in Kabale and Kampala, imposed heavy fines with long-term rigorous imprisonment, deported without trial, and so on. It destroyed property and created utmost insecurity. It extradited resisters and suspects and intensified retribution. There was also the joint Anglo-Belgian cooperation in intelligence and sharing of information about rebels, the military and patrols:

> While foreseeing at the time the possibility of further disturbances ... I had hoped that the recent severe blow to the movement would preclude active preparations for at least some months.... Meanwhile as the storm-centre is invariably reported to be the same frontier forest areas as before, in proximity to the KIGEZI-RUTSHURU road through British Ruanda, I am again closing that county to all but your regular armed courier. I should be grateful if you give publicity to this order.

... 'This measure in conjunction, with surveillance of paths, was one of the principal means which enabled us to prevent NDOCHIBILIS' communications with his main body in the forest, thus isolating him and facilitating his destruction.[53]

Early in 1919, we were constantly threatened by the armed raids of Ndoki-mbili and his murderous bands. Their headquarters were, near the frontiers, in the mountains north-west and south-west of Lake Bunyonyi. So, soon as one ordered porters or moved out from Kabale, they were informed before hand of one's movements. I, therefore, conceived of the idea of establishing myself on a small centrally situated island in Lake Bunyonyi, whence, under cover of night and the usual dense mists, one might be able, unostentatiously and by canoe, to strike at either extremity of the lake. The secrecy and mobility thus attained was in fact a principal factor in the final cutting off and wiping out of Ntochi-mbili.

In order that the island could not be regarded as a Public Rest Camp and its Chief Value (namely secrecy of movement) thereby destroyed, I paid (and gladly) from my own pocket both the compensation to occupiers and for the clearing, planting and building which I undertook. It was thus regarded by everyone merely as a not very serious hobby... (*op. cit.*)

Rewarding Local Collaborators as a Strategy

The colonial state broadened local allies, collaborators and spies among the peasants, with attractive remuneration, promises, favours and exemptions from certain obligations and demands. Religious converts played a significant role as informers. As will be recalled, agents from outside Kigezi formed the social base of colonialism right from its invasion.

However, due to increased Nyabingi attacks, the state realised the need to dispense with these alien agents by creating and broadening a local social base. Consequently, it gradually created a social base, first among peasants under lineage leaders like Mutambuka, Rwagara, Mushakamba, Mizerero, Ruhayana, Duybumba, and Ruzindana. These were remunerated with political posts, livestock, and so on. Gradually, it began recruiting individuals in its service from all sections of society. Spies, like Sebisorora Sowedi and Mutasa, were instrumental in gathering intelligence information on Nirimbirima, Ruzira-

---

53   The Ag DC of Kigezi, to the Commissaire de district, Ruzizi-Kivu on 5 July 1919 and copied it to le Resident du Rwanda, Kigali and to PCWP on movement of Nyabingi-ites. This was in pursuance of Philipp's earlier letter to him dated 24 June 1919.

kuhunga and Kabango. Their incrimination of the three in the complicity with the Nyabingi Movement testifies to the success of this colonial scheme. The new social base was recruited mainly by Baganda agents, or under their recommendations and the missionaries' recommendation.

By 1923, the district colonial authorities were including some local people in the chiefly service but at the lower levels as the table below shows;

Table 2

County	Sub-County	Names of Head	Region of Origin
Rukiga	County Agent	E.W. Kagubala	Buganda
	Bukinda	Stephen Musoke	Buganda
	Butale	Alikiso Zikale	Buganda
	Kikungiri	Stephano Alibaziwonnye	Buganda
	Nyakishenyi	Abdullah Namunye	Buganda
	Maziba	Aliseni Walusimbi	Buganda
	Kitanga	Alipo Salagumba	Buganda
	Nyarushanje	Ibrahim Njuba	Buganda
	Ikumba	Joseph Kalimarwaki	Kigezi
Rujumbura	County Chief	Kalegesa	Kigezi
	Ruhinda	Erasto Musoke	Buganda
	Kagunga	Benedicto Daki	Buganda
	Buyanja	Nadanairi Muwereza	Buganda
	Kassese	Leo Mabulo	Buganda
	Kebisoni	Yafesi Wavamuno	Buganda
	Nyakagyeme	William Biteyi	Kigezi
	Kivumbo	Ndabahwerize	Kigezi
Kinkizi	County Agent	Sulimani Ntangamalala	Buganda
	Kirima	Mukombe	Kigezi
	Kambuga	Lwamusisero	Buganda
	Rwanga	Nekemiah Kityo	Buganda
	Kayonza	Muginga	Kigezi
	Rugyeyo	Tilugira	Kigezi
Bufumbira	Country Chief	Nirimbilima	Kigezi
	Bufundi	Gelazi Kimenya	Buganda
	Kigezi	Kanyamihigo	Kigezi

County	Sub-County	Names of Head	Region of Origin
	Nyarusiza	Mizerero	Kigezi
	Busanza	Kisanabagabo	Kigezi
	Chahi	Ndemeye	Kigezi
	Bukimbiri	Ziribugiri	Kigezi

Source: *File: Counties – Chiefs – Divisions and Titles of, Uganda National Archives*

The domination of chiefs from outside Kigezi continued to create discontent among the colonised people.

The informers and those who remained neutral in the struggles were opposed to the Nyabingi Movement. Many sold out for opportunistic reasons. Some wanted immediate wealth in form of livestock, posts, and so on. It was this group that claimed to be pragmatic and argued that they saw nothing wrong with the British forces that were better than Belgians and Germans. However, they undermined the Nyabingi Movement as they sold out, and gave away most important secrets about Nyabingi to the enemy. This facilitated the enemy to understand its adversaries' strengths and weaknesses and how to defeat it. On the other hand, resisters could not get access to vital information about the colonialists.

The state was receptive to any individual, group or lineage that collaborated or showed positive signs to cooperate. There were collaborators from different lineages and ethnic groups like *Abatutsi* and *Abahutu*, who had deep-rooted differences, being united by one colonial master.

Another important thing to note is the role of religious converts. The Muslims played a dominant role among its first cadreship. This was mainly because the first foreign religion in Buganda was Islam. Islam had been introduced hand in hand with trade. When colonialism came, these converts had a broader knowledge and experience of the world than others. This was a windfall for the colonisers.

On the other hand, the Catholic and Protestant Missionaries that came just before colonialism spent much time in wrangles with each other and also wasted too much time at the palace instead of carrying out their work.

On their arrival in Kigezi, the colonisers used Protestant converts headed by Sebalijja to cause crises by fuelling enmity there. These included Sulaimani Ntangamalala, Abdulla Namunye, Saidi Bitensi, Sowedi Sabada, Zambatisi Jute, Luvayagwe, and so on. (*op. cit.*) These remained very useful in the running of the state machinery until the colonial state and the new European religions had created a new cadreship from the area. The colonial state had to forcefully use the new religions to carry out their ideological role.

The colonialists, being far-sighted, did not entertain illusions. They expected that 'a further religious war of revenge will be undertaken by this cult at a not very distant date'. The PCWP suggested a new site for Kigezi Headquarters with a '*Boma*' in July as he was 'fully alive to the fact that incendiarism on the part of fanatical followers of the late Ndochibiri, the late Luhemba and the still existing witch doctoress Kaigirwa is a real danger and not to be scoffed at' (PCWP to CS on 7 July 1919).

They were certain that the leadership under Kaigirirwa would be able to explain the causes of this death in light of religion as the will of Nyabingi for delinquencies in religious duties and would call on all the membership for revenge. 'It is the same dangerous and illogical problem of religious fanaticism world over'. They anticipated an attack.

Intesification of the Persecution of the 'Nyabingi-ites'

There were new developments in response to colonial appeals 'that all indications of Nyabingi, witchcraft or incantations be reported immediately to the DC in person'. This was contained in a document entitled 'Detail of Events leading to implication of NIRIMBIRIMA WITH NABINGI CONJURATION by DC including evidence'. Local allies like Sebitaka, Rwakazina, Mizerero, Sebisorora had incriminated Nirimbirima, Ruzira-kuhunga and Kabango of the Nyabingi Movement and for allying with Ndochibiri against colonialism.

The Belgian Authorities' wrote to the ADC on 16 April 1923 attesting that they had discharged Kabango from chieftainship at KITAGOMA for political reasons, that they had always had apprehensions as to his connections with the Nyabingi Sect without obtaining positive proof. Lulebuka and Lwakazina gave similar evidence on 21 April 1923. DC/DM reported to PCWP on 23 April 1923 that the two persons that he had sent to gather information on the above case, Sowedi and Mataza gave a lot of incriminating evidence.[54]

Ruzira-kuhunga[55] was arrested on these charges. His arrest caused some disturbance. They were attacked by eight peasant resisters while bringing him

---

54   Also see the DC's letter of 23 April 1923 to le Resident du Ruanda Kigali (See evidence of the three signed by E.E. Filleul as DM on 24 April 1923).

55   The name Ruzira-kuhunga was variably spelt as Luzira-kuhunga.

(*idem*. Also see communication of DM to PCWP of 27th April). Colonialism was resolved that Nyabingi, witchcraft or *'okubandwa'* activities should be nipped in the bud and not be permitted to pass without the most exacting secret enquiries being made about Ruzira-kuhunga's practice of Nyabingi (DC to PCWP on 28 April 1923.)

Ruzira-kuhunga's conviction under 'The Criminal Law (Witchcraft) Ordinance 1912 was certain, only awaiting evidence from Kigali and Bufumbira 'to prove anti-European inclinations against him'. He argued that 'such beliefs against Nirimbirima that have been proved to exist amongst *Abahutu* can have nothing but a retrograde effect on the general native administration in Rwanda. The native government here is only in the embryo stage and is very fragile and easily disturbed, and the fact that they do not trust their chief can have nothing but a deterrent effect on the advancement of these people' (DC to PCWP on 23 April 1923). He was convicted and sentenced to three years RI at Kampala gaol with a fine of Shs. 100/=. On his release, he was to be deported for at least another year in a distance not less than 250 miles from Kigezi. However, Ruzira-kuhunga maintained his struggles while in prison. He attacked a warder with a hoe, hit him in the head and neck and split his skull. These led to his death sentence, which was later commuted to twenty years RI (KDAR 1924).

Kabango was considered to be 'a pawn in the Nabingi game, but at the same time a deterrent influence to the rapid advancement of this part of the district...' He, too, was accused of leading Nirimbirima into resistance, 'laziness, and bred the distrust of his District officers'. He was, therefore, repatriated to Belgian territory.

The DC concluded: 'And thus ends the reign of another 'Nabingi' authority whose evil influence is so retrograde to the natives of the district'. The colonial sanction of banishment for witchcraft was only abolished by the Constitutional Court in Abuki's case. Among the panel of the judges was Justice P.M. Tabaro.

The PCWP discovered too late how deep Nirimbirima had penetrated the colonial system and the political implications of deposing him and charging him in court. The colonialists wanted to avoid unnecessary grievances which would form bases for Nyabingi resistance. After all, Nirimbirima was a colonial creation. They dropped all charges against Nirimbirima. The explanation was that Nirimbirima had been in office for only two and half years:

The history of Kigezi does not go back very far (Sic!) and... action in a similar case essential in another District might be unwise in the present state of development that yours is in ... no great harm if we leave this matter for another two months ... it might be advisable to issue propaganda to all chiefs in Bufumbira that as a result of Luzirakuhunga's case the Government believe that other chiefs and people in Bufumbira were partly implicated and warning them that the government are determined to put down Nabingi and severely punish anyone practising it whether chief or peasant.

We want to teach these chiefs rather than turn them out and that it would not be easy to find others and if we did they might not be any better. Dismissal as rule makes a native hopeless punishment and maintenance in his position sometimes makes him strongly...

PCWP cautioned the DC against the use of force. He disclosed how he had learnt through 'experience how difficult they are... although a prosecution is justifiable and a conviction probable we have made any great progress in the District and might we not be at rather a dead end?' (PCWP to DC of 24 August 1923).

There were some important developments. The first one was that despite the missionary education and his friendship with Dr. Sharp of CMS, Nirimbirima still worshipped Nyabingi religion and communed with its *abagirwa*. Secondly, he managed to penetrate the colonial system through the DC's Clerk, Yoasi, to get access to important information about himself. This gave him the opportunity to prepare himself and hide all traces of Nyabingi practices. The state realised this too late. It was Yoasi who got dismissed (*idem*).

It should be stressed that the colonial state was incapable of addressing correctly the causes of the struggle, as colonialism was the problem. Peasant resisters were challenging its existence. To solve such a problem would have required it to dissolve itself, which it was incapable of doing. Secondly, it was dictatorial by nature and could never engage in democratic discussions. It remained confronted by resistances under Nyabingi. 'Every local grievance, whether real or imaginary, and every apprehension or misapprehension, is greedily exploited, hence the need of going slow, constant personal contact with the peasantry, and seeing under the surface, in Kigezi. NyaBingi and all its works are unlikely to die out except with the present generation' (*op. cit.*)

The colonial state took steps to revert from forced food contribution to forced food production for sale. The former had been collected by the chiefs under the supervision of agents. Gradually, this took root as peasants began to bring things voluntarily for sale.

The state also took steps to ensure food security for the peasants. Among the measures was the introduction of famine crops and communal granaries as food reserves. It intensified communal food reserves and granaries in its administration centres.

This increased the peasants' resistance. They did not understand the rationale of these communal granaries while households had their own granaries at household level. Secondly, they did not trust the colonial state in this. They suspected that it wanted this food for its troops, porters and for selling. This was not baseless as some food was sold without consulting the owners, and agents embezzled some of it.

The peasants knew that these famines were neither caused by Nyabingi, nor by devils but by the colonial state, which was now forcing them to pool food together. To peasants, colonialism had proved to be evil. The pooling of food was also resisted as it had the effect of undermining men's position in society. While men were the political heads of their households, colonialism reduced them tremendously. In default of any state demand, it was these family heads and other men who were harassed or punished. This undermined their political and social status in society; and as the main generators of ideas, ideology, teachings and as the initiators of moral standards. Colonialism made men become more or less fugitives in their area. The food pooling was aimed at expropriating the end product, usufruct and distributive control at the family level, and to disable the social system and reorder the production relations. It went counter to the concept of indirect rule.

This had the effect of recruiting more peasants into active anti-colonial struggles. The colonial state was, therefore, forced to reform policies on communal famine granaries. Top colonial officials also began touring the whole district, inspecting records and the granaries, and so on.

The colonial state was forced to abolish *kashanju* due to peasant resistance to it. Its abolition was followed by peasants withdrawing their labour as there was no legal basis to force them. Sullivan reported their response thus:

> Under the 1920 Ordinance, offenders render themselves liable to imprisonment or to work in custody. Previous experiments have shown the futility of such people to work on plantations, as they merely vanish. The abolition of Kasanvu has removed any form of compulsory labour, with the result, that these people who have no wants, (Sic!) and who can grow their food without any effort, do not undertake voluntary labour. There is apparently a passive movement against tax paying, the natives saying 'Kasanvu is now abolished,

the Government will not kill us, and the jail cannot hold us all' (File: Native Affairs. Poll Tax in WP).

The state was forced to revisit taxes and their collection in the area. It desisted from taxing women. It relaxed *potoro* (patrol) aimed at netting tax defaulters. It also began to alleviate the tax burden both on the young men and on the aged. The first one was to fix the age limits for tax-payment, and the category for those to pay partial taxes. The PC pleaded for tax exemption for 'elderly men whose earning capacity is exhausted to contribute tax even at a partial rate; actually the sum due has generally to be earned by a younger member of the family' (PCWP to CS on 6 May 1937).

In fact, it ensured a continued tax-assessment annually, basing on individual's capacity to pay, age, amount of resources one owned, and so on. The colonial state went ahead and made reforms on forced labour. It allowed peasants to commute *oruharo*. Gradually, it phased out *oruharo* by consolidating it with poll tax. In addition to this, it was forced to make other concessions.

This section has shown that there were many changes with the World War. These were in reaction to colonial demands, impositions, punishments, and so on. These demands and brutal coercion, massacres, tortures, and so on, had forced peasant resisters to adopt new forms of recruitment, conscientisation and struggle. They adopted new methods and raised more or less standing forces.

This was also the time when this Nyabingi Movement took a broader internationalist line. They began attacking all the imperialist powers in the whole region. They incorporated the enemy's technology and weaponry into the resistance, trained peasant resisters into new military warfare and gave them access to use of these new weapons. It is not surprising that colonial forces got defeated in some skirmishes and were forced to flee. This was also the time when many grand military plans were foiled and intelligence agents were rendered useless by resisters.

Faced with the imperialist war on a broader scale and this Nyabingi Movement domestically, the colonialists were forced to seek other solutions in addition to militarism. They were forced to make a series of reforms, based on the prevailing social grievances so as to undermine the Nyabingi Movement. They accomplished this through material rewards and posts, promises, promotions, and so on. Another method they used was direct de-militarisation of Nyabingi, drawing from malpractices of *abagirwa*. Although this phase evidenced the climax of the Nyabingi Movement, it also witnessed the beginnings of its demise.

6

The Role of Women in Anti-Colonial Struggles

'Witchdoctors (females) have been a source of great trouble to the native administration of the Kigezi District for years by inciting the natives to disobey the chiefs and leading armed forces against authority ... If Kanzanyira returns to Kigezi District for the next three years, her influence is likely to cause a recrudescence of such armed revolt'.

The Nyabingi Movement was neither constituted by one gender, nor by one generation. This chapter attempts to locate the females in this movement. It examines how the Nyabingi Movement addressed the issues of gender and of outsiders in leadership and membership. It seeks explanations for the activeness and staunchness of many women in Nyabingi's service at all levels both prior to the invasion and during these new struggles. It explores the internal reforms which were demanded and which ones were initiated during and after these struggles, and their consequences.

As mentioned earlier on, women were very instrumental in the leadership of the Nyabingi Movement. This was mainly because of their leadership role in Nyabingi religion. Women took an active role in military adventures. This chapter deals briefly with their role in this movement, and factors that facilitated them to play this crucial role and their limitations.

The prohibition of women from owning weapons and active participation in war was premised on the argument that women were weak, lacked experience in wars, and had their specified roles. A more plausible explanation seems to have lain in the question of whether men were ready to allow ownership of weapons to all sections of society. Could such a process have facilitated these other sections of society to resist men's domination and oppression or the whole arrangement was symbolic - to preserve the status of men as heads of households? This calls for revisiting the restrictions of women and children to go to forges, let alone touching the raw materials like charcoal. This, therefore, meant that the oppressed sections of society had to be protected from any external aggression. Monopolising the protective role had the effect of legitimising the oppressive position of men, their magnanimity, infallibility and indispensability in society.

However, this did not mean that these other sections of society did not contribute to the defence of their society. Field research shows how women and children equipped men with stones during these fights and threw stones at the enemy while shielding themselves with winnowing trays (*entaara*). Women used their staves (*emihunda*) to stab their enemies. In case of attacks, women and children could use men's weapons for self-defence. This was not directly condemned by the lineage elders as they would be defending themselves and their *enganda* from external aggression. In such instances, there would be no condemnation and no purification rites. Any defeat or victory affected all people, their economy and social set-up. In other cases, they would poison the enemy or make them drunk and then kill them with daggers (*endiga*) or other weapons. This did not apply to *Abatwa* ethnic grouping, where all sections of society had their instruments of production which were at the same time, weapons.

It was through the Nyabingi Movement and such charismatic leadership that a spirit of comradeship developed. This had the effect of sealing together various peoples in the struggle. All other practices and cultural initiations contributed to this. Another development was that women in leadership discussed with men on equal basis and commanded all membership in the fight. Combatants had realised that the issue at stake was to combine efforts of all members of society to defeat the invaders. As such, every contribution was welcomed. The role of *abagirwa* was also critical in the treatment of injuries sustained in the struggle. It was *abagirwa's* role to invoke Nyabingi to threaten with curses and death penalty or actually arrange the deaths of the saboteurs.

The peasants who did not take up arms to resist gave logistical support in food and arms supplies, transport, scouting, intelligence, keeping secrets, making arrangements, guiding and directing resisters in movement, transmitting information, hiding the resisters and confusing the enemy, recruitment, morale-boosting and encouragement, harassment of collaborators, and so on. All these contributions were critical in sustaining and promoting the struggle.

The Kivu Mission and the Boundary Commission were confronted militarily by peasant resisters. The first two main anti-colonial resistances were led by Muhumuza and Kaigirirwa. Muhumuza, mother of Ndungusi, was widow to the former King Rwabugiri of Rwanda. On her husband's death, both Muhumuza and Ndungusi got involved in power struggles against Musinga. Musinga got the backing of colonialists and took the reins of power. These events and the subsequent ones forced Muhumuza and her son to flee to Rutobo, which was soon to be made the border between the new Ankore and Kigezi Districts. So, they joined peasant life and developed new relations with these peasants after falling from the ruling class in Rwanda. Also, Kaigirirwa came from the peasantry and was *omugirwa* of Nyabingi.

What is worth noting here is that while female *abagirwa* like Kaigirirwa were selected into the service of Nyabingi in their girlhood, got initiated into Nyabingi secrets and rites, and so on, and had more religious faith in Nyabingi religion, Muhumuza and her son adopted this religion, after leaving the palace. Their choice of Nyabingi religion was a conscious one, unlike other *abagirwa*. Nyabingi religion, became a powerful ideology for mother and son to gain legitimacy and credibility among peasants. Like other *abagirwa*, Nyabingi religion was important for them to extract surplus from the peasants through *okutweija* and *okuterekyerera* to Nyabingi and to declare war.

Owing to their historical origin, Muhumuza and her son were more conscious politically, ideologically and militarily than these peasants. Furthermore, they had encountered German colonialists and European missionaries in Rwanda. Both son and mother had no illusions about colonialism. In addition to that, they had been beneficiaries of the Rwanda state and understood the need to defend land and independence.

It is no wonder, therefore, that her struggles against Germans led to her capture and deportation to German East Africa (GEA). However, she struggled and managed to return soon after. This was also the time when other *abagirwa* were mobilising peasants into resistance against colonial invasion in the whole region. These resistances led to massacres and Kaigirirwa's deportation to Mbarara. The absurd encounters of *abagirwa*, like Muhumuza, with colonial forces in Rwanda and GEA and Kaigirirwa with British forces while in detention at Mbarara were very important for their future military and organisational purposes. These provided them with insight into the mechanics of the enemy, the need to resist and methods to accomplish it. Colonialism had set the terms.

The deportation of the leader did not cause them to disband. Instead, they became more determined to emancipate their society. They learnt more about the adversaries: their ways of life, their motives, methods of struggle and strengths, weaponry, military tactics, and protection from the weapons. They learnt the importance of mobility, retreat, broader unity, the role of the masses in self-emancipation, the need to study both the enemy and their members with a view to choose capable and dependable ones into leadership positions to keep the struggle going, as well as the need to conscientise the members. In fact, the separation was very important to the leadership. For instance, Muhumuza's separation from the ruling class in Rwanda and then from the peasants to GEA helped to cut her ties to the aristocracy.

In a similar manner, Kaigirirwa's deportation to Mbarara was a time of reflection. It helped to cut her roots from the geographical and social environment. It was this weakness which had led to the heavy losses and massacres.

Peasants would hide in swamps, bushes, caves and rocks in their geographical environment and be besieged by the colonial forces for weeks. Faced by hunger or misjudging that the enemy had left, they would fall easy prey to the enemy while trying to return. Their main problem was that they had not known that the new adversaries were skilled professional fighters. This was evident in the Nyakishenyi resistance. The colonial officer reported how a large number of rebels had become tired of hiding in the swamps and had tendered their submission, while others were following suit daily.

It was thus a time for gaining a rich experience for the forthcoming struggles, in which they were to apply most of this knowledge and skills. It also helped them meet many other oppressed people from other areas. This gave them opportunity to share their experiences about their new enemy and the need to fight to final victory. All these developments became the bases for their charismatic and forward-looking leadership in the struggles that they led thereafter. And their religious and political leadership roles made them the conscience of society.

Inauguration of the Nyabingi Movement

Muhumuza took the first initiative to mobilise peasants in the region against the invading forces. Her past rich experience enabled her to take the first initiative and mobilise peasants in the region into resistance. She was the first known woman resister who mobilised a cross-section of peasants into armed resistance against colonialism in Kigezi. She took the initiative to sensitise the peasants about colonialism and its dangers. This was proved practically at Rutobo. There, she intercepted a convoy of White Fathers destined for Mulera. After interrogating their porters, she denied them food and passage (1911 BCR).

In the same area, these peasants resisted the Boundary Commission from carrying out demarcations. They disrupted the border demarcation exercise, uprooted border pillars, attacked the commissioners and occupied some of their camps. The Commissioners were compelled to step up security and move under tight protection.

The peasant resisters attacked all those in colonial service. These included mail runners and messengers. Although the colonial forces hit back - leading to deaths and injuries, the peasant resisters maintained their stand. The state attributed all these to Muhumuza's political work (*idem*).

Preparations for the War

As already noted, the major problems for the natives arose from the low level of productive forces and absence of an organised armed force to engage and repel the invaders. There was no established institution to mobilise peasants for self-defence. The only way was through collective armed resistance.

It was in these circumstances that Muhumuza assumed leadership and mobilised peasants into armed resistance against colonialism. Knowing the weaknesses of peasants in relation to religions and witchcraft, she exploited the situation by promising them the protection of Nyabingi. She used Nyabingi religion for ideological purposes to unite and encourage them. She applied a militaristic approach to whoever refused to join the resistance. This way, she was able to raise a big force composed of various ethnicities and lineages. Some of these were formerly hostile to one another. Through her politics and invocations to Nyabingi, she was able to convince many peasants into unity against the common enemy. She showed them that the only way to defend their land and interests was through collective armed struggle.

Aware of the dangers of guns, she encouraged the resisters that she would render the European guns harmless by turning them into water. These were some of the promises that the subsequent leadership was to uphold and modify. Muhumuza was also able to incorporate lineage leaders and other influential personalities into the leadership. This had the advantage of bringing in various peoples under such lineage leaders into the movement, even if they had not initially accepted Nyabingi religion.

She tried to rid the area of all those who formed the internal enemies of the struggle. She had no patience with this category of people. To this cause, she sharpened and carried three stakes for staking alive Mutambuka, Rwagara and Basajjabalaba, 'who had brought the British into the region'.

Though she was able to mobilise a large peasant force, her militaristic approach to individuals, lineages and peoples that refused or hesitated to join the movement led to negative consequences. By attacking them and looting their livestock, they alienated many of them and forced them to join the enemy forces. This was detrimental to the movement as it swelled the enemy's forces. In isolating and attacking them before attacking the principal enemy - colonialism - this peasant movement lost a credible force. The force could have been neutralised through dialogue, diplomacy, and other methods. This would have led to fewer isolated enemies. Yet, thousands of armed peasants under Rwagara and Mutambuka joined the colonial forces after being beaten by the resistance forces. Cap. Reid wrote to Maj. Jack in August 1911 that the situation was getting worse:

> Mumusa was preaching an anti-European Crusade and collecting a considerable following in Rukiga, Mumusa or Muhumusa is a well-known personage in Ruanda, and has formerly given a great deal of trouble to the Germans. She is one of the 'witch-doctors' who are found in this part of Africa, and who are regarded with superstitious reverence by the native. Mumusa at one time had enormous power and still has (*idem*).

Given the struggles that she had organised and waged against the German colonialists in the German East Africa, the German colonialists also pledged military cooperation against the movement.

The leaders after Muhumuza tried to overcome this limitation. The leadership that emerged later tried to involve more people into the movement. We find that both the leadership and membership of the Nyakishenyi resistance were composed of both peasants and local people, who had been in colonial service as chiefs, *askaris*, messengers and porters.

The new approach had advantages. It weakened colonial forces at the time of the armed struggle, as many of its local chiefs defected to the Nyabingi Movement. It also increased the resisters' morale, courage and inspiration in the resistance. As the chiefs came with their followers, the colonial numbers reduced, augmenting the ranks of the resisters with experienced, hardened fighters.

Realising that some members were likely to lose faith in the leadership and desert the struggle or defect to the enemy or even turn against the leadership, Muhumuza drew lessons from the characteristics that people attributed to Nyabingi. One of these was to transform herself into a Nyabingi personification.

She was leading a big peasant force of various ethnicities and lineages. And she was not blind to the fact that some of them were likely to challenge her military plans and legitimacy to lead men to war. Even some of her membership had been allies or friends of Mutambuka and Rwagara. This, then, called for the creation of a solid ideology, which would unite them, and keep them, under indirect fear, from rebelling or questioning her legitimacy or refusing to carry out orders. People needed to be convinced that her line of action was the correct one as it was the Nyabingi line. She was able to marshal all these by combining her knowledge from the palace and that from the peasantry.

Other *abagirwa* were to capitalise on Nyabingi personification in the subsequent resistance. This was still prevalent by 1928 as the colonial officer reported Nyabingi's subversion to state and church with the local personification, heavily concentrated in Ndorwa (KDAR 1928). Unlike the pre-colonial personification, the new form was precipitated by the needs of war.

This transformation into a Nyabingi personification scared those who would have betrayed the struggle. Here was Nyabingi, in human form, defending their interests. It elevated her above other members of society. It gave her more powers and legitimacy to act decisively and created room for manipulation and command. It also bestowed on her more powers to dictate and deal with individuals and situations promptly as she deemed fit, especially those with dissenting views, wavering behaviour, traitors, and so on. It legitimised her to compel people to resist colonialism and to wage war against anyone who refused to heed the call of Nyabingi. Her decisions were claimed to be the decisions of Nyabingi. It also became a basis for increased encouragement, bravery, unity and comradeship among the peasant resisters. It had the effect of restraining more people from withdrawing from the struggle. It increased the confidence of the membership in the leadership for both temporal and spiritual interests. The membership became more determined to fight when they saw her more resolute in her promises, actions, and her spiritual claims.

Her fears were not unfounded. Some of the elders despised and feared this initiative and leadership by a woman. While some felt that it was degrading to be led by women to war, others felt that their position as men and leaders would be undermined if women led them to war. Others feared the consequences of such leadership and resistance after the battle. They envisaged a situation of turmoil - where women and children would disobey them. These would challenge the existing social relations. There were those who did not understand the gravity of the situation. Some resorted to outright collaboration with the enemy for wealth and power, while others decided to sit back and wait rather than join forces led by women. Even others refused to join them because their former enemies had joined them.

In response, the resisters decided to attack such people before attacking the principal enemy. This also forced the leadership to increase propaganda, ideology, thinking, planning, secrecy and ruthlessness with the weak, the wavering, the traitors and informers.

Another development which united the peasant resisters under her leadership was her broadening the leadership of the struggle to unite the former hostile lineages and incorporate them into one strong peasant force. Lineage leaders were part of the leadership.

The Course and Consequences of the War

As she was organising a major war against the British forces, the British forces defeated her forces in a surprise attack under Cap. Reid and Sebalijja jointly with peasant forces of Mutambuka and Rwagara on 28 September 1911. In this surprise attack, masses of armed peasants were massacred. The colonial forces had to use 66 guns, 1,680 bullets and one canon. Sebalijja put it melodramatically thus:

> I opened fire on them and they fled towards Effendi Marijani. He opened fire and they fled towards Captain Reid... the battle was won and Muhumuza was captured... Many unknown Abakiga were killed in the battle... We set fire to all the houses. We buried about forty corpses in one deep grave... On our side, one man was mortally wounded, while trying to plunder a house... The Abakiga on our side doubted the utility of carrying enemy wounded on their heads. They killed them and threw them down and moved on (Sebalijja, *op. cit.*)

His account is inaccurate and full of self-praise. This can be shown by the length of the battle. It lasted for six and half hours, with losses on both sides. As the report showed, Dr. Marshall, of the Commission, had led a force to Kumba. Though he found the war over, there were a good many wounded and he did most useful work in attending to the wounded colonial troops. He transferred the acute cases to Kamwezi (*op. cit.*)

Although he did not explain the causes of this war, Sebalijja recounted how the peasants, who had been shouting that they were going to turn guns into water, had been wiped out through a surprise attack. He reported that *Abakiga* collaborators killed many unknown peasants.

Ngorogoza (*op. cit.*) records a mass grave of 40 people while others were devoured by vultures. This constitutes a minute window into how the colonialists were violating people's rights and international conventions over prisoners of war (Sebalijja, *op. cit.*) In his account, the peasant resisters had burnt Sebalijja's camp and then fought Mutambuka. After the final battle, Reid gathered peasants and threatened them that Muhumuza actually meant turning bullets into her men's blood not water.

The significance of this battle is that it was an inaugural battle for peasant armed resistance under Nyabingi. It should be noted that the first recorded resistance was in Mpororo Kingdom, led by King Makobore in 1899. He was arrested and fined in 1899 for allowing two trading caravans from GEA to be cut up (Sebalijja, *op. cit.*; Vide File: A6/17/1904: Annual Reports. General Report on WP 1904).

British Strategy of Separating the Leadership from the Membership

While Ndungusi and others managed to escape, Muhumuza was wounded, captured by the colonial forces, despatched to Mbarara and then deported to Mengo. There followed a hot pursuit of other members in the leadership. However, they could not catch them as they had escaped into the hills. Even peasants resisted Cap. Reid's investigations about the resistance (Cap. Reid's Report of 5 March 1912. *op. cit.*)

Her return was blocked as she was a military and political threat - 'high priestess of revolutionary religious-political cult Nabingi'. The agents feared her political-religious powers and military attacks. Her return would mean loss of their newly acquired lucrative jobs with tributes, incomes, bribes and prestige. On her part, Muhumuza continued sending messages that she would soon return to chase away the Europeans (PCWP to CS on 4 October 1917).

Fearing that she would organise the resistance through messengers, the state denied her visitors from Kigezi. It also stopped Nyindo's herdsboys from contacting her while taking Nyindo's cattle to Gulu (PCWP to CS on 16 July 1917. Vide File: Historical and Political Notes [West] 1941).

The PCWP's memorandum of 1 May 1922, vide minute 28 in SMP 5409 asked about Muhumuza's repatriation so as to relieve government of maintenance costs. The district and provincial administrations remained emphatic against her return until her death in 1944. The PCWP communicated this position to the CS on 25 May 1922 that the District Administration was opposed to the return of both Muhumuza and Nyinabatwa. The KDAR 1932 noted that Muhumuza was receiving presents from her people.

This colonial strategy of separating the leadership from the membership had some basis. The state had realised that the return of such a deportee would be taken as testimony of Nyabingi's triumph over the state. The 1926 incident confirmed the fears when *abagirwa* mobilised peasants on the theme that Muhumuza was returning. Hundreds of 'people came from all parts voluntarily to build a large fence in an area 200 yards by 200 yards... to welcome her back as queen of Nyabingi since her 'Nyabingi' had obviously overcome everything causing her return to the district - even though she had been exiled for the last fifteen years!' (*op. cit.*)

What threatened colonialism most was that not a chief reported it but a Roman Catholic Father. Obviously, the colonial agents feared Nyabingi, and the peasants' wrath and vengeance.

Despite objections to her request for visitors, the peasants devised methods of visiting her secretly in Kampala for initiation into Nyabingi institution and its secrets and took her presents and tributes (*op. cit.*). This made the state more vigilant against the Nyabingi Movement.

The Buganda Resident, who went to Rwanda on this mission in 1939, discovered that the Nyabingi Movement was still active. The colonialists were shocked to learn that many people from Kigezi, Rwanda, Congo and Ankore came regularly to Muhumuza for initiation.[56] They, therefore, took strict steps to stop these missions.

All these prove the effectiveness of this weapon of separating the leadership from the membership. Had she been in Kigezi, then, it would have been easier for her to effect a better organised resistance as Kaigirirwa was later to do.

56   Memo of the Buganda Resident Commissioner to CS on 14 April1939 and his report on Ruanda dated 13 April 1939.

This dismisses the narrow view presented by the colonialists that Muhumuza was just fighting to establish herself as ruler. Even this official view had changed by 1941 to the view that her special aim was to form a kingdom for her son Ndungusi (*op. cit.*). The problem with such presentation is that the resister is projected as using peasants to fight and die for her personal interests. This fails to show what popular interests were being advanced, the progressive nature of such a struggle and its achievements.

Women in Leadership Post-Muhumuza

There were many *abagirwa*, whose role in leadership and struggle led to their death, capture and deportation. Others had to disappear among the peasants. The Nyabingi Movement proved a military and political challenge to colonialism.

Muhumuza's deportation was not the end of the movement. In fact, that was the launching of the Nyabingi Movement. Colonial authorities were soon to lament that 'the female witches of the Mamusa type' were at work in the whole district, mobilising people with 'anti-European ideas'. It was not long before colonialism learnt the charismatic and effective character of these women - *abagirwa*, their political and mobilisation capacity, their capacity to provide leadership, ideology, interpretation of phenomena for people's cause, and so on. It responded by intensifying repression, applied all ruthlessness it could marshal to hunt them down. Among those killed was Wahire. Chandungusi was captured and deported to Mbarara. She died on her way back. She was the mother of Katuregye (KDAR 1914-15. Vide Reports of WP of August and September, 1914). Mukeiganira was arrested, deported and her cattle seized. Nyinabatwa[57] and Kanzanyira were also arrested and deported.

The Court Subjugation Strategy

Both Nyinabatwa and Kanzanyira were arrested and charged like the rest under Section 2 WC Ord. 1912. Nyinabatwa was charged under Criminal Case No. 56 of 1917 while Kanzanyira was charged under Criminal Case No. 6 of 1918.[58] Judgment was based on D.C's oaths and evidence. The Colonial Court deemed it imperative to deport each of them to a place more than 250 miles away as 'witchdoctors (females) have been a source of great trouble to the native

---

57   The name Nyinabatwa was variably written by the colonialists as Ninabatwa.

58   Vide Files: Native Affairs: Ninabatwa (Witch doctor) Died 23 March 1923; & Native Affairs. Kanzanyira d\o MAESI (Witch doctor) Deportation of.

administration of the Kigezi District for years by inciting the natives to disobey the chiefs and leading armed forces against authority... If Kanzanyira returns to Kigezi District for the next three years, her influence is likely to cause a recrudescence of such armed revolt'. DC Gervoise swore to this Affidavit at Jinja on 31 March 1919. Nyinabatwa had been convicted on 6 December 1917.[59]

Colonial administration applied its *modus operandi* of setting up administrative and legal barriers to block their return to the membership. The state decided that they were not to return until conditions became more settled and the authority of the chiefs was less likely to be undermined by such perverse persons.[60] It is not surprising that this separation also became their tragedy. Kanzanyira died on 28 July 1919 at Entebbe, a few days after arriving in deportation. Nyinabatwa died on 23 March 1923 at Mengo. Available records and correspondences reveal that both died of neglect, hardship and cruelty by the colonial authorities (*op. cit.*).

The intensity of colonial repression to the resisters forced the leadership to change tactics and operate among the people with utmost secrecy. For some time, the state retained maximum repression to suppress the 'fanatical witch movements... essentially anti-European and need to be put down with a firm hand' (KDAR 1915-16). It was forced to post a wardress at Kabale because of 'increased number of female prisoners, chiefly Nabingi offenders' (KDAR 1921). The leadership was forced to change their methods of mobilisation and struggle. They increased secrecy of movement, plans and operation, and thus broadened their work. More *abagirwa* sprung up and intensified their work with zeal. They travelled to other places to conscientise the oppressed peoples into resistance despite the intensifying repression.

New languages developed in form of *Orupikya*, which was a product of mixing syllables and twisting words and ideas to produce new meanings. Others included parables and allegories. Resisters also utilised the pre-colonial art of speech to communicate certain secrets without being understood by the enemy. The colonialists concluded that this was a Nyabingi language. They were also forced to expand their geographical terrain to Masaka and Karagwe. The colonial state arrested *omugirwa* in Masaka, charging her with 'her disturbing and pernicious influence over the more ignorant natives'. She was deported. Another

---

59   DC to PCWP on 9 January1919 and PC's reply on 27 January 1919. Also see their Deportation Orders in the same files.

60   Governor to Secretary of State for Colonies on 2 September 1919. Also see excerpt from PCWP's memorandum of 1 May 1922 Vide Minute 28 in SMP 5409. Also see his communication to the CS of 25 May1922.

was 'deported from Bgugi to Usumbura for dangerous propaganda'. It captured another one in Karagwe, and burnt all her appliances with the exception of her specially designed spears. It then convicted her on a number of charges.[61]

One of the limitations of these *abagirwa* was their failure to delineate clearly the objective and subjective conditions within the new areas. Although they raised pertinent issues of foreign occupation, impositions, demands and restrictions, the people in these areas responded differently to their call. Nyabingi religion lacked a historical and social base in the new areas. Yet, the subjective factor was very critical. So, the people's response in these new places tended to be slow and lukewarm to *abagirwa's* gospel of resistance. It should also be mentioned that some peasants had lived relatively peaceful lives, and were not ready to accept anything that could create more trouble for them.

In places like Masaka, Nyabingi religion and its *abagirwa* were newer than colonialism. Worse still, this area had been under the Buganda state. It had been subjected to various forms of state exploitation prior to colonialism. As such, these appeals by *abagirwa* could not be accepted so easily. It required time to gain legitimacy and social acceptance in these societies.

The state was vigilant and denied them the chance. However, it was clear that the peasants had great fear of both Nyabingi and its *abagirwa*. The colonial officer recounted the impact of one *omugirwa* on the peasant public in Bukoba:

> During the course of the Baraza at Bagene it was interesting to note the effect she produced on the assembled natives. The chiefs, with scarcely any exception, trembled whenever her look was directed towards them. She also made most noticeable efforts to exercise some form of hypnotism over me (*op. cit.*).

Kaigirirwa's Leadership of the Movement

On their part, both Kaigirirwa and her husband Ruhemba underwent serious transformation during their separate deportations. Ruhemba had been deported in 1912 for his role in the movement. On his return, he was put under the supervision of Nyakishenyi's agent. This gave him advantage to monitor their activities and spy on them. It enabled him to learn their weak points and then choose appropriate methods for the attack, the timing, and so on. Even more so, his resolve was concretised by the murder of his brother by an *askari*. It must be understood that

---

61   Uganda Intelligence Report No. 12 May, 1922 (13) No. C 515. WP on Tanganyika - Native Affairs by R.C. Stuttaford, Lieut I.O. Uganda.

neither of the two *abagirwa* compelled the other to join the movement. It was their religious and political roles that led them to this leadership.

While Kaigirirwa's initial methods of struggle were not very much different from those of other members like Muhumuza, she underwent a major transformation during her deportation. She was able to learn the importance of training, preparation, and sophistication; the necessity to keep away from the enemy so as to preserve the forces while tiring the enemy; the importance of avoiding to fight on the enemy's terms; and the importance of hitting the enemy by surprise and at its weakest point.

It should be noted that the conditions and methods of struggle had changed from those prior to the 1914 war. Before that war, the leadership had been predominantly from the peasantry, with little or no wide experience. Peasant resisters were still rooted in the habitat like their crops. (This excepts Muhumuza.) Even the objectives of the struggle had changed. It should be recalled that PC had reported in 1912-13 that the natives, who had been recently in a state of semi-rebellion had become peaceful and were cultivating their crops and that 'the clans who a month or two ago were defying the government have submitted and are similarly employed' (WPAR 1912-13).

The first struggle that Kaigirirwa headed, after her return, was the Nyakishenyi resistance in 1917. The leadership for this resistance was broadened and included four women *abagirwa*, Ruhemba, seventeen chiefs and other influential personalities. Colonial reports show that this plan was made three months before the actual day and was kept a top secret. It is important to note that she, with others in leadership, studied the whole colonial situation in the area; understood its weaknesses and those of its local allies. They understood the need for broader alliances of peasants and those in colonial service. This was done by first identifying the conflicts between the colonial state, its Baganda agents and the local chiefs, and then exploiting them. These chiefs had grievances against the state. The local chiefs were marginalised in their own country by both the British and the Baganda agents. This included discrimination from ranks, status, income, and so on. The local chiefs could not benefit like their Baganda counterparts through accumulation of wealth from tax rebates, court dues, corrupt practices, and so on. They were excluded from all these. Kaigirirwa was able to exploit the situation to mobilise these chiefs.

The strength of the leadership was its capacity to understand the social grievances of different sections of society and then incorporate them into its programme. Among these was the hated taxation, forced labour, in form of *Ruharo, Kashanju,* head porterage, and so on. Others included abuse of office and direct abuses, corporal punishments and other arbitrary decisions and punishments, land alienation, forced contributions, and so on. The female *abagirwa* identified with men on these social grievances. Other social grievances arose from the rampant corruption, oppression, unfair court judgment, witch-hunting of Nyabingi followers and imposition of both British demands and Baganda language and norms onto the peasants. This was worsened by unfair court proceedings, heavy fines, denying peasants services and court judgment because they were incapable of speaking Luganda, and unfair land cases. These grievances had the effect of raising the peasants' sentiments for nationalism.

Even chiefs, like Kisyagari and Ruzindana, who later betrayed the resistance at the critical time could not leak out the secret before that time. This was because, they had initially believed in the explanations and plans given by *abagirwa.* They, too, had suffered the naked oppression and discrimination in the system for political and economic resources. Furthermore, they feared the wrath of Nyabingi and its *abagirwa,* and of the people. They also realised that even if they had succeeded in betraying them and the colonialists pre-empted this resistance, they would be wiped out through revenge. However, they failed to marry theory and practice.

Abagirwa bound together all these resisters with an oath of secrecy and commitment under Nyabingi, and offered a solid ideology for the struggle. All this was accomplished secretly and selectively. The state conceded that, 'No suspicion however of even disaffection or unrest leaked out until one daybreak when the massacre began though the victims had connections in peasantry through birth, marriages, blood brotherhood, and so on. Nyabingi enforced among them discipline, unity, courage, determination, confidence and comradeship. The leadership carried out secret organisation among Nyakishenyi peasants for self-emancipation under its guidance and protection. It was through this capable leadership and high level of organisation with a solid programme, that they mobilised over 1,400 armed peasants into the armed struggle. This occurred on 12 August 1917 at around 6.30 a.m. when they attacked all in the service of colonialism and destroyed all the symbols of colonial oppression and exploitation.

According to reports, 'hordes of Abakiga and Bahororo from the adjacent country... attacked the residence of Abdulla Mwanika... all his enclosures and houses were totally destroyed by fire, 64 dwelling houses of Baganda, Banyankole and loyal Abakiga were also burnt. The CMS and Moslem Mosque suffered similarly'. The agent's life was saved by, 'loyal Mukiga Chief Kisiagali and others with their people... 63 men, women and children were massacred by the insurgents, 15 men, women and children were wounded, some severely. ...All lived near the agent and some of them were assisting him in his duties.'

Although all those people had wives, followers, or blood brothers among the local population, nothing ever leaked until the daybreak when the insurrection began. The insurgents seized 64 cattle and 330 goats from the agent and others. They looted or destroyed much property, including five Poll Tax Registers, Case Books of the Native court and Five Books of Poll Tax Tickets.[62] The state was quick to learn that the resistance 'was directly due to the machinations of witch doctor Kaigirirwa and possibly others with her due to superstitious influence of a native witch doctor who unfortunately succeeded in escaping. The 'Nabingi' cult has never failed to find a following in this district'. Colonial intelligence reports argued that 'certain of the disloyal chiefs some months ago paid a visit to Ndochibiri, who is believed to have entrusted Kaigirirwa with the task of fomenting mischief in Nakishenyi' (KDAR 1917-18).

It became clear that '...the rebellion was an attempt by a section of the residents in Nyakishenyi to free themselves from European rule, and to restore former conditions of independence; and absence of obligations, - in the shape of Poll Tax and Labour. Rebel opinion supported the belief that the overthrow of authority and the removal of the chiefs appointed by Government and the European officers was a task within their powers' (*idem*). Abdulla testified that 'five hordes of Abakiga' shot at him and said, 'We do not want you here. The Nyabingi has ordered us to kill you or drive you away'. The court evidence by Kasenene, a Nyakishenyi peasant resister shows some of the issues around

---

62   Communication from the Ag DC of 31 August 1917 on 'Native Rising in Nyakishenyi'. Vide the PCWP's telegraph to CS of 20 August 1917. Also see PCWP to the CS on 24 September1917 & C.S' telegraph to PCWP of 12 October 1917 on the same issue. Report of the DM/DC to the Chief Justice on 8 September 1917. Report of the DM/DC to the Chief Magistrate of 8 September 1917; and the DC Kigezi to the PCWP on 26 June 1919.

which the peasants were mobilised, how they were mobilised, the theme of the struggle, and Nyabingi's context:

> Our Chiefs told us 'we see you are tired of work we have made a plan to kill the Baganda and the Europeans, so that they may leave the country and we shall be independent as we were before. You will pay no more tax and we will serve Nyabingi who used to rule over us before'. When we heard what the chiefs said, we agreed, as we did not want to do any work, so we attacked Abdulla (Court evidence by Kasenene, rebel peasant forwarded by DM/DC on 21 September 1917).

Wavamuno, one of the agents that narrowly survived the onslaught testified that over 1,400 Bakiga peasants came shouting; 'We have come to pay tax!' They carried spears and other weapons in their hands instead of money (Court evidence by Wavamuno, forwarded by the DM/DC). This was a veiled statement of resistance to exploitation through an alien taxation system.

This testimony demonstrated that the colonised people were fed up with colonial exploitation in form of taxes. Given that the colonialists were far removed from the scene of exploitation and oppression, the peasants had to attack the representatives of colonialism. That was the object of indirect rule – using the proverbial *omwiru* rope to tether fellow *abairu* for the oppressors and exploiters.

The testimony further reflects the impact of Nyabingi on the followers. They did not only use it for struggle but also believed in it and worshipped it. The spears were not only symbols but actual weapons for resistance. Nyabingi religious philosophy inspired them against colonial power and its impositions including taxes, laws, alien chiefs, and so on. By that action the religious/ideological perceptions were influencing, albeit negatively, the economic policies of the colonial regime, which were represented by the taxation imposed and collected by the chiefs. That marked the interface between the religious clashes, represented by 'modernity' versus 'traditionalism'. The former represented by the colonial government and its agents were pushing for taxation to sustain economic activities and, therefore, political base.

Cecil Rhodes' quotation is very instructive. This so-called modernity imposed an alien capitalist set of exploitative technologies on peoples with different modes of existence. The courts were part of the colonial system. As such, the courts' rulings, representing and protecting modernity had to impose mercilessly heavy punishments on whoever challenged the colonial order. This was the source of the legitimacy, mandate and the right of existence of these courts. Courts, therefore, had to facilitate colonialism instead of crippling it. It was on this basis that the Governor instructed the Attorney General to conduct these prosecutions. This was accomplished and all the accused were sentenced heavily.

In this particular legal scenario, three of the accused were convicted and sentenced to death through public hanging. Two were subsequently hanged in Kabale while the third was executed in Kampala.

Colonial Reactions to the Nyakishenyi Resistance

It should be understood that by 1917, the whole district was characterised by resistance through covert and overt methods. It is important to review briefly the peasant resistance that took place at Butare, four days before the Nyakishenyi resistance. Lwampomo, of Mukaranga, organised peasants into armed resistance. The actual resistance took place on 8 August 1917. They blocked passage of the agent Butale who was touring Mukaranga, attacked him and shot one of his followers. They forced him to retreat and chased him and his entourage. The DC had noted in April that Butare peasants were among the most truculent, who were averse to forced labour and any taxation (DC's report on Kanyarwanda on 22 April 1917).

Faced with the Nyakishenyi resistance, the state was forced to shelve counter-insurgency for Butare until after resolving the major resistance in Nyakishenyi. This finally took place on 24 August 1917, when the DC and his team led a force of 20 policemen and other followers to Butare to crash it. The peasants 'whereof fled at the first signs of approach, and hiding themselves in the swamps'. They captured peasants' livestock which were treated as a Collective Political Fine. After two days, they were forced to retire after burning down all the peasants' houses. Given this real threat to colonial power and its agents at Butare, the colonial authorities left behind four armed policemen to guard the agent and government property (Telegraph of Ag. DC to PCWP dated 20 August 1917 & letter of 31 August 1917 on 'Attack on Agent, Butale').

In response to the Nyakishenyi resistance, colonial forces from all over the district headed for Nyakishenyi. The forces from Kinkizi and Ikumba arrived early and saved Kisyagali's village from destruction. Peasant resisters had attacked it as reprisal for his betrayal. The forces came with all force to smash the resistance, restore colonial law and order. It unleashed state terror, used arms against the resisters. 'Energetic action was at once taken and the natives dispersed... a number of Bakiga were shot in action with the police and a considerable amount of stock captured' (KDAR 1917-18).

In the five days of intensive counter-insurgency, over 100 peasants were killed, including three chiefs. They captured 479 cattle and 764 goats and sheep, recovered one Poll Tax Ticket book of the previous year and 2 Poll Tax Registers (*op. cit.*)

However, resisters fought back and the state was forced to confess that it was 'impossible to arrest persons wanted owing to the armed resistance' (DC to PCWP on 21 September 1917).

Peasant resistance intensified. Casualties in colonial forces included Dr. Webb, who was speared (DC writing to PCWP on 21 September 1917 about Native Rising in Nyakishenyi).

Agents and local allies played a significant role in this counter-insurgency. During this exercise, DC Ankore sealed off the border and patrolled it to net any rebels running into Ankore. The peasants crossed these borders, fleeing from state demands and repression (*idem.* Vide DC's Report of 8 April 1912). That was the new colonial technology of power. Seven chiefs were still at large while seven chiefs had refused to join the peasant forces.

Colonial intelligence reports indicated that Kaigirirwa and her forces were operating near the Belgian frontier. The DC concluded his report that they 'left Nakishenyi for Kabale 19th. the country having been restored to a peaceful condition'. The KDAR of 1917-1918 noted re-establishment of colonial order in Nyakishenyi.

In inviting the Chief Justice to the court trial in Kabale of the rebels, the Ag DC/DM underlined the need to create a frightening impression to the peasants:

> This rebellion is a serious affair, and in its results the most deadly I have known, or heard of in this district. It seems to me to be an affair in which the trial of the principal prisoners by the High Court would be an eminently desirable feature; such a course would have a decided impression in the district (Vide KDAR 1917-18)

On 19 September 1917, the Ag Governor suggested that the Attorney General should conduct the prosecutions. This was aimed at inflicting fear into the peasants. So, while three rebels were executed, the rest had long term R.I.

It would be erroneous to argue that the resisters were only against Baganda agents for imposing their language and demands on them. They wanted the alien, oppressive, exploitative system to go. That was why they took away the Poll Tax Tickets, Tax Register records and case books, which symbolised the oppression and exploitation by the new system.

The looting of the livestock of the allies of the state was another testimony. In a region where livestock was sparsely distributed, on an average of 3-5 head of cattle per household, Agent Abdulla had accumulated 64 cattle and 330 goats in five years. Agents were busy using the system for their economic gains. On the other hand, this counter-insurgency led to disastrous famines in the two following years. KDAR, 1917-1918 commended the great work by Agents: Stephani Musoke, Zambatisi Jute, Sowedi Sabadu, Zakaria Barake, Namunye and Sulimani. The names clearly suggest three things. First, all these agents were foreigners to this area. Secondly, they had been converted to the new religions – either Mohammedanism or Christianity. Thirdly, they were all men.

There are various reasons why different parties participated vigorously in the counter-insurgency. Colonialists wanted to smash the resistance before it spread in the whole area. They had to protect their political and economic interests. They had to punish the resisters and restore some order while also teaching them never to resist again. They also had to prove to their agents and local allies that they had a strong state which could smash any resistance, and protect them.

Similarly, Baganda agents had also to prove to their masters their ability to serve the system. They did not want to lose their lucrative, privileged positions by being replaced with new agents. They were beneficiaries of this colonial system and any threat to overthrow it threatened their interests. At the same time, they had some scores to settle with the peasant resisters who had murdered their relatives, friends, and so on.

Seen from a narrow perspective, it appeared as an ethnic conflict between Nyakishenyi peasants, Baganda and Banyankore. This was what the colonialists presented persistently in their communication and later capitalised on to reform the system.

Many people saw Baganda and other agents as their enemies. These included the small, local chiefs. These were rivals to the alien agents and wanted to take their positions. They had opted for collaboration earlier on for various reasons. They did it for material gains in form of rewards from looted property, jobs and promotions, and social status. There was also an element of ignorance, especially among the new converts and agents' followers.

The DC handed over some livestock and other property to agents and collaborators, settled claims and he asked sanction to give out rewards to collaborators, compensate others and sell the surplus livestock. The most important point was his request 'for the sanction to offer a reward of 20 head of cattle for the capture of the witch doctoress Kaigirwa alias Musige'. PCWP wrote to CS on 26 September 1917 about these issues and the CS sanctioned all these in his telegraph to PCWP on 12 October 1917.

This brutal suppression did not cow down the movement, as the PC hoped: 'I trust there will be no further trouble of this sort amongst the Bakiga, who are a fine race but unfortunately intensely superstitious as regards the powers of the 'Nyabingi' and at certain seasons of year addicted to excessive beer drinking, which frequently leads to fighting among themselves' (*op. cit.*).

Mutation of the Resistance

The role of Kaigirirwa did not end with the Nyakishenyi resistance. This was a step towards stronger and longer peasant guerrilla warfare under Ndochibiri and others. This new development cannot be attributed merely to the fear of colonial repression unleashed in Nyakishenyi or to the fear of the price on her head. It can be explained from their new programme for the movement; their patriotic objectives and impact of intensive repression on the peasants. It should be understood that peasants were not ready to betray her to the colonialists. The opportunists, who would have ventured to earn those cattle did not know her movements and programme. Even those who could have known, feared revenge and mysterious deaths.

However, the price on her head led to other consequences. Peasants became more vigilant to protect her. Others were forced to harden and join the struggle by her charisma, realising that a woman had threatened this colonial force. Her capacity to elude the enemy's traps, intensification of militancy, organisation and determination, transformed her into a hardened, seasoned fighter, who, with other resisters shed all attachments to home or village life. They joined Ndochibiri's guerrilla forces actively. It was her long experience in resistance and commitment, courage, military training, leadership qualities and charisma that brought her to top leadership after the tragic death of Ndochibiri and other three top leaders.

In pre-colonial times, she would have been expected to withdraw from all activities for days to mourn her husband and comrades. She would have had to wait quietly having been widowed and wait for one of her brothers-in-law to inherit her. Instead, this hardened her, made her more resolute to fight colonialism. However, it should be noted that it was impossible for her to mourn her husband, even if she had wanted, since she was on the run as colonial forces were pursuing her. Right from joining ranks with Ndochibiri, her programme of emancipation had extended beyond the colonial borders.

Kaigirirwa had distinguished herself in her capacity to organise peasants, inspire in them courage and lead them to war. Her capacity to understand people's grievances and problems went beyond gender limitations. Women began identifying with men's cause, seeking appropriate solutions and implementing these solutions. Their capacity to study the whole situation, integrate themselves into it, then come out with correct solutions of self-emancipation through armed struggle and then carrying out the task of mobilising a cross-section of society into militant resistance was a testimony to their leadership role. This charismatic leadership inspired and united the combatants.

It was these *abagirwa* who purported to alleviate people's burdens from colonialism and then change the order of things in their favour. They had the capacity to identify people's rights and the methods to regain them, to unite with men leaders to plan struggles and convince local colonial agents to cross to the people's side and fight for their popular rights. This forced the state to intensify brutality, witch-hunt them and impose deportation, executions, long, rigorous imprisonments, and prices on some of them.

Kaigirirwa, Ruhemba and others joined forces with Ndochibiri. In the struggles that ensued, Kaigirirwa played a key role in military training of the fighters, organisation and planning, spying and other intelligence network, and the actual struggle. She contributed a lot in training these peasant resisters in the use of lethal weapons, and so on. It is no wonder, therefore, to find that she was commanding a peasant force of over 600 fighters by 20 June 1919.

It is of interest that the deaths of Ndochibiri, Ruhemba, Rumuri et al. did not discourage her from the struggle but instead strengthened her into more resistance. She took on the new tasks of providing the fighters with arms and food; training; creating and strengthening friendship between the resisters and the peasants; creating more brotherhood; recruiting more combatants, and so on. The state hurried to change the site of the administration headquarters with a new *Boma* at Kabale, re-roofed the buildings with corrugated iron sheets since it was 'fully alive to the fact that incendiarism on the part of fanatical followers of the late Ndochimbiri, the late Ruhemba and the still existing witch doctoress,

Kaigirwa, is a real danger and not to be scoffed at' (PCWP to OC Police on 7 July 1919).

She led an attack on the colonial forces within two weeks after her assumption of top leadership. She led another attack from the Kisalu area. This 'was driven off by a Police Patrol in Nakishenyi-Kinkizi area and; 'in retiring they announced that they would wait for vengeance until the Government relaxed their precautions and forgot their presence.'[63] They waged other attacks in the subsequent period. It was in combat in 1921 that she was shot and killed, after twelve years of active anti-colonial struggles (*op. cit.*).

The other challenge to colonialism was that while all actors in its service were men, Nyabingi had both men and women in the membership and leadership, with women playing a dominant role in the leadership. The same applied to the new religions which came with it. Men dominated their ranks, both at home and in these colonies. Back in Europe, the European woman was discriminated against in public roles like the military, active politics, religions, and so on. Yet, here was a locally established religion dominated by militant women, addressing people's spiritual, temporal, military, physiological and psychological needs. This complicated matters for the colonialists in terms of both armed struggle and justification.

Continued attacks and heavy losses in terms of personnel and expenditure forced colonialism to make certain reforms, aimed at removing some of the social grievances.

---

63   PCWP's Report of July, 1919. Ag CS to the Director of PWD Kigezi Station. File: Western Province, Kabale Station, Defence Precautions.

7

Contributions and Limitations of the Nyabingi Movement

Any unaccountable incident is put down to 'Nyabingi' and is at once seized upon by the witch doctor as a proof of his powers which all helps to foster any agitation he may have in mind. The recent dry weather causing the matama crop to begin to wilt of course lent colour to the general rumour that a new Sultan would arrive in the country in the place of Government and would bring 'nyabingi', new seed, rain, etc (op. cit.)

We shall find it extremely difficult to effect his capture since he is always informed of our slightest movements. He is held in terror by the native population by reason of his supernatural associations, and no one dares to denounce his gatherings from the additional fear of reprisals ... he seldom risks remaining in villages and takes the precaution of establishing his camps in places which are far from population and kept secret, these rendezvous even he changes frequently.

The Nyabingi Movement resisters were able to defeat colonial forces in some of these battles because of some advantages they had over the latter. These included numerical strength, commitment, methods of struggle and timing, knowledge of the terrain and its effective utilisation, people's support and involvement, and so on. However, being masses, at a low level of production and with a narrower outlook than their counterparts, they could not press home for more successes to final victory. Neither did many of them develop beyond mass resistance and create a regional, armed force to fight for their rights and defend their successes.

Many of them saw these wars in the same way as pre-colonial wars with other *enganda*, where the initial defeats meant final victory. Yet, the state attacked in succession with no attachment to production, no family responsibilities, no shortage of supplies, and so on. It did not first make war preparations which built up to climaxes through dances or beating drums. It did not even first challenge its enemies to fight as these peasants did. Its rules of the game were different and overwhelmed the resisters. So, the peasants' military success were short-lived.

The peasants' defeat arose out of their objective weaknesses. These included lack of organisation and broader unity of all peasants in the region to resist at the same time. They failed to neutralise collaborators, either politically or militarily. This excepts the Nyakishenyi resistance and the one under Ndochibiri. Most of them failed to learn and master the enemies' military methods and weaknesses. This was worsened by their crude pre-capitalist weapons and military methods, which made them vulnerable to advanced capitalist ones. Stones and spears are no match to the repeated fire of self-loading machine guns. These measures contributed in undermining the Nyabingi Movement.

By the mid-1930s, Nyabingi resistance was declining, taking new forms such as avoidance of poll tax, forced labour or other obligations (KDARs 1933-38). The state had penetrated deep into the peasantry (*idem*). By 1939, the Nyabingi Movement had been weakened considerably (Buganda Resident to CS on 14 April 1939. Vide File: Historical and Political Notes [West] 1941).

Despite the eventual defeats, the armed violence had great impact. The natives knew that this was their collective responsibility. It helped them to patch up their conflicts and join forces for self-emancipation. Right from the beginning, the more they were beaten, the more resistances flared up. They did not surrender but were conquered militarily after bitter wars. However, successive defeats, massacres, tortures, imprisonments, public executions, deportations, and so on, demoralised the resisters. They came to terms with reality and learnt the invincibility of colonialism. They gradually began to use it from within and to appeal to the state for arbitration.

Effect of Nyabingi Movement on Colonialism

The state had learnt that militarism alone could not last long. It, therefore, resorted to political solutions, reformed its administration, made changes in its demands, promoted some local institutions to undermine Nyabingi, reduced witch-hunts and punishments to the culprits. It changed its approach and policies and adopted a cautious approach in dealing with them.

Faced with the insurgency, the state was forced to import an anthropologist in the person of Mandelbaum to study the peasants and devise measures to control them. Gradually, it made peasants form councils up to village level in which they would discuss colonial policies and air their grievances. The new reforms were not outrightly hostile. On their part, the peasants, tired of continuous defeats, punishments and famines, wanted to settle down to production.

The state embarked on the programme of 're-construction and soothing a volcanic people by explaining or removing causes of potential upheavals rather than by initial punishment and by substituting, where possible, indigenes for aliens in the control of local affairs' (*op. cit.*) It was also forced to shift its administration centre, first from Kigezi to Ikumba[64] and then to Kabale. In 1919 alone, it had to spend more than a thousand pounds to change the Kabale Station. All these were from real fears of the Nyabingi Movement (File: 146: Native Administration: Nabingi and Kabale defence (1919-1923).

It gradually began to remove any grievance that would form a basis for peasant resistance. This included warding off missionaries from exploiting peasants in different ways under the blessing of the state. These malpractices revolved around taking away peasants' resources such as land, labour, food and exposing them to diseases.

The state, however, made policies outlawing carrying spears and any other object, which could be used as a weapon. Secondly, it made policies against local smithing, and inflicted heavy penalties on anyone that violated this. Punishments included imprisonment and cutting of thumbs. This was worsened by forced labour, labour migration and massive importation of cheap manufactured goods. These undermined the local industry and tied the area to the new economic order. Yet, the new weapon of making war - the gun - was never available to the local population. And there were restrictions against free political organisation.

---

64   The colonialists variably spelled Ikumba as Kumba.

Changing from an Insurgent Religion to a Revolutionary Movement

It should be noted that in all these struggles, these resisters put their faith and protection in Nyabingi; even those households and lineages which Nyabingi religion had not permeated. Confronted by colonialism, peasants accepted that Nyabingi had sanctioned this struggle. Nyabingi was their leader and protector in this war. Nyabingi religion, therefore, transcended its spiritual roles to address peasants' temporal needs. As such, the leadership of this resistance had to use Nyabingi religion, even if it might not have believed in it.

Resistance had to be given a solid faith to hold on to. This gave *abagirwa* a vital role in increasing the resisters' faith and fear in Nyabingi, encouraging them to fight, threatening the waverers and the weak to become strong and fight. Nyabingi gained more legitimacy and expansion among the peasants and the area freely, without threat of internal opposition. It also helped in undermining the passive religions.

While some of them were pro-established orders, all of them offered no practical solution to secular, psychological and spiritual problems confronting peasants. With colonial invasion, these religions could not come up with any solution either. It was only *abagirwa*, who attended to these problems and offered some solutions and explanations.

At the time of invasion, Nyabingi confronted two enemies, the external and the internal. It became clear that while the main enemy was external, to confront him required internal reforms. Internal reforms were demanded both in the society and the Nyabingi institution. It was necessary to use instruments of violence and subordination to different sections of society regardless of gender, age, lineage, historical origin, and so on, and allow members to come into leadership and address issues of gender, minorities, among others. With colonialism as a new oppressor, various sections of society found the solution in the Nyabingi Movement. All were forced into anti-colonial struggles at various levels, in various forms. While some took to arms, others supported them with information, logistics, like coverage and shelter, arms, food, guidance and messages.

New Changes from the Anti-colonial Struggles

It was in these anti-colonial Nyabingi struggles that women took up a critical leadership role in armed struggles - not only as mediums of Nyabingi but as defenders of society; directing the fighters and participating fully in combat both in leadership and among fighters, planning, providing ideologies, encouraging fighters and administering invocations of secrecy under Nyabingi. In addition to holding local weapons, women held guns and taught other resisters how to use them. This was the first time that they stood with men in battle, fought side by side with men and died together. The active participation of women - both in membership and leadership - fostered an atmosphere of commitment, dedication and comradeship among the resisters without any discrimination. This ensured sustenance of the resistances.

This great leap from pre-colonial period demonstrated clearly that a solid, long-lasting defence for society depended on all members of society, and that in time of crisis, every member had something to contribute. This called for all sections of society to defend it. In other words, defence for society could not be based on gender differences but on all who lived in it. It showed that basing on gender to determine defence of society spelled out peril since all sections of society were needed in this struggle and that unity had to be built on equality and comradeship rather than basing on inequality, oppression and discrimination. This new development became the basis for the development, sustenance and longevity of the Nyabingi Movement. Hence, the struggles that ensued gradually had shed away spontaneity and developed into arduous, protracted, sharp struggles of mobile peasant resisters.

While these internal reforms were made, they did not extend deep to household level. In other words, they did not permeate the whole society, beyond the immediate requirements of defence of society. Even those who did not engage in resistance did not experience them. The same old hierarchy remained with the colonial state on top. Such reforms, therefore, remained superficial, without any profound effect on the existing relations.

Secondly, even these reforms were not long-lasting. After the military encounter, the various sections of society resumed their social positions in the existing framework. Meaningful, profound reforms would have to address the existing social relations, address issues related to gender, youths and other minorities. In this context, equality and comradeship was experienced only in the battlefield. The narrowness of these reforms finally contributed to the defeat of the Nyabingi Movement.

The natives did not incorporate the new ideas completely. While *abagirwa* accepted sacrifices in monetary terms and applied foreign military technology and science, they restricted their fold from accepting certain innovations being preached by the state. A situation developed where *abagirwa* brought forward explanations to counter any colonial move. The colonial state brought forth counter-arguments in defence of such moves. These colonial explanations were backed by coercion while those by Nyabingi were backed by fear of the supernatural and the unknown consequences. Force, therefore, compelled peasants to implement these programmes, against their will and the wishes of *abagirwa*.

However, as the colonial programmes produced positive results in conformity with what colonial authorities had earlier explained, the Nyabingi religion was undermined. In issues related to health, sanitation, production, soil protection, medicine and vaccines for people and cattle the state's explanations and policies proved most successful and convincing.

The sacrifices to Nyabingi in form of alcohol, daughters and foodstuffs were gradually abandoned due to the dynamics of this war. Secondly, the long, pretentious process of selecting *omugirwa* was abandoned. With the new continuous struggles, it became clear that any rigidities or delays in leadership-formation, or initiative-taking spelled out peril for Nyabingi and the people. Nyabingi, therefore, became very flexible to the membership in joining its ranks. Since all *abagirwa* were busy mobilising peasants into resistance, and on constant run from colonial repression, there was no time for a systematic initiation of new *abagirwa* into Nyabingi secrets.

War conditions demanded continuity in leadership. Where one *omugirwa* got killed or arrested, another had to emerge promptly, take up her place and continue the struggle. As such, many more people became *abagirwa* and sustained the struggle.

That paralysed colonialism. The dynamic process had the advantage of bringing in different people with different leadership qualities, military skills and experience into leadership. Most of them would never have qualified in normal conditions to become *abagirwa*. Many of them were men, formerly in colonial service. Such would never have qualified to join its ranks due to gender bias and their former role in the colonial service. Most pre-colonial *abagirwa* were women. Yet, during these struggles, even personalities with royal origins like Muhumuza and Ndungusi became *abagirwa*. It was this new leadership that emerged after 1914; became instrumental in the resistances and led peasant resisters into long, protracted struggles. The new leadership had new skills and politics to teach them.

These events showed that even non-believers had something to contribute to save society and Nyabingi religion. It demonstrated that beliefs were not enough.

Effects of the Changes

The fluidity and flexibility into the ranks of Nyabingi led to its undermining. Many who replaced the old *abagirwa* had not undergone any initiation into the secrets and rituals of Nyabingi. Neither had they been chosen in the usual way. This hampered them from managing adequately the spiritual aspects and defending Nyabingi outside the resistance. They were not committed to the spiritual aspect like the initiated *abagirwa*. Their main object was to struggle, although they feared and revered Nyabingi. It was this type of leadership which came to understand some weaknesses of Nyabingi and either exploited them for personal gains or disorganised the movement. In colonial language, they became 'charlatans masquerading as Nyabingi'.

Separation of leadership from the membership through death, imprisonment or disappearance did not wipe out the movement although it affected the course, magnitude and momentum of the resistance. This was because the Nyabingi Movement did not depend solely on individual leadership, which would have made it incapable of bringing up new leadership. New leadership always sprung up and led the struggle.

The limitation of this type of leadership was that it was handicapped by lack of experience, absence of prior records of the struggle and a consistent programme, strategies, lack of continuity, experience and lack of the capacity of the former leadership. These had negative consequences. It was also hard for the new leadership to know the connections in the enemies' camp, all the codes used, their contacts, and so on. This gave the advantage to the state as it was organised, had records, with a systematic programme, and so on (KDAR 1928).

This explains why the death of Ndochibiri and his comrades was followed by the weakening of the resistance. Their attacks on British forces under Kaigirirwa's leadership were easily defeated although they were well armed with 28 rifles. Worse still, they began showing other weaknesses to the enemy. One of them was when 'they announced that they would wait for vengeance until the Government relaxed their precautions and forgot their presence' (WP July Report).

While the dialectical process of Nyabingi was very important in sustaining the struggle, it also became a weakness. Before the emergence of the new leadership, peasants believed in religion so much that they failed to advance ahead to make longer, comprehensive planning against the enemy. Similarly, they did not study the situation after any defeat to learn from such experiences. This denied them opportunity to understand the enemy and his skills, strength and weaknesses and the necessary internal reforms and planning before attacking.

Another critical point was of timing. The wholesale belief in the invincibility of Nyabingi contributed heavily to a series of defeats. While the process was very crucial and timely, with the effect of paralysing the enemy, still, it had weaknesses. It increased the death toll, arrests, mistakes, political fines, among others. This decreased the morale and forced peasants to re-think and re-assess the whole situation.

Continuous peasant attacks that resulted in humiliating defeats also contributed to the undermining of the struggle. There was no time to study the enemy's resources, tactics, methods of struggle, strategies and weaknesses. They did not have time to make comprehensive reorganisation and modifications of strategies and arms. In many of the struggles, no attempts were made to capture or acquire the enemy's weapons and master his skills so as to defeat him. Repeated defeats and massacres of peasants depleted them numerically and demoralised them. It also depleted their weapons and livestock while the enemy increased in strength and numbers.

Many peasants came to understand the invincibility of the enemy and the weaknesses of Nyabingi. Some came to recognise their weaknesses vis-à-vis the enemy and decided to withdraw from resistance, or to migrate across the borders while some resorted to other individual solutions like suicides, murders, joining the enemy forces, and so on. In other words, they began to withdraw their faith from Nyabingi as they could no longer continue dying for beliefs. Others began to understand the need for more and better organisation and preparation for a general mass resistance by all the peasants. Some resorted to sending their children to learn the enemy's knowledge but objected to their conversion into new religions.

By the 1930s, many peasants had dropped the option of militant resistance and were joining the new religions. Others were being recommended to join the colonial ranks by missionaries and agents. In fact, the CMS had proposed in 1914 to the ADC, 'to appoint only Protestants as chiefs in a certain district, a proposal which I was unable to accede to. I have yet to learn that Protestants make superior chiefs to those of other denominations.' (Sullivan to MacDougall, ADC Kigezi on 13 March 1916).

Other Forms of Resistance

There were other various forms of peasant resistance, which were not under the Nyabingi Movement. These included resistance to colonialism by crossing both internal and international borders, with all their property for new settlements. The best example was in 1912, when 132 peasants crossed the Ankore-Kigezi border. The second effective and frequent form of resistance was through cutting and stealing telephone wires and smashing the insulators. While the stolen wire was used for manufacturing anklets and other ornaments, the whole act disrupted communication between Kigezi, Mbarara and Entebbe. Another related resistance was the interception of messengers and looting mail and parcels. Silence was another main weapon. In other cases, they would deceive the colonialists, aiming at derailing them.

Peasants developed a hostile attitude towards collaborators, sell-outs and the wavering. They punished collaborators through ostracisation, killing, and so on. It is not surprising that even some individuals took to committing suicide. Faced with the new invincible force, the peasants complicated their method of communication and speech. This denied colonialists and their local allies vital information. Confronted by this invincible adversary, the peasants had to build a secure, coherent internal system aimed at keeping out the enemy.

Even at the level of local languages, there was a problem of communication. There was a lot of distortion or misunderstanding by both parties, which was worsened by alien people being employed as interpreters and intermediaries. The peasants would decide to misunderstand certain commands and do the opposite or what was not wanted to be done. All this increased the dilemma of the state.

8

Transformative Processes of the Movement

Many people going to him for Nyabingi from all parts of the district and all being informed by him that his Nyabingi was more powerful than the Government, that no work should be done on Mondays in the shambas, that no taxes should be paid, and that the Europeans would be driven out (DC to PCWP on 29 May 1930 about Komundu, a Nyabingi Mugirwa).

The 1920s witnessed the decline of the Nyabingi Movement simultaneously with the increasing anchoring of colonialism, Christianity, Mohammedanism and alien legal regimes in the GLR. *Abagirwa*, like Komunda, Ndemere and others, went on the defensive to prevent its decline and the consequent erosion of its status, power and privileges by proclaiming its greatness vis-à-vis the state and the new religions.

The DC gave an interesting narrative of events between Komunda and Zaribugiri, a colonial agent. He narrated how the latter had arrested Komunda for witchcraft. The DC released him due to lack of evidence. Komunda then testified to the peasants that his 'Nyabingi' had defeated the government and left him free. The chief's wife and child fell ill immediately and nearly died. This proved to the peasants Nyabingi's greatness and powers of revenge.

It had become clear to the state that Nyabingi was 'above all revolutionary political... chief among chiefs, a state in the state. Its aim is to free the country of Europeans and of all authority other than 'Nyabingi'...All the agents of Nyabingi with their pretended mysterious and occult power give themselves out as liberators of the country' (PCWP to CS of 17 July 1928: 'A Supplementary Report on Nyabingi Movement Kigezi District').

The colonial state's predicament was its failure to distinguish between Nyabingi as a religion; Nyabingi as a supernatural force; Nyabingi as a revolutionary movement; Nyabingi as an ideology; its character and dynamism, and so on; and other practices like witchcraft, prophesying, healing, curing, rain-making, and so on. It lumped all of them together. This was advantageous to the resisters. It helped them to recruit all those that the colonialists persecuted, even those who would have refrained if the state had first made a theoretical and analytical study of this society's movement. Thus, by 1927, the DC reported a large amount of Nyabingi practice (KDAR 1927).

Threatened by religious and political persecution of Nyabingi leaders, worshippers and resisters, by the state and the new religions, and lies by missionaries of the imminent arrests of peasants who did not join Protestantism, *abagirwa*, like Komunda, began to create propaganda to wield together the disintegrating Nyabingi Movement.

They issued declarations against colonialism and proclaimed the supremacy of Nyabingi over all people, state, other religions and institutions. They called upon all peasants and chiefs to adhere to Nyabingi's teachings, work on Sundays and observe Mondays and Tuesdays as Nyabingi days. No work was to be done on those days. Peasants feared to die and followed this decree. This was challenging European religions, which had set aside Sunday as a day of worship and rest.

What compounded the problem was their weapon of secrecy: 'Direct evidence is always difficult to obtain as the pursuit of witchcraft is carefully screened from chiefs who are regarded as the eyes of Government' (DC to PCWP on 1 March 1928). The colonial dilemma still remained:

> It is, therefore, in Rukiga that NyaBINGI presents a peculiar character
> with more persistent and more dangerous aspirations than elsewhere.
> It pretends moreover to sovereignty. The principal verse of their
> hymn in Rukiga is ... 'The king (or queen) has come to his country'
> (KDAR 1928).

In pursuit of their resistance, the *abagirwa* called upon all peasants in Belgian Rwanda, Kigezi and Congo to bring in votives and sacrifices for Nyabingi in form of money, beads, and so on, in preparation for a broader resistance. This money was meant to be for sustaining the resistance. However, it cannot be ignored that the *abagirwa* would have appropriated most of it for their personal ends. This was the phase when Nyabingi became known as *Muzeire-Kasente* - a parent that needed or accepted money. They also called upon peasants to smith more weapons, sharpen them, and begin intensive military training for an imminent resistance. The theme was 'now *Omukama* (Nyabingi) is coming in the country'.

The CMS evangelist also testified that he and his Mkungu (Sub-Parish Chief) Busisiri had reported to the Gombolola Chief (Sub-County chief), when two hundred persons under the Nyabingi 'priest' Ndemere marched through his garden. The DC noted that the Sub-Chief was away as he 'had knowledge if not complicity in the Organisation' (*idem*).

DC Trewin warned all Saza Chiefs of an imminent Nyabingi resistance thus:

> The affair of 'Nyabingi' is wanting to increase in this district, also I think that all the chiefs are not aware of everything which is going on in this country. Because I see that many chiefs do not want to converse with peasants.
>
> I know that witchcraft is going high, and that someone is telling people not to do their work on Mondays and Tuesdays. Not one single chief has told me of this... people are afraid to go to work on Mondays and Tuesdays because they are obeying the 'Nabingi'. Why do you all not put strength to find out about the 'Nyabingi'? (DC Trewin to Saza Chiefs on 28 January 1928).

Indeed, anti-colonial resistances followed in the first quarter of 1928. The leadership mobilised peasants and they began war preparations in Kagarama Mountains opposite Kabale. They aimed at centres of colonial oppression and exploitation: the CMS, Kabale Station and Kikungiri. Their object remained to chase away the oppressive, exploitative system and all in its service. This was well-brought out in the Memo by CS to the Governor on Nyabingi, Criminal Case File No. 4, in which two peasants were found guilty and sentenced to five years RI.[65]

---

65   Also see the CS' telegraph to the DC, Kabale dated 24 February 1928 and DC's reply to the CS on 28 February 1928 about this matter. File: Raids and Punitive Expeditions.

The leadership organised peasants in Kigezi, Rwanda, Congo and Ankore, under the theme of self-emancipation. The leadership urged peasants to contribute something to the movement. Over a thousand peasants from the whole region were said to have participated and contributed in cash, livestock, beads and bracelets. Acceptance of sacrifices in money and beads was another qualitative change of Nyabingi religion. There was a movement to build more shrines for Nyabingi and peasants began military training with bows, arrows and spears. Peasants came from different parts of the region, in preparation for an attack on Kabale Station. It was during this time that they were surprised by colonial forces. People came from Karuzanga and Kumba to attend to these 'Nyabingi' chiefs and give their offerings.

The whole resistance began in January to March, from Kabale (Kagarama) to Karujanga and across in Rwanda, under the leadership of Ndungusi, Ndemere, Mweyahusi and others. The first was betrayed by a Protestant convert Senyange, who reported to colonial authorities. The one near Kabale was organised in mountain forests and the hills of Kagarama, four miles (and in sight) of Kabale. The resisters screened all events and secrets from a Muganda agent although over 300 of them passed through the *Gomborora* (sub-county) compound that day. The local agent had been informed of this resistance and had left the area to avoid being blamed as an accomplice of the resistance. DC wrote to PCWP on 13 September 1928 about 'Unlawful Assemblies and Incitement to rebellion by 'Priests' of NYA-BINGI Society, 1928':

> The principal objectives were the Government Station and the Protestant Mission whose houses and contents were definitely allocated by the leaders. At roughly the same time, exactly a similar manifestation under some of the same escaped leaders took place 15 miles South of Kabale on the other side of the frontier.

Resistance in Karujanga and in Belgian Rwanda developed faster and in a more organised manner. Peasants crossed from Uganda and joined others in Belgian territory, murdered collaborators, burned many villages, and threatened to burn the *Gomborora* headquarters. Inside Belgian Rwanda, resisters were reported to have killed 24 Belgian Police (Ag PCWP to the CS on 4/4/1928).

The colonialists went on the offensive on both sides of the border. The Belgian authorities deployed 100 police who subdued about 2,000 peasant resisters. They burnt many villages, killed or injured many of them. British forces suppressed the resisters on the Ugandan side, disarmed them and detained them.

The colonial authorities became alarmed on learning that the revolt was organised from Kagarama to Rwanda under the leadership of Ndungusi. Sending in a reinforcement of ten policemen and one officer from Mbarara, they were determined not to show any leniency to anyone linked to Nyabingi as it would be ascribed to Nyabingi's powers and indestructibility regardless of time. The colonialists were aware of the political dangers the Nyabingi leadership posed. In their words: 'it involves the fundamental basic anti-European element whereby all Europeans must be driven out in order to make way for their god and king and queen Nyabingi to rule their country and who for the time being has entered into, and is depicted in that particular person' (*idem.*) (sic):

> Any unaccountable incident is put down to 'Nyabingi' and is at once seized upon by the witch doctor as a proof of his powers which all helps to foster any agitation he may have in mind. The recent dry weather causing the *matama* crop to begin to wilt of course lent colour to the general rumour that a new Sultan would arrive in the country in the place of Government and would bring 'nyabingi', new seed, rain, etc (*op. cit.*)

Colonial Strategies to Defeat Resistance

The two colonial states used all means at their disposal to suppress it. Some members in the leadership were captured, convicted and sentenced heavily. The DC wrote to PCWP on 30 November 1928 about the Extradition Proceedings following Nyabingi rebellion on Belgian East Africa (Mandate) and Uganda Frontier, March 1928. He reported that he had arrested the following additional accused against Belgian Arrest Warrants of April:- Maheranni, Lupfumu, Bariganengwe and Kagambirwe. Ndemere and Mweyahusi were given five years RI each.[66]

There were new colonial reforms, based on the weaknesses of Nyabingi institution. The state had learnt the exploitative character of 'Nyabingi cult to enable it to impose its character of liberator, strikes the imagination of the simple. Thus it preys on the people demanding payment of cows, goats, foodstuffs and money.' In his supplementary report on Nyabingi Movement Kigezi District which he sent to the CS, the PCWP acknowledged that Nyabingi belonged to all tribes with its headquarters at Omukyante (Report of PCWP to CS of 17 July

---

66   Extradition to Belgian East Africa (Mandate). Diary of events 1928/29. File Nyabingi (1928).

1928: 'A Supplementary Report on NYABINGI Movement Kigezi District'). The state exploited this coercive taxation to mobilise peasants in its own favour against Nyabingi. It preached against Nyabingi, suspended taxation and other demands in Butare, Bufundi and British Rwanda. It should be noted that by this time, peasants could see some tangible results from communal labour in form of roads, hospitals, and so on. On the other hand, there was nothing tangible by Nyabingi *abagirwa* that they could cite. All peasant contributions to Nyabingi were consumed by those in its service.

The state devised a gradualist strategy to undermine the Nyabingi Movement. Peasant resistance was prevalent even after arrests. Peasants were hostile to the colonial system and were not ready to incriminate their fellow peasants. They '...had to be forcibly brought to Kabale on order to obtain their evidence which was given reluctantly in awe of the presence of accused. It was clear they were endeavouring to suppress incriminating evidence and had they not been brought in their evidence would not have been obtained' (*op. cit.* PCWP's communication to the CS on 23 May 1928).

After this, peasants refused to give information about the captured leadership. Even those who were dragged to court still refused to co-operate. The DC, therefore, recommended that Kagarama be fined 75 head of cattle under Section 2 Collective Punishment Ordinance for conniving in these witchcraft dances; well knowing their nature and illegality, and suppressing and combining to suppress all evidence which would cause the leaders to be apprehended. He argued that this would serve as an example and deterrent to other local areas should they at any time contemplate similar acquiescence in holding these Nyabingi agitations. He stressed that it was '...essential to impress on these people that the government will not tolerate these Nyabingi outbursts' (DC to PCWP on 1 March 1928).

It was due to the vigilance of agents like Zaribugire and Ndyabahika that Komunda and other resisters were hunted down. When Komunda received news of his imminent arrest, he moved camp with his followers to the Kayonza Forest, and he continued his political and religious work for two weeks. His arrest caused marked resistance. One of the *askaris* was wounded and a peasant resister shot dead. Komunda was arrested with peasants from the vicinity. The peasants in the neighbourhood were fined fifty head of cattle under Section 2, Collective Punishment Ordinance.

The colonial view, presented by the DM, was that 'any waiving of punishment on these people in those areas can but have the most serious and deleterious effect and would probably endanger the safety of others in future'. Chiefs who failed to track the resistance were dismissed. (DC to PCWP on 29 March 1928. File: Nyabingi 1928.):

> In the native mind the forfeiture of cattle causes a deep and everlasting impression, well-heeded and observed by others, but a contribution in the shape of work is merely a phase which is ephemeral, possibly irksome, and will by no means be stamped on the minds of onlookers as a deterrent. *'Emandwa'* is of much more personal a nature - and infinitely less harmful - than 'Nyabingi'. Nyabingi may extend to the attempt at expulsion from the land of any form of government: Emandwa is not anti-Government in characteristic (*idem.*)

The convicted appealed against the judgment. This alarmed the colonial state. One of them won the appeal and was released, while Ndemere died under harsh prison conditions (DC to PCWP on 29 May 1930. File: Nyabingi 1928). The appeal was a testimony of the waning of the Nyabingi Movement. Many peasants began to join the new religions. This was partly due to the religious persecution of local religions and the political threats while at the same time promoting the European religions, and partly due to the rewards, privileges and favours that colonialism accorded converts to these new religions. This would be on recommendation of Missionaries and agents.

By the late 1930s, the Nyabingi Movement had been undermined. A new peasant movement occurred in form of *Ruvaivuro* 'Revivalist Movement', whose membership and leadership were pre-dominantly women. They lacked any other organised forum around which they could organise to express their interests and wishes. The colonial policies had developed Kigezi into a labour reservoir. So, most men had to leave the district annually for wage labour for taxes and for other political, economic and social demands. As such, it was mainly women and children who remained in the villages, practising the religions.

By then, the colonial state was sure of itself. The balance of forces had tilted in its favour. The local allies, most of whom had been incorporated into the colonial system, were promising. The colonial assessment was that 'they are slow to learn new methods but, once learnt, are steady and reliable, with the notable exception of fear of the supernatural as represented by the organisation known as NYABINGI. I know no African race who retain their social equilibrium and mental stability so well under modernising influences' (*idem*).

Resistance began to take more individualised forms like arson, murders, suicides, and so on. As an instance, they burnt the house of the District Clerk in July, 1932 and the culprits escaped (KDAR 1932). The same happened to

Mandelbaum's hut in 1933 in Bufuka. Colonialism had brought her to study these peasants so as to know how to control the Nyabingi Movement. However, these peasants refused to be objects of her anthropological study. The choice of Bufuka was based on the fact that it was taken as part of the headquarters of Nyabingi. She carried out an anthropological research between 1932-33 (KDAR 1933).

Nyabingi Movement and Colonial Reforms

Confronted by the Nyabingi Movement, the district colonial officers were able to examine their policies and practice. They came to realise that Baganda agents were causing unnecessary social grievances among the peasants. This practice had been employed in all forms of colonial administration as highlighted below:

> Judicially Baganda endeavour to force their language upon the local population. In a recent case an old woman was refused a hearing for three months being told she must speak *Luganda* in Court - which she was unable to do. Indigenous peoples are insufficiently consulted by the Baganda caucus (who in Rukiga have the overwhelming majority in court) on cases arising from local usage and tribal custom...

> Following the compulsory use of *Luganda* by the Government; and the consequent association of officers with it, Baganda lords, customs and outlook are gradually becoming fastened... peaceful penetration, upon the local people whose point of view is largely lost sight of in Native Courts where Baganda preside or predominate much natural resentment is felt by the indigenous population with which I entirely sympathise. I consider it almost entirely due to the GANDA atmosphere created by the use of Baganda interpreters, and the *Luganda* Language which is imposed by the Government in Districts where it is as alien as it is unnecessary (KDAR 1919-1920).

As such, colonialism tried to reduce Baganda agents and their powers. It re-introduced Swahili as the official language. It accused Kago (a Muganda) of nepotism; 'forwarding unduly the interests of his own family and advising DC to introduce alien (Baganda) customs resented by the indigenes which formed inflammable material for the incipient fires of rebellion organised by powerful witchcraft associations, under capable leaders (*op. cit.*)

Philipps pursued this issue further to show that Baganda had become a liability to colonialism:

> The District has been almost entirely in the hands of the Baganda (who have been steadily increased) since its opening. The mediums

of communication between the Government and the local population have been *Luganda*, though heretofore Agents have always to employ Kiswahili in personal intercourse with officers - i.e. both being on terms of equality in using a medium of speech which was not their own.

The compulsory use of *Luganda* has been the most material influence in misleading the indigenous population as to the Government's attitude towards alien (Baganda) customs, in misleading the Baganda as to their own position in the country... I cannot but consider its employment in this district to be a distinct political error (*op. cit.*)

The state had two options - either to retain the Baganda agents or to dispense with them. It opted for the latter option. This would have the effect of hoodwinking the colonised peoples that this was a transformation to self-rule. This would make the position of the state even more obscure and secure. At the same time, it reverted to Swahili language as the official language, brought in more personnel from Tanzania of Baziba ethnic grouping to replace Baganda as agents, interpreters, and so on. It was made compulsory for all government personnel to learn Swahili and the state offered a bonus to whoever accomplished this task.

British colonialists used these proxy administrators from other nationalities and later from the local ones for various reasons. It was handicapped in terms of British personnel, wanted to keep low the administration costs and also minimise contradictions between colonialism and the colonised by using these proxy administrators as shields.

The Nature of Colonial Justice: Networks and Syndicates

Local agents had been learning from Baganda how to man the system. The state embarked on reforming the political system, reorganising the political leadership of the district by removing the less indispensable Baganda agents and replacing them with the local agents. It gave them necessary rewards and privileges (*op. cit.*) By then, both the major and minor chiefs were salaried. However, the role of Baganda as instructors and advisors was still important. So, many of them were retained (*op. cit.*)

The colonial ploy was to disassociate the state from the crises and attribute all of them to Baganda agents. However, it could not shy away from the question of responsibility as it was the one in command, formulating policies and supervising their implementation. Real power lay with the colonialists, not the agents. Baganda agents did not have the autonomy to act as they wished, or to formulate policies. Furthermore, the system represented British and not Baganda interests. Baganda agents could not be considered at the same level with British colonialism as these colonial accusations do.

Available facts prove that they were an indispensable tool for British colonialism in invading, conquering, penetrating and setting up the first administration system in this area. Even after phasing them out later on, neither colonialism, nor the post colonial governments tried to abolish the system.

It had become clear to the state that 'the Nabingi organisation cannot be dealt with by military measures' (PCWP to CS on 13 November 1920). The new colonial proposals for remedies and safeguards against it were: general civilisation of the District, the levelling up of administration on both sides of the two international frontiers, abstention from pressure of tax or labour in frontier areas, increased tolerance of the Ruanda *Emandwa* (anti-Nyabingi institution), and employment of *Abatutsi*, the hereditary rulers whenever possible and increasing the police force (*idem*). The PCWP considered the first two proposals as a matter of time while the last three proposals had been laid down and placed on record as general policy (*idem*).

In a bid to accomplish this, it increased educational grants to missions, began pushing religious missions to carry out their ideological and educational work and to tolerate the passive *Emandwa*. In this line, it criticised the CMS' method of work and hostilities against animists and other religions, their lack of tolerance with them as a basis for social grievances. The PCWP warned:

> One of the dangers of these illegal aggressions by native proselytisers, mistaught by Europeans ignorant of the nature of the religions or cults which are endeavouring to destroy and replace is not only the creation in Africa of a feeling of persecution and antagonism against Europeans in general, but also the natural possibility of exasperated reprisals on local churches. The latter are mostly grass huts and easily inflammable (PCWP to CS on 15 October 1930 about CMS' Mission Methods).

Drawing from the protest in the newspaper the previous year, Philipps advocated the recognition and respect of animists (as in modern China and ancient Rome) who practised the same cults of the ancestral spirit and of great men now with the gods - *Emandwa*. He argued that these religions could not be mistaken with the little shrine within the enclosure or behind the house:

> 'It is unthinkable that English or native mission-teachers should forcibly penetrate the residence of a Japanese officer or official and set fire to the shrine or even utter threats about it. In Africa, however,

even under the British flag and religious liberty, mission teachers have been and are known to trespass on private residences of Africans, chiefs and peasants, to destroy or molest their shrines.

He exposed the CMS and their teachers who accused the colonial state for its new position of hindering the burning of 'devil-huts' in the district. Philipps criticised one of the teachers for this view published in the vernacular newspaper thus: 'He doesn't add whether he considers the spirit of his own father an animist, to be a devil... Animists in Africa are set down contemptuously as heathen. A sense of both history and realities of the world as well as perspective, seem still to be relatively rare.'[67] Colonialism had moderated its position and was advocating the freedom of *Emandwa* and other mild religions.

Philipps' criticism was multi-barrelled: criticising malpractices of CMS and their greed, their failure on the ideological front, and also pushing forward the political programme to defeat peasants under Nyabingi.

The state found another solution in deliberate creation of social distinctions in the society. This was conceived by Western Province administrators in 1921:

> The question of getting into close touch with younger and more educated natives with a view to giving them some vent for their aspirations and preventing them by *practical measures from becoming revolutionary or disloyal...* To form a club or reading room in each station for the native clerks, interpreters, young chiefs and other native youths of similar education.... *The idea is to enable these natives to have a place where they can meet to pass their spare time, and providing papers and suitable literature to endeavour to curb those ideas which are at present making headway in the country...* The club should be managed by a committee of natives under the guidance of the DC, who would draw up such rule as local conditions found necessary, and *see that only suitable natives are permitted as members* (Emphasis Mine)[68]

---

67   Extract from 'The Japanese Mystery' (1930), *Atlantic Monthly*, Sep. 1930. p. 290. Also refer to J.E.J.P. Philipps' work of 1October 1930. File: C. 1605 Missions: Ruanda (CMS) Mission Methods.

68   File: Provincial Administration: District Commissioners Conferences:- Minute of Meetings:- Meeting at Mbarara on 4-8 August 1921 of DCs of Toro, Ankole, Kigezi and ADC Kigezi and Secretary.

The objective of giving a club to this new category of people – *évolue* class – was to uproot them as a privileged class from the rest of the colonised peoples. The colonial concern was on how to stem the nationalist thoughts and ideas which were rising in the country. Which class would they depend on for this project? They thought that providing these *évolue* with newspapers and selected literature would depoliticise them and mould them within the fold of colonialism and the trappings of Western modernity. That way, they would stem the insurgent nationalist ideas.

To ensure discipline, conformity and to discriminate against many people, they set up rules, which prohibited access to the club of women and children. They were to set up a committee to screen and bar unsuitable people from entering, to check on political or religious discussions, inter alia (*idem*).

It should be noted that colonial authorities had learnt clearly the insurgent character and influence of women in Kigezi. They also understood that the mixing up of different sections of society would lead to the revolutionary tendencies that were developing in the district and the world over. Class creation was at the same time aimed at undermining women, and their improved position in society. It aimed at entrenching or exacerbating inequalities through isolationism and social distinction based on gender, age, religion, education and employment.

Fears of the past resistances, and the prevalent revolutionary feelings demanded that the state should create such a club of docility, of non-active political membership, and so on, who would form a dependable ally. The colonialists did not mince their words on the anti-revolutionary role of this club, 'intended as a rendezvous for the educated type of young natives and as a check on revolutionary tendencies' (*op. cit.*)

All these colonial measures had some impact on the movement. Colonialism spelled out that the matter was one of general administration, which would always require watching. But as the district progressed, any possible danger to Government would disappear and all cases harmful to natives would be dealt with by law (DC to CS on 17 January 1922 & PC to CS commenting on Philipps' report *op. cit.*).

The Politics of Christian Revivalism

The ideological, political and cultural contributions of European religions to colonial interests were quite clear to the state. Being the most interested party, the state could not leave this important work unplanned. Yet, missionary work was hotly challenged by peasants. In 1915 the religious and secular work by both missions had been retarded by the Nyabingi Movement. This had climaxed in the murder of a CMS teacher (WPAR 1915-16).

The state wanted a planned education for the 'natives'. The creation of a semi-literate and unskilled class of natives was most undesirable. It, therefore, planned a strategy for the success of this work through compartmentalising the District, basing on ethnicity, language and other differences.

Protestantism had been rejected in Rwanda where they stuck to their religion. The White Fathers had nine Catholic missions manned by priests in Rwanda. Its personnel spoke the local language and had a wide experience with the people. The state correctly understood that Baganda Protestant Teachers would hinder this valuable work by Abanyarwanda teachers and White Fathers. This also applied to the Abakiga, who disliked Baganda but liked Abanyarwanda and were accustomed to them. The state saw it as 'politically and tribally desirable' that 'these two counties which are ethnologically, historically and geographically part of Rwanda' be under the spiritual charge of the vicariate of Sud-Nyanza. Rujumbura of Bahororo and Kinkizi of Batumbi, who were 'not unsympathetic to Ankole and Protestant influence' had to be left for Protestants, whose personnel spoke Runyankore language.

The plan was implemented successfully. One of its achievements was to create deep-rooted divisions amongst nationalities in the region based on religions. It sharpened these differences, undermined local religions and increased religious animosity amongst the new converts (*idem*. Vide KDAR 1961 on District politics and Provincial Reports from 1956-1962 on religion and politics in Kigezi).

As the military option had failed, the state began to combine various methods to defeat these resistances. It saw education as important 'to combat the influence of the witch doctors. The intelligence of the natives generally could be much improved by widening their outlook, and education would prove of much assistance in this and in making the chiefs independent of alien clerks' (KDAR 1917-18). In pursuit of this, it maintained its supportive programme to these missions. By 1930, it offered £ 500 as educational grants, and raised it to £ 547 the following year. In 1933, the total educational grants had been raised to £ 656.12 (KDARs 1930-1933). Although these figures cannot tell how the money was used, they still show a commitment of the colonial state to education.

Riding the Unruly Horse: From Christian Revivalism to Christian Revisionism

The new religions created new antagonistic contradictions between the whole colonial train and the colonised. There is a school of thought which argues that the coming of the missionaries was a blessing for the pagans. Among these are Rwampigi (1980), Ngorogoza (*op. cit.*) and Sebalijja (*op. cit.*). These contradictions revolved around material resources, notably land, labour and livestock. These increased peasants' resolution to wage an armed struggle.

In Kigezi's context, the cross followed the sword. It was the colonialists with the Kivu Mission, who paved way for Christianity. The White Fathers, who had arrived earlier in the southern part of the region, did not extend their work to the Ndorwa-Mpororo-Kajara areas. Colonial administration embarked on hoodwinking peasants to allow the missionaries in. In 1913, the Provincial Commissioner, Western Province (PCWP) disclosed that chiefs had said that peasants would allow missionaries to come provided they did not deprive them of their plural wives or their land (PCWP Report, 1913-14). It was in the following year that White Fathers and CMS selected plots around Kabale (KDAR 1914-15). The so-called conditions laid by the peasants were violated immediately.

Continued peasant resistances necessitated intensive ideological work. In this pre-literate, peasant society, religion would play an important role. The problem facing colonialism was that Nyabingi, the dominant religion, was against it. Worse still, peasants did not and could not understand or accept British interests, let alone represent them.

The duty fell on European religions, as was happening elsewhere on the continent. It had its own religions which people believed in, revered and feared. In such a context, the new religions could not be accepted wholesale. This was aggravated by misconduct by the missionaries and their new converts. Their association with the murderous state and its forced demands exacerbated the situation. Eventually, the activities of these new missions caused a lot of conflicts with the peasants. This called for the state to come in and control their activities.

The Politics of Land Grabbing and New Forms of Ownership

The first major conflict revolved around land. On his first visit, Lewin of the CMS 'marked out the choicest pieces of cultivated land for his plots'. Instead of compensating the peasants for their gardens and land, he deceived them that 'if they resigned their claim to the land and became mission people that they would be released from all obligations to their chiefs, the government, and also from road work.' He forced them to supply free food to mission teachers. The state had to come in to resolve it. (ADC writing to Governor on 23 August 1914 in defence against CMS accusation 'Obstruction in the Granting of Plots to CMS in Kigezi'. Vide Sullivan to ADC on 13 March 1916):

> Owing to the density of population and extremely strong feeling among the clans as to alienation of their land whether fallow or cultivated it has been explained to the indigenous population that such lands will not be alienated without their consent (obtained after individual explanation to those interested that lands then granted would cease to belong to them) missionary societies were simultaneously informed that applications for unoccupied lands (not cultivated or fallow) would receive sympathetic consideration (KDAR 1919-20 & WPAR 1919-20).

The subsequent years witnessed an intensification of the scramble for land by missions. By 1928, the colonial state was alarmed. Missions had 407 Temporary Occupation Plots, of which 272 belonged to CMS. In addition to that, they had three miles of freehold land. This land had been acquired through force, intimidation and deceits to peasants. The CMS later deceived the state that all its plots were bush schools. Because of that, they were able to get educational grants from the state for these unoccupied plots (DC to PCWP on 1 August 1929: 'Land, T.O.L., Missions.' Sub-grade [Bush] Schools).

Politicising Land Ownership for Colonial Ideology

However, the state realised that the CMS was failing to execute its ideological duties. Most of its plots lacked teachers while the rest were manned by young boys, 'practically illiterate, irresponsible... unfit to teach the doctrines of Christ'. To the DC, their presence was doing more harm to the community. The colonial argument was that, these evangelising classes made children 'develop a contemptuous insubordination to both domestic and tribal discipline' (Report of DC on '272 Temporary Occupation Plots. Plots at Kihi'). On its part, the CMS preferred to exploit the cheap labour as it paid only a shilling a month and freedom from forced unpaid labour (*oruharo*).

While the CMS was receiving enormous educational grants for these empty plots on the pretext that they were schools it was exporting teachers to Belgian Rwanda, where its outlook and main interests lay (DC to PCWP on 1 August

1929. Also see KDAR 1933). The state was forced to spell out its educational policy in no uncertain terms, thus:

> We owe it both to a contented continuance of English trusteeship, and in fairness to the men with whom we shall have to deal in the new Africa of ten and more years hence, that the rising generation should either remain under a proper African or a proper European influence. Unless such conditions are rectified, we would appear to be drifting aimlessly (if not dangerously between the two) (*op. cit.*)

The state limited the amount of land acquired by missionaries. It also forced them to visit these plots regularly and staff them with qualified personnel. It did not want these plots to develop into centres for dissention, resistance and insubordination to disrupt colonial order. It threatened to withdraw educational grants, deprive them of most of the land and the privilege to church teachers if the CMS did not fulfil its ideological obligations. It demanded accountability of the CMS, stopped them from exporting teachers to Rwanda, and accused them of embezzling most of the resources received for educational purposes. 'Money granted to White Fathers seems to go much further (Sic!) than an equal amount given to Protestants, who encumber themselves with large families.' (KDAR 1929 & 1930).

Exacting Forms of Slavery and Servitude

In 1931, the Roman Catholics had nearly twice the number of converts of Protestants. The former had 9,186 converts and the latter had 5,087. It reported that 232,603 peasants were still worshipping their pre-colonial religions (1931 Returns on Converts, KDAR 1931). This was also reflected by the enrolment at school. In 1930, CMS had less than half the enrolment number of the WFM. It had 109 pupils while the WFM had 230 pupils. This worsened the following year when WFM had 287 pupils while the CMS had 96 pupils. By 1933, WFM had 525 pupils while CMS had 164 pupils.

The colonial state continued demanding accountability from CMS as it was receiving more money than WFM. The CMS was forced to respond. By 1960, it had narrowed the gap. It had 8,817 pupils while WFM had 11,398 pupils (KDARs 1930-33 & 1960).

Secondly, it discouraged the CMS from using crooked, cunning and deceitful methods to extort peasant resources in form of free labour. The first example is Seseme Church, which was struck by lightning. The CMS demanded its replacement by *oruharo* labour, lying that it was 'burnt by incendiarism'. It received and used *oruharo* labour worth a hundred pounds to build a bigger and better one. The oruharo labour was worth more than a hundred Pounds (Dr. Smith CMS to DC on 23/9/1927: 'The CMS 'Freehold' at Seseme (Kisoro), Bufumbira (Rwanda)' DC to Dr. Smith on 13 October 1927 and Dr. Smith's reply on 3 November 1927).

Conflicts between state and the CMS arose when the church was being completed. Dr. Smith informed the DC that he had made a sad 'discovery' that he had been appealing for help 'under false pretences. Apparently, it was not destroyed by incendiarism, after all, but struck by lightning' (Dr. Smith to DC on 3 November 1927). The DC was angered by this duplicity and exploitation; 'an act of god and not of naughty natives,' though it was the latter who had to suffer for it... the CMS asked (and obtained) 'unpaid forced labour' against the existence of which they inveighed so forcibly public (*op. cit.*). He warned them against this malpractice.

The CMS created lies and promised converts rewards, absolution from work and other obligations and punishments. One of the lies it created was that natives that were not Christians would be considered sympathisers with Nyabingi and would be thrown into prison and that safety lay in the 'religion of the Government', namely Protestantism. It was reported that 'a few pagans, oscillating alarmed between Scylla and charybdis, betook themselves to Islam'.

The Roman Catholics retaliated by creating a rumour that the PCWP had become Catholic and that Catholics alone could and would communicate to him and would be the ones to get jobs. The DC had to disprove this publicly that 'there was no religious 'reservations' mediaevalisms which would get them into or keep them in any post...' (KDAR 1915-16, 1928).

Resistance between peasants and missions arose over school fees. The best case is of Ruhara's three children, who were expelled from school for failing to pay church dues. What complicated matters was that they had paid school fees. The state accused the Catholic Church of manipulating school fees to exploit resources for the church. After a lot of correspondences, the colonial state concluded thus:

> Education, is after all a social service. In Uganda the Protectorate
> Government has entrusted it, almost entirely, to the Mission Societies.
> ... Responsibility still rests with Administrative and Education Officers
> to exercise, in the name of Government,... who wish to make use of
> educational facilities, provided largely by public funds, in spite of

statements to the contrary, and are willing to behave themselves, must be allowed to do so; and to attend Mission schools until state schools are established. Schools must not be used as instruments for enforcing Church discipline against children or parents, especially when it appears to be only a matter of tithe payments.

Uganda has suffered since 1890, or earlier, from the political and religious rivalry of the Mission Societies... (*op. cit.* Vide Memos of 10 February 1941 and of 15 February 1941 on the same issue).

Protecting Flora and Fauna for Political Tourism

The colonial authorities called Kigezi the Switzerland of Africa. They knew that it had the best climate, and that it was free of diseases that affect cows. Their aim was to preserve it for their settlement. The colonial state, therefore, had to take practical steps towards this important project.

It stopped the CMS' activities of hunting and shooting game for ivory and meat in the outlawed Sleeping Sickness (S.S.) belt. In addition to violating S.S. laws, they were depopulating the animals. To make matters worse, the colonial state had prohibited peasants from going there, let alone hunting there or killing animals. During their hunting expeditions, the CMS personnel exploited unpaid labour of peasants on these trips. They took an average of 50 porters per trip to these S.S. areas for an average of twelve days.

The colonial state accused the CMS of exposing these porters to sleeping sickness, overloading them without remuneration, separating these peasants from their households for twelve days, forcing peasants to contribute food and milk without pay, and then forcing men to carry them for long distances and many days, and inhuman exploitation, without feeding these porters on these trips, inter alia (DC to PCWP on 15 May 1929).

Not only were these grievances bases for Nyabingi resistances, but they also had the effect of teaching peasants to defy government laws and go into the S.S. areas to hunt as the Whites were doing. This came to be known as poaching. Peasants saw this as a racist move to block the Africans from hunting and keeping it exclusively for Whites. The state threatened to prosecute any missionary violating this rule. This was a strategy for resource consolidation. It marked a gradual movement from antagonism to consolidation to achieve economic benefits for political sustainability. This was vivid in these fresh strategies of protecting animals and plants for tourism, health reasons, and so on.

Peasant Resistance to Super-Exploitation by Non-State Actors

The state intervened when peasants appealed against forced milk contribution. When peasants changed from militant armed struggles to legal methods, appeals, and so on, the state seized the opportunity and came in with a pro-peasants' face. It began to address some of the social grievances.

Peasants appealed to the DC against forced milk contribution (*ezekibeere*) by the CMS. They had been compelled to take one cow each to the CMS at Kabale, three days' march away. They were compelled against their will to remain on the CMS Mailo for 30 days and to supply milk. They had to take their own money for food and cook the food themselves while so detained. To make matters worse, the CMS gave them two shillings per cow for one month's milk. An average of thirty peasants were thus compelled every month to take, each, a milk cow, to the CMS, principally from Nyarushanje and Nyakishenyi Gombololas (DC to PCWP on 28 September 1928. File: CMS). The DC explained this super-exploitation, by showing that a Kiga cow produced as much as three bottles of milk. The standard price of milk was 20 cents a bottle, which meant Shs. 9/= per month, per cow.

We find that in sanctioning this forced milk contribution, the colonial state, which was still in its embryonic stage, was too careful to antagonise the organised large cattle owners. The victims were peasants owning an average of two head of cattle apiece. The agent received orders of the needed cattle and he then acted. There was very high mortality among the cows and calves, thus, brought to Kabale due to great climatic differences and pasturage which were injurious to the cows and their calves.

The DC recounted to the PCWP the hazards these cattle and their owners were exposed to: the marked climatic differences (damp-cold) in Kabale; differences in composition of both water and pasture between the valleys of the Edward watershed and those of Victoria (For example, Kabale). On pasturage, he argued that MBULALLI[69] and RUMBUGU[70] formed the staple pasture, while the latter was relatively rare and the former practically did not exist:

'The MBULALLI grass at Kabale was injurious to cattle when unaccustomed to it, leading to high mortality among cows and their calves brought to Kabale (*idem*). This is a source of grievance among

---

69   The word Mbullali was used to refer to a particular grass locally known as Emburara. It is nutritious for cattle.

70   Rumbugu means couch grass or *agropyron repens*.

the peasantry. The average price of a cow in milk is about Shs. 100/=.
No compensation is paid by the CMS in case of deaths.

Worse still, there were relatively very few cattle. The DC explained that 'the proportion of cows, and in milk, at any one time was small, and nearly all Rukiga cattle were owned in ones and twos, which made the taking of the only cow a man had, and any death, a matter of real hardship':

> To gain a sense of perspective, one might reasonably say that the loss of a cow to a mKiga (Omukiga) is equivalent to the loss by fire to a poor European, who has neither income nor bank balance, of his house and all its contents ... uninsured! A cow to a mKiga frequently represents the savings of a life time (*idem*).

The PC ruled against the practice: The assistance of chiefs and the native courts cannot be invoked in this matter. He stressed that it was not equitable that the peasants of Rukiga should be forced to bring the cows for providing the milk and ghee for the 16 Europeans on the CMS Hill (PCWP to CS on 23 October 1928 and C.S' comments on 30 October 1928). The practice was abolished that December.[71] The DC then castigated the criminal nature of forced milk contribution:

> It should however be placed on record that throughout the past eight years the cattle have, in point of fact, had to be brought in by ORDER of the DC supported by criminal convictions (flogging and fines) in Native Courts, all of which are now stated to have been illegal. The question of influence has never arisen. The matter is now seen frankly to have been one of illegality, profiteering on and discrimination against, the native. Had the cattle belonged to a White man, this state of affairs would clearly never have occurred (DC to PCWP on 14 February 1929 on 'Compulsory Milk CMS').

Peasants needed the milk for themselves. Besides, it led to the detention of men, who commanded respect in society and were heads of households on the mission station for a month. It forced them to carry out roles which were hitherto considered in their customs to be exclusively for women. These included cooking.

---

71   Telegraph of CS to PCWP of 22 December 1928 and telegraph of PCWP to Districter, of 24 December 1928. Also see DM to the Attorney General on 13 January 1929 and the Solicitor General to CS on 22 January 1929.

This degraded and humiliated the men. It had the possibility of undermining their social position in society. It disorganised their households and their production plans, their defence system, and so on. Worse still, they had other compulsory state obligations to meet (DM to Attorney General on 13 January 1929 & Communication of the Solicitor General to CS on 22 January 1929).

In fact, the state was able to assess the effectiveness of its reforms the following year by attributing the confinement of NYA-BINGI to 'a *MAGNI NOMINIS UMBRA*' to be principally the 'removal of a number of grievances, petty enough to the European who is not touched by them but acute and infuriating to the African, and easily exploitable by the Nya-BINGI, *laudator - temporis - acti*' (KDAR 1929).

In all the aforementioned conflicts, the state sided with the aggrieved peasants. This shows that the colonialists were not willing to condone the crooked ways of the missionaries, who constituted a crucial ideological wing of colonialism. At the practical level, it did not want to leave unattended to, any grievances which could constitute fertile grounds of insurgencies.

While this approach exposed divisions amongst the Europeans before the eyes of the colonised, it ended up creating an alliance between the colonialists and the peasants versus the missionaries. It constituted a strong basis for forging state-peasant alliance. It also exposed the class of interests between the colonial administration and the missionaries over economic interests. The administration wanted the missionaries to concentrate on the ideological front and vacate the economic domain.

This helped to deconstruct religious-political alliances while reinforcing the forging of a *nouveaux* (new) political alliance between the colonialists and the peasants. Above all, the colonialists could not condone the corrupt practices by the non-administrators which had high possibilities of refuelling and igniting peasant resistances. Another compelling motive was that the colonialists could not sanction corrupt privileges for a nonentity group which, they themselves, were not enjoying. They, therefore, used political power to tame religious power. State power had to reign supreme over spiritual powers and preclude it from involving and benefiting from temporal domains.

9

Conclusion

*...it is difficult to realise the immense importance locally of the death
of this rebel who has defied two Governments for five years and was
a leader of an anti-European Secret society which has terrorised the
RUANDA - RUKIGA county for four generations.*

This study has shown how the Nyabingi Movement arose on the various social
grievances from both within society and from outside. Within society, the
Nyabingi Movement was against ruling classes in areas with states like Rwanda,
Mpororo and Kinkizi. In other areas, it was against the privileged members of
society, like heads of households.

What became evident was that to confront the principal enemy, colonialism,
there had to be internal reforms. Secondly, it also became clear that in the absence
of an organised political forum and an armed force to defend the peasants' rights,
they had to do it themselves. *Abagirwa* took up the initial initiative to mobilise
them.

With a dynamic armed force, the colonialists posed a direct threat to
abagirwa's privileged positions, social status and religion. To protect these,
abagirwa had to mobilise their fold. This led to the flaring up of the Nyabingi
Movement up to the 1930s. Nyabingi institution transcended other religions by
its active politics. *Abagirwa* of the Nyabingi credence devised new ideologies
and practices to retain and encourage their fold.

It is important to note that, unlike other religions in highly developed class societies, where religion is an ideology of oppression and exploitation, Nyabingi became a solid ideology for the peasants' struggles. The successive leadership recognised the importance of religion in the area. Even the most advanced and sophisticated guerrilla movement under Ndochibiri and others recognised this and exploited it intensively. Another important thing was that the leadership tried to incorporate some of the pre-colonial practices, methods of struggle, language, and so on, to enrich the movement.

One of the major weaknesses lay in strong belief in Nyabingi religion. This was dominant between 1910 and 1914. The peasant resisters put too much faith in the Nyabingi institution. This was worsened by *abagirwa* claiming to be personifications of Nyabingi. While this transformation had the positive effect of encouraging resisters, it led them to defeats and massacres by the colonial forces.

In the same manner, the dialectical character of the Nyabingi Movement of bringing up new leadership, whenever the existing one got separated from the membership, had positive and negative effects. While it encouraged and sustained the resistance, it led to defeats due to lack of continuity.

The Nyabingi Movement developed with the World War I. The movement got new leadership from those who had been recruited in the colonial army, and those who had been deported or detained. They brought in the enemy's military hardware and methods of struggle, planning and commanding. They exposed the enemy's strengths and weaknesses, and devised new methods. It was this new leadership which paralysed colonialism and forced it to make various reforms. However, the Nyabingi movement was not an organised armed force. While the supply of resources to the state was compulsory, those given to the movement was by the peasants' willingness. They withdrew from the struggle when they realised that the movement was not likely to defeat the enemy.

Gradually, the Nyabingi Movement got defeated though it was not wiped out. The colonial state achieved this through combining various methods. These included the military option, which it sustained throughout, and various reforms that it was compelled to make. In administration, it was forced to replace proxy administrators with local ones, and avoided taxing women. It was careful to make Kigezi a labour reservoir instead of introducing production of cash crops and high technical skills, industries or any other major investments. It had to modify its demands in taxation, forced labour, and so on. The state also intensified deportations, deprived resisters of resources to fuel the movement and maintained its scorched-earth policy.

On the ideological front, it encouraged and financed the new missions to promote their work. It broadened its social base among the peasants using pecuniary and non-pecuniary incentives. The latter categories included medals and honours. It also intensified its propaganda. With time, peasants were able to compare results of colonial policies vis-à-vis the blind opposition of *abagirwa* to these policies. Through all these, the state managed to anchor into the peasantry while undermining the Nyabingi Movement. It increased legislations against Nyabingi religion. Gradually, peasants began to withdraw into the new religions.

The Nyabingi Movement is a concrete testimony to people's persistent struggles to defend their rights and independence. It demonstrates that no matter how backward a people may be perceived by others, they will always resist any threat to their rights, irrespective of the level of advancement of the adversary. The Nyabingi episode demonstrated practically why and how religion could be instrumental in providing a platform for struggle, theories, ideology and leadership. It also showed that in a situation characterised by backward forces of production, with no state or other strong social or political organisation, people would find a base in any form of organisation like religion to advance and defend their interests. It is in such a situation that we find religion taking on a progressive role. On the other hand, we see colonialism using Christianity to penetrate and control these new colonies. It is in the latter case that religion gets introduced for reactionary purposes as 'an opium of the people' for oppressive and exploitative purposes.

The defeat of the Nyabingi Movement was a landmark to their loss of independence and incorporation into the broader capitalist system. It was a turning point for the pre-capitalist area. On the other hand, the fixing of borders and lumping together of different peoples under one administration was a step forward. Former antagonisms were dropped and peasants began to cooperate towards self-emancipation.

However, the colonial state was quick enough to understand the effects of such nationalism and began fragmenting them. It denied them rights to grow and develop crops for export, killed their industries and developed them into labour reservoirs. Furthermore, it disrupted their social set-up, and outlawed their socio-economic, political and military practices.

Peasants gradually became more scared of colonialism and tried to combine both pre-colonial religions with the new ones. They took on European names as an external sign of conversion to European religions while maintaining their pre-colonial religions in secret. This became the genesis of the synergism between European and African religions. This segmentation of the resistance groups fragmented the fighting forces. It became a handy weapon and strategy for the colonialists to nip these resistances in the bud.

What needs to be observed is that appealing a ruling per se cannot signify the end of the Nyabingi rebellion. Rather, it is the theoretical signification of the action of capture then prosecution from which an appeal was sought that shows political surrender and submission to the new political alignment of which the court system was a vital part.

The Nyabingi Movement showed, in concrete terms, the need for leaders of religious organisations to get involved in solving people's problems; the need for them to give courageous and untiring leadership. It showed that dependence on any single section of society spelled out peril for that society.

Though the Nyabingi Movement got defeated, it still represented popular interests. It faced the limitations of circumstances and leadership. The circumstances of peasant life were highly fragmented. No wonder, their unity was overly shaped by ideological factors. While the religious vision articulated by the leadership emphasised the unity of the people, it could not conceal the conflicting aims of the leadership for long. Its anti-colonial aims were intertwined with its aspirations to safeguard its internal dominance. Its alternative to colonial control was its own control within the context of safeguarding the *status quo*.

Of course, the nature of the leadership changed, as did circumstances. New types of leaders kept on arising from the ranks of peasants, particularly from amongst those who, like soldiers, had had a close colonial encounter. While their influence could not reverse the fortunes of the movement in the immediate run, it did steer the course of resistance in Kigezi into the fold of Uganda - the larger entity the British had created to satisfy their own appetite.

Emerging Issues and Policy Recommendations

One of the intersecting issues that emerges from the study is the important influence of a shared common language in uniting people to network in the pursuit of a common cause. Nyabingi Movement was able to withstand colonial assault because of the use of a shared language among its supporters across the region. The same female prophetesses ruled in the Bantu-language speaking areas extending up to South Africa.

Arising from the above was the influence of and role of networks, vivid in the patterns observable across the African continent, especially among the peoples who were led by female prophetess. The Maji Maji rebellion versus German colonialism in Tanzania was also religion-based, with religious beliefs and practices.

The popular belief that cut across most of these movements was that water and concoctions could kill fire power. The Maji Maji taught that sprinkling water mixed with millet seeds would stop bullets from killing the believers.

Such networks demonstrated the power of religion to unite people and provide them with political hope. This clearly demonstrates that the concept of networks and power had developed in Africa long before colonialism. As such, they formed an ideal political model for emulation in developing political territories and control.

The policy implication is the potential and relevance of religious and other forms of networks in political leadership and control which can be exploited. Networking as a concept is a policy tool worth replicating in political science and in the exercise of political administration.

The other implication emanating from the above is a comparative one. That is the centrality and fusion of religion with political control, both within medieval Europe and pre-colonial Africa. The same model was continued by the colonial administration in executing the imperialist project. This raised the policy implication of the relationship between political power and religious prophecy which is used as a tool of ideological conviction. Even within the contemporary political dispensation, this is still the case. Instances as the inclusion in the national constitutions of state religions, the use of religious symbols in the national slogans and mottos such as 'for God and my Country' in the case of Uganda, are vivid examples.

The role of 'king makers' played by competing religious denominations in campaigning and convincing their followers to elect a given candidate during election time and going to the extent of intimidating with death some candidates and the wavering voters is further testimony of the influence and power of religious prophecy and power. These demonstrate how the new religions were able to seize the ground, push to the background the pre-colonial African religions and dominate the scene with state support.

The implication of this reality, for political and development studies, is that religious power has to be watched, controlled and harnessed in the exercise of political control. There is a mutually exclusive relationship between religious activity and political power. Both strive to control each other, for gain, influence and access to economic resources. These influences have to be delicately controlled and promoted to ensure a successful political activity.

Failure to do this can result into the use of religious activity to mobilise for conflict and destabilisation of the power relations and technologies of power. It can also lead to regime change. Such conflict can take a number of forms as evidenced in the various guerrilla strategies employed by the Nyabingi Movement at the various moments in time; they sprang up with various effects. The most damning conflict manifested is in The Movement for the Restoration of the Ten Commandments of God cult that wreaked economic and social havoc and led to the loss of thousands of lives.

The role and the emancipation of women are stressed in the leadership roles they played. These demonstrate that ignoring a section of society in the economic and political activities becomes a recruiting ground for rebellion and ethnic conflicts, reflected in the various movements in Africa. The most recent examples in Uganda include the Holy Spirit Lakwena Movement and its successor, the Lord's Resistance Army, and the Allied Democratic Forces. These have to be checked.

An important policy implication should be deduced from the colonial use of religion to fight religion; that is, using Christianity, Mohammedanism and *Emandwa* as state religions to fight and finally dislodge the Nyabingi Movement. This shows the use of ideology to fight ideology. The state resorted to use *Emandwa* religion to fight Nyabingi religion amongst similar people, who shared language, customs, norms, habits and cultures.

In actual fact, this was another form of the use of proxies. In other words, it was another form of using indirect rule through another type of agents. Indirect rule was an effective weapon used against people resisting political control and domination, as other African experiences show. It was a divide and rule strategy that effectively worked in the short term and continues to be practised even in contemporary leadership styles in different countries.

The colonial government, as part of the general strategy to fight Nyabingi, used formal law to outlaw the Movement. As in other countries Africa, it declared Nyabingi an outlawed organisation and characterised its activities as repugnant to morality and good values based on Western Christianity. Within this framework, the colonialists also put in motion a propaganda campaign of legally representing the Nyabingi Movement as a criminal syndicate.

All over Africa, this was the label given to such movements. The use of the term – criminal syndicates – was instructive. The syndicate was the networks or political network across Africa. The unity and wide coverage harmony was possible because of such attributes as trust which underlies all literature on such networks.

The resilience of the Nyabingi culture in the face of legal suppression, use of law and police indicates an empirical divergence such that the Nyabingi persisted in spite of colonial bans. This resilience demonstrates the incapacity of law as a tool to rout out other cultures and tradition of a people unless they accept it. The other factor was religious beliefs. Whereas it is not written anywhere, still, it is vivid in the primary data of this book.

The heinous human rights violations and atrocities were perpetrated through the supposed spread of Christianity, which claimed to espouse and claim high morality and adherence to the 'Almighty God'. The practice in the GLR was that political struggles manifested in the use of 'modern' religions in forms of Christianity and Mohammedanism and later the colonially integrated traditional '*Emandwa*' versus the 'traditional' Nyabingi Movement.

Religion manifested enormous contradictions. However, these contradictions placed in context of the Capitalist developments elsewhere, were a true reflection of the 'primitive accumulation' which were witnessed elsewhere in the operations of capitalism, the forced taxation, and so on.

Incidentally, the human rights violations were being perpetrated with state sanction as was witnessed in the corresponding (coincidental) passage of national laws to give effect to these practices. Examples are the 1902 Order-in-Council that declared the majority of practices such as religions and movements as Nyabingi Movement 'repugnant' and, therefore, illegal in Uganda. Mohammedanism also got its laws (as some rewards) such as the Marriage and Divorce of Mohammedans Act. This is the same period of increased activity of these religious and political contestations as highlighted in this work. The two religions enjoyed substantial state funding to undertake their ideological functions.

Significantly, there is no evidence that these human rights violations legitimated by the laws enacted by the very perpetrators - the colonial administration - were ever reproached or their victims compensated in form of reparations as provided for under International Law. Instead, the colonial establishment, in protracted fashion, succeeded in ideologically presenting it as a fight of 'modernity' against 'traditionalism' or 'primitiveness'; of 'good' versus 'evil'. It is an issue that such bodies as the UN and other human rights bodies, national and local, have to take up. While this was being presented simplistically as a fight against primitiveness, it was in reality a political struggle.

That was the network or syndicate trust that was used in guerrilla warfare including the Mau Mau and the NRM to effectively operate political belts unnoticed or undetected and the use of religions, rituals, symbols and practices derived from those similar to the movements. Syndicates survived on legend figures and mythology such as cats to claim the NRM leaders' magical and supernatural powers that made them supernatural beings. This was used to fortify and morale-boost the rebels to scare the enemy and to mobilise support for the rebellion that effectively succeeded in five years, thus setting a global record.

The pre-colonial Abachwezi and their offspring in the GLR plus monarchical claims based on similar supernatural ideological forces provided strong foundations for similar claims by the *abagirwa*. Museveni's current references to the Abachwezi and his protection of their historical sites need further reflection. Could it be a continuation of the African spiritual power being invoked for political purposes? Could it be that the past is being blended with the present political and spiritual practices to address the current and future needs?

The Nyabingi *abagirwa* who ably exploited those supernatural claims included Muhumuza, Ndungusi, Ndochibiri, Kaigirirwa, Komunda and those other individuals who were arrested in Bukoba and Masaka. It is this that presents reverence of leaders as charismatic. This comes from Nyabingi works such as the stone with feet – foot prints, and so on. Others practice this in their quest for political power.

The implication of the division of the areas to fight religious prophets had a lasting impact. This was the division of the peoples of the same ethnic origins, shared languages and history into smaller ethnic entities by putting them in different countries, regions and borders. This is one of the causes of contemporary ethnic divisions and conflicts noted in Rwanda and Burundi, the Sudan, Uganda, the DRC and Kenya. This is a political question that has to be grappled with, resolved, understood and rediscovered in order to explain African politics and to set foundations for political and constitutional stability.

Summarily, this study has demonstrated that the real contestations for colonisation of the GLR, as it is currently known, took place largely in the Kivu-Mulera-Ndorwa-Rukiga-Mpororo region. All the contestations and negotiations marked the forging of the Great Lakes States as they are known today. Put differently, the Great Lakes States resulted from the 1909-1926 compromises in Rukiga to divide the territory. This is the history of the Great Lakes States that has been ignored and marginalised in speech, discourse and writing.

Bibliography

Archival Sources

11209: Native Affairs: Visit of Uganda Chiefs to U.K. 1947-1948

12,741: Lease of Habukara Island in Lake Bunyoni to Dr. L.E.S. Sharp

12,921: International Touring Congress of Africa - Archaeological and Historical Sites

12567: Mbarara-Kabale-Congo Belge Road

131: C.M.S. NI CMS

1450A: Kigezi: Monthly Reports 1911

1450B: Kigezi: Monthly Reports 1912

146: Native Administration: Nyabingi And Kabale Defence (1919-1923)

146A: Native Administration, Nyabingi (1928)

147/09: Mfumbiro District, Occupation of: [3 Vols.]

1682: Part II: Sleeping Sickness Toro: Salt Traffic At Katwe And District: Measures

1700: Western Uganda Census, 1911

17083: Trespass Belgian

1981: Kigezi: Fighting by Natives. Sentences Passed on Natives of Makuburri's Country

2205: Reorganisation of Administrative Units

237: Economic Crop: Encouragement of the Reproduction of

2471B: Western Province Monthly Reports, 1914

2471G: Western Province Monthly Reports, 1919

2471J: Western Province Quarterly Reports, 1920; 1927

273/1907: Murder by Bagishu of Two Chiefs of Batandiga

2923: Western Province Districts and Boundaries

29381: Anglo-Belgian Boundary Commission, Mahangi Strip [2 Vols.]

301/2/2: East African Production Committee

306/2: Labour Routes: Conditions of Immigrant Labour Not in Employment: Food Supply, Shelter, Medical Care etc.

306: Labour: Immigrant; South Western Route

308: Veterinary. Tsetse Survey of Uganda

3092: Sleeping Sickness - Kigezi: Infected Area, 24/4/14

3111/1: Native Affairs (Native Councils) - Uganda

3173: Kigezi: Ndungutzi - Native Chief: Deportation of, Death: Settlement of Estate

3174: Kigezi: Kumba, Police Officer for

3176: Kigezi: Murder of a Native Captured in German Territory

3226: Boundary Commission: in Reference to Mfumbiro-German-Uganda-Congo [2 Vols: Pt I-II]

3314-3314P: Western Province Annual Reports 1912-1927

3634: Military: Western Province Movement of Troops, 18/11/13

42/99: Western Province: Annual Report 1905-06

438: Western Province, Kabale Station Defence precautions

4522: Native Markets: Dues on Livestock

4526: Raids and Punitive Expeditions in the Kigezi District

4572: Public Works Department: Roads in Western Province: Construction of

47: Missionary Societies and Mission Land, Churches (General)

4754: Kigezi Chieftainships

5113: Land Policy in Bugishu: Bugishu Land (3 Vols.)

514: Western Province: Annual Report, 1905-06

516/08: Crown Land Rents and Poll Taxes - Appointment of Collectors [2 Vols.]

53 (1941): Historical And Political Notes (West)

5339: E.A.R. & H. Extension from Kampala to Belgian Congo. Physical Considerations

5355: E.A.R. & H. Extension From Kampala to Belgian Congo: General Correspondence With The Provincial And District Commissioners

5359: K.U.R. Extension from Kampala to Belgian Congo. Communications from the General Public

5972: Provincial Administration: Provincial Commissioner in Council Proceedings of Meetings 1919

60/1910: Boundaries: Anglo-Congolese, Anglo-German Negotiations (Mfumbiro)

651: Cattle Keeping in Uganda, Veterinary Department 1929

657: Ankole - Attack on an Askari Between Kigezi and Kagamba

657: Military: Board at Kigezi on Bayonet Scabbard No. 52 & 110

7032/2: Native Affairs, Deportation Ordinance, Susani s/o Tabyabwiza

7998: C.M.S. Annual Reports

8849: Premature Burial of Natives Before Extinction of Life

9430: Education: Grants From Native Governments

9727: Treasury: Calculations of Subvention: Western Province

A27 1906-7: General Reports in Districts of Ankole, Toro And Masindi

A43/257: Elgon Administration

A43/295: Expedition Against the Bagishu in November 1907

A43/50: Murder by Bagishu of two Chiefs of Batandiga

A6: Annual Report 1904, 1904-5

A6/17/1904: Annual Reports & Co.

A6/18/03: Reports 1901-1903

ACS's Copy: Agricultural Survey Committee: Memoranda for Consideration of
    Members

Agriculture: Native Coffee Industry - Kigezi District - Arabica

Ankole Kigezi: Monthly Reports 1910

Annual Report - Uganda Police 1928-1934

Annual Report of Kigezi District 1961

B61: Provincial Administration: Report of the Departmental Organisation
    Committee 1933. Comments of Provincial Commissioners

Blue Books 1910 - 1945

Book for 1947 Material Tax

C1429: Missions. Temporary Occupation Licence Plots

C. LAN 8/3/2 Land Policy: Mbale Land Tenure - Bugishu. [2 Vols.]

C/2 Annual Report General

C1040: Omugabe of Ankole Claims Ruzumbura

C15/15 (L. LAN. 8) Land: Land Tenure - General

C1605: Missions Ruanda (CMS) Mission Methods

C1916: Boundaries: Southern Protectorate Boundary [2 Vols.]

C22 561: Luwalo: Abolition of

C404: Church Dues and Deflection of Fees

C465: Legal: Native Authority Ordinance

C54: African Affairs, Emigration of Nations from Belgian Congo to Neighbouring British Territories

C706B: Boundaries: Uganda-Kigezi-Rwanda

Census Returns - Uganda 1911, 1921 & 1931

Colonial Government (1955) "The Uganda Protectorate Land Tenure proposals."

Colonial Office (1945) "Native Land Tenure in East Africa." London: Her Majesty's Office

Colonial Office (1952) "Land and Population in East Africa." London: Her Majesty's Office

Colonial Office (1955) "East Africa Royal Commission 1953-1955 Report."

London: Her Majesty's Stationery Office.

Colonial Protectorate (1950) "The Land Policy of the Protectorate Government in Uganda."

Crown Land: Leases, Individual Cases

F78/65/11: Roll of Honour - Casualties, Kigezi District

File District Book

File: The District Commissioner, Kabale (4 Vols.)

Foreign Office: Annual Series, Africa, Report on the Trade and Industry of Uganda, 1897

G3/9: Telegraph and Telephone Communications, Mbarara-Kabale Line

General Report By His Majesty's Special Commissioner on the Protectorate of Uganda March 31, 1904

H132: Coffee Schemes to Further the Consumption of

H174: Agriculture: Records of Experiment Stations

H175II: Agriculture: Advisory Committee For The Native Agricultural Production: Constitution, Policy etc.

H197: Co-ordination Between Agricultural, Forestry And Veterinary Departments

H202/2/1: Agricultural Developments

H225: Agriculture: Restriction of Production

H241: Grass Fires

H293/1: Industries: Pyrethrum Extraction

H 295/1 Flax Industry: Compulsory Acquisition of a Flax Factory at Kigezi

H 310/5: Development and Welfare Committee

H 43/5 Native Coffee Industry: Arabica Coffee in Ankole and Kigezi, Marketing of Crop

H 57 Agriculture: Imperial Agricultural Research Conference

H 87/1 Game: Pests - Crows - Destruction of, For Damaging Crops

H301/2/1: Agricultural Production: Minutes of Meetings of the Eastern African Committee on Production

H301/2: Agricultural Production: East African Production Committee; Constitution, Functions

H316: Veterinary. Report by Mr. J. Smith, Adviser on Animal Health in Colonial Office on his Visit to East Africa – 1940

H336: Agricultural Production Programmes, 1943

H375: Agriculture. Prizes for Agricultural Production

H.R. Wallis, "The Handbook of Uganda," 4, Mill Bank, London S.W. 1, 1920 Intelligence Reports - Uganda, Feb. 1907-1914, [2 Vols.]

K30/12: Congo: International Border: Administrative Proposals

K30/10: Congo Belge: Claim by Mr. F.H. Rogers

K30/12: Congo: International Border: Administrative Proposals

Kigezi (Kamwezi) Mpororo, 1929

Kigezi District Annual Reports, 1911/12 - 1962

Kigezi Native Administration, Kabale, Personnel 1930

Kigezi: Agents; 17 April 1914

Kigezi: Nindo And His Sub-chiefs Paying Tribute to Msinga, Sultan of Ruanda

Kigezi: Nyindo - Deportation of

Kigezi: Punitive Expedition Against Ndochibiri

Kumba: Murder in Rukiga

L22/1: Land: Leases of Native-Owned Land to Non-Natives: Principles and Policy

L79/1 Land: Native Land Tenure Systems

LAN 4/1: Boundaries Interterritorial. Ruanda

Land Acquisition Act 1894 - Action Under No. S 8

Legal: Native Courts in Kabale

LJ 45/1 Vol. II: Crown Land Leases, Individual Cases

M/5/2I: Exclusive Prospecting Licences: Application for Kigezi District

M5/211 Vol. II: Exclusive Prospecting Licences: Application for Kigezi District

Ministry of Agriculture: "Bean Crop Protection."

Native Affairs: Kanyaruanda

Native Affairs: Kanzanyira d/o Maesi (Witch-doctor) Deportation of

Native Affairs: Mginga - Deportation of

Native Affairs: Ninabatwa (Witch-doctor) - Deportation of

Native Affairs: Poll Tax in Western Province

Native Coffee Industry: Arabica Coffee in Ankole and Kigezi Marketing of Crop

P14/16: Bufumbira Water supply, Kisoro

Personal 1930 Kigezi Native Administration, Kabale

R.31/5: Luwalo Labour: Luwalo Commutation Fee: Western Province

R.31: Labour: Luwalo Labour Policy And Principles

R.25/711: Native Administration and Native Government Finance, Eastern, Western and Northern Province Accounts Auditors Reports 1933-1939

R.3/4III: Chiefs: Western Province: Appointments And Dismissals

R.30/3: Labour: Immigrant Labour - Buganda

R.306/6: Immigrant Labour: Southern Route: Feeding of Labour

R.61/1/II: Native Affairs: Native Taxation And Expenditure on Native Services

R.66 (1930): Native Administration Estimates, Western Province, 1930, 1931, 1932, &1936

R.66 (1993): Native Administration Estimates, Western Province, Kigezi District, 1933

R.95/1: Native Industries, Mat-Making in Kigezi

Report By His Majesty's Special Commissioner of the Protectorate of Uganda, Africa No. 7, 1901

RR.66/3(1938): Native Administration Estimates: Western Province, Kigezi District 1939; 1940

S.2122: Honours: Circulars and Instructions on Award of Honours [2 Vols.]

S.M.P. 22351: Counties - Chiefs, Divisions and Titles of

S61: Missions: Miscellaneous Correspondence

The District Commissioner, Kabale 1929

The District Commissioner, Kabale, Personal: Missions. C.M.S. [2 Vols.]

The District Commissioner, Kabale: Royal Geographical Society

The Governor of Uganda (1939) "Uganda Protectorate: Native Administration." Entebbe: The Government Printer

U2/14 (1931): Annual Reports: Inspector of Labour (1931)

U2/14 (1935): Annual Reports: Annual Report on the Western Province 1935

Uganda - Uganda Protectorate Annual Reports of 1936-1959

Uganda Congo Boundary

Uganda Government, The First Five-Year Development Plan 1961/62 – 1965/66 Entebbe: Government Printer

Uganda Labour Department, Annual Reports 1947-1959

Uganda Protectorate (1912) "Report on the Work of the British Section of the Anglo-German-Belgian Boundary Commission, 1911." London: Darling & Son Ltd.

Uganda Protectorate (1922) "Crown Lands (Declaration) Ordinance 1922."

Uganda Protectorate (1938) "Report of the Committee of Enquiry into the Labour Situation." Entebbe: Government Printer

Uganda Protectorate (1939) "Native Administration." Entebbe: Entebbe: The Government Printer

Uganda Protectorate (1946) "Annual Report of the Department of Agriculture for July 1944-June 1945." Entebbe: Government Printer

Uganda Protectorate (1951) "Progress in Uganda 1950." Entebbe: Government Printer

Uganda Protectorate (1955) "Land Tenure Proposals." Entebbe: Government Printer

Uganda Protectorate (1958) "Crown Lands (Adjudication Rules 1958": Entebbe: Government Printer

Uganda Protectorate "Soil Conservation Report", Entebbe: Government Printer For the years 1939-1950

Uganda Protectorate Annual Reports, 1900-1956

Uganda Protectorate Annual Reports, 1905-1924

Uganda Protectorate Reports, 1939-1946

Uganda Protectorate Secretariat Minute Paper

Uganda Protectorate, (1953) Kigezi District Western Province Plan, (Revised and Amended to Dec. 1952) Entebbe: Government Printer

Uganda Protectorate: "The 1953 Labour Report on "Estate Labour, Suggestions for the Management of African Labour with Particular Reference to Agricultural Estates." Entebbe: Government Printer

Uganda Protectorate: Annual Reports of the Western Province, 1936-1946

Uganda Protectorate: G.4: Matrimonial Causes (War Marriages) Act 1944

Uganda Protectorate: Soil Conservation Report for 1943

Uganda Protectorate: The Uganda Agreement, 1900."

Veterinary Annual Reports: 1929-1969

Veterinary: Glossina Morsitans: Presence of in South Ankole

War in Germany: The Kavu Incident

Western Province Annual Reports - 1909 - 1959

Western Province File

Western Province, Kumba: Declaration of as a Township

Secondary Sources

Adas, Michael, 1979, *Prophets of Rebellion, Millenarian Protest Movements Against the European Colonial Order.* London: Cambridge University Press.

Alson L. des Forges, 1986, *'The Drum is Greater than the Shout: The 1912 Rebellion in Northern Rwanda'*; in Crumney, D., ed., *Banditry Rebellion and Social Protest in Africa.* London: Heinemann.

Amadiume, Ifi, 1997, *Reinventing Africa: Matriarchy, Religion and Culture.* London and New York: Zed Books Ltd.

Amin, Samir, 1974, *Accumulation on a World Scale.* New York: Monthly Review Press.

------, 1974, *Neo-colonialism in West Africa.* New York: Monthly Review Press.

-------, 1975, *Unequal Development.* New York: Monthly Review Press.

------, 1977, *Imperialism and Unequal Development.* New York: Monthly Review Press.

Arvind, N. Das, ed., 1982, *'Special Issue on Agrarian Movements in India: Studies on 20th Century Bihar'*, The Journal of Peasant Studies, Vol. 9 No. 3 April.

Aseka, Eric Masinde, 2005, *Transformational Leadership in East Africa: Politics, Ideology and Community.* Kampala: Centre for Basic Research and Fountain Publishers.

Bamunoba, Y. K., & Welbourne, F. B., 1965, *'Emandwa Initiation in Ankole'*, Uganda Journal, Vol. 29, Vol. 1, pp. 13-25.

Banerjee, Sumanta, 1980, *India's Simmering Revolution, The Naxalite Uprising*, London: Zed Books Ltd.

Baran, Paul, 1968, *The Political Economy of Growth*. New York: Monthly Review Press.

Barone, A. Charles, 1985, *Marxist Thought on Imperialism*. London: The Macmillan Press Ltd.

Bates, Robert, 1981, *Markets and States in Africa*. Berkeley: University of California Press.

Bayart, Jean-François, 1993, *The State in Africa: The Politics of the Belly*. London and New York: Longman.

Bayart, Jean-François, et al, 1999, *The Criminalization of the State in Africa*. Oxford: James Currey.

Beaud, Michel, 1984, *A History of Capitalism 1500-1980*. London: The Macmillan Press Ltd.

Ben-Jochannan, A. A. Yosef, 1991, *African Origins of the Major Western Religions*. Baltimore: Black Classic Press.

Bernal, Martin, 1987, *Black Athena: The Afroasiatic Roots of Classical Civilisation*, Vol. I. London: Free Association Books.

----------, 1991, *Black Athena: The Afroasiatic Roots of Classical Civilisation*, Vol. II London: Free Association Books.

Bew, Paul, 1987, *Conflict and Conciliation in Ireland 1890-1910*. Oxford: Clarendon Press.

Black, George. 1984, *Garrison Guatamala*. London: Zed Books Ltd.

Bessell, M. J., 1938, *'Nyabingi'*, Uganda Journal, Vol. 6.

Bianco, L., 1975, *'Peasants and Revolution: The Case of China'*, The Journal of Peasant Studies, Vol. 2 No. 3 (April).

Bogumil, Jewsiewicki, 1980, *'African Peasants in the Totalitarian Colonial Society of the Belgian Congo'*, in Martin A. Klein, ed., *Peasants in Africa: Historical and Contemporary Perspectives*. Beverly Hills and London: Sage Publications.

Brazier, F. S., 1968, *'The Incident at Nyakishenyi 1917'*, Uganda Journal, Vol. 32.

Brizan, George, 1987. *Grenada, Island of Conflict, from Amerindians to People's Revolution 1498-1979*. London: Zed Books Ltd.

Cabral, Amilcar, 1969. *Revolution in Guinea, The African People's Struggle*. Kent: Whitstable Litha Ltd.

Chilcote, H. Ronald, 1991, *Amilcar Cabral's Revolutionary Theory and Practice*: *A Critical Guide*. Boulder & London: Lynne Rienner Publishers.

Crummey, D., ed., 1986, *Banditry Rebellion and Social Protest in Africa*. London: Heinemann.

Campbell, Horace, 1987, *Rasta and Resistance*. Trenton: Africa World Press, Inc.

---------, 1987, *'Popular Resistance in Tanzania, Lessons from Sungu Sungu'*, Mawazo Workshop, Sept. M.U. (Unpub.)

Caplan, Lionel, ed., 1987, *Studies in Religious Fundamentalism*. London: Macmillan Press.

Cardoso, Fernando Henrique & Enzo, Faletto, 1979, *Dependency and Development*. Berkeley: University of California Press.

Carothers, J. C., 1954, *The Psychology of Mau Mau*. Nairobi: Government Printer.

Castells, Manuel, 1996, 1997, 2000, *The Information Age: The Economy, Society and Culture* (3 Volumes). Oxford: Blackwell Publishers..

Chatterjee, Partha, 2004, *The Politics of the Governed: Reflections on Popular Politics in Most of the World*. New Delhi: Permanent Black.

---------, 1993, *The Nation and its Fragments: Colonial and Postcolonial Histories*. New Delhi: Oxford University Press.

Chchachchi, Amrita, 1989, *'The State, Religious Fundamentalism and Women in South Asia'*; Economic and Political Weekly, Vol. XXIV No. 11. (Mar. 18).

Chilcote, H. Ronald, et al eds., 1983, *Theories of Development: Mode of Production or Dependency?* Beverly Hills, London and Delhi: Sage Publications.

Connah, Graham, 1975, *African Civilizations: An Archaeological Perspective*. Cambridge: Cambridge University Press.

Cooper, Frederick, ed., 1983, *Struggle for the City: Migrant Labor, Capital, and the State in Urban Africa*. London: Sage Publications.

Coote, J. M., 1956, *'The Kivu Mission, 1909-10'*, Uganda Journal, Vol. 20.

David, Lan, 1985, *Guns and Rain, Guerrillas and Spirit Mediums in Zimbabwe*. London: James Currey.

Davidson, Basil, 1959, 1960, *Old Africa Rediscovered*. London: Victor Gollancz Ltd.

------, 1991, *Africa in History*. London: Orion Books Ltd.

---------, 1992, *The Black Man's Burden: Africa and the Curse of the Nation-State*. London: James Currey Ltd.

Daily Monitor Newspaper, Kampala.

Diop, Anta Cheikh, 1974, *Black Africa: The Economic and Cultural Basis for a Federated State*. Westport: Lawrence Hill and Company.

---------, 1989, *Great African Thinkers*. New Brunswick: Transaction.

---------, 1978, *The Cultural Unity of Black Africa: The Domains of Patriarchy and of Matriarchy in Classical Antiquity*. Chicago, Illinois: Third World Press.

---------, 1981,1991 *Civilization or Barbarism: An Authentic Anthropology*. Chicago: Lawrence Hills.

---------, 1974, *The African Origin of Civilization: Myth or Reality*. Westpoint: Lawrence Hill.

---------, 1966, *Tales of Amadou Koumba*. London: Oxford University Press.

---------, 1987, *Pre-colonial Black Africa*. New York: Lawrence Hill.

Dhanagare, D. N., 1983, *Peasant Movements in India 1920-1950*, New Delhi: Oxford University Press.

Ddungu, Expedit, 1989, *'The Crisis of Democracy in Africa: A Case of Resistance Councils in Uganda'*, M.A. Thesis, University of Dar es Salaam.

Emmanuel, Arghiri, 1972, *Unequal Exchange*. New York: Monthly Review Press.

Fanon, Frantz, 1966, *The Wretched of the Earth*. London: Penguin.

---------, 1965, *Studies in A Dying Colonialism*. London: Earthscan Library.

---------, 1967, *Black Skin, White Masks*. New York: Grove Press, Inc.

Fetter, 1970, *The Creation of ElizabethVille*. Stanford: Hoover Institution.

Fleming, W.G., 1964, *'The District Commissioner and Tribal Administration in Uganda'*, PhD Thesis, Northwestern University.

Foster, G.M., 1967, *Tzintzuntzan, Mexican Peasants in Changing World*, Little Brown.

Foucault, Michel, 1977, *Discipline and Punish: The Birth of the Prison*. New York: Random House.

---------, 1980, *'The Confessions of the Flesh'*, in Gordon, Colin, ed., *Power/knowledge: Selected Interviews and Other Writings by Michel Foucault, 1972-1977*. New York: Pantheon Books.

---------, 1991, *'Governmentality'*, in Burchell, Graham et al., *The Foucault Effect: Studies in Governmentality*. Chicago: The University of Chicago Press.

Frank, Andre Gunder, 1969, *Capitalism and Underdevelopment in Latin America*. New York: Monthly Review Press.

---------, 1984, *Critique and Anti-Critique: Essays on Dependence and Reformism*. London and Basingstoke: The Macmillan Press Ltd.

Freund, Bill, 1984, *The Making of Contemporary Africa: The Development of African Society Since 1800*. Bloomington: Indiana University Press.

Gakaara, wa Wanjau, 1988, *Mau Mau Author in Detention*. Nairobi: Heinemann.

Gashegu, Rutiba Eustace, 1982, *'Traditional/Modern Therapy and Christian Ministry of Healing, With Special Reference to the Bufumbira of Kigezi'*, PhD. Thesis, Makerere University.

Gebre-Medhin, Jordan, 1989, *Peasants and Nationalism in Eritrea*. Trenton: The Red Sea Press, Inc.

Guha, Ranajit, 1983, *Elementary Aspects of Peasant Insurgency in Colonial India*. New Delhi: Oxford University Press.

Guha, Ranajit, Partha, Chatterjee and Shahid, Amin, eds., *Subaltern Studies*. New Delhi: Oxford University Press.

Gutkind, P. C. W., and Wallerstein, I., eds., 1985, *Political Economy of Contemporary Africa*. London: Sage Publications.

Horowitz, L. Donald, 1985, *Ethnic Groups in Conflict*. Berkeley, Los Angeles, London: University of California Press.

Huntington, S. P., 1968, *Political Order in Changing Societies*. New Haven: Yale University Press.

Hill, Christopher, 1981, *The Century of Revolution 1603-1714*. Hong Kong: Van Nostrand Reinhold.

Hill, Christopher, 1986 *Religion and Politics in 17th Century England*, Sussex: Harvester Press Ltd.

Hobsbawm, E. J., 1959, *Primitive Rebels*. New York: Norton Library.

---------, 1969, *Social Bandits*. Harmondsworth: Penguin.

---------, 1973, *Revolutionaries*. London: Quartet Books Ltd.

---------, 1973, *'Peasants and Politics'*, in The Journal of Peasant Studies, Vol. 1, No. 1.

Howe, C. H. W., 1961, *'Colonial Policy as a Major Variable Force Shaping Political Change in Africa: 1905-1945'*, PhD Thesis, Boston University Graduate School.

Hountondji, J. P., 1983, *African Philosophy: Myth and Reality*. London: Hutchinson & Co. Ltd.

Hrbek, I., ed., 1988, 1992, *General History of Africa III: Africa from the Seventh to the Eleventh Century*. California, UNESCO: James Currey.

Hyden, Göran, 1980, *Beyond Ujamaa in Tanzania: Underdevelopment and an Uncaptured Peasantry*. London: Heinemann.

---------, 1983, *No Shortcuts to Progress: African Development Management in Perspective*. London: Heinemann.

Jack, E. M., 1914, *On the Congo Frontier*. London: T. Fisher Unwin.

Jackson, G. John, 1970, *Introduction to African Civilizations*. New York: Carol Publishing Group.

Jaffe, Hosea, 1988, *A History of Africa*, London: Zed Books Ltd.

Jewsiewicki, Bogumil, 1980, *'African Peasants in the Totalitarian Colonial Society of the Belgian Congo'*, in Peasants in Africa: Historical and Contemporary Perspectives, Klein, A. Martin, ed. Beverly Hills, London: Sage Publications.

Kabwegyere, B. T., 1974, *The Politics of State Formation*. Nairobi: East African Literature Bureau.

Kanza, Thomas, 1972, *Conflict in the Congo: The Rise and Fall of Lumumba*. London: Penguin Books.

Karugire, R. S., 1980, *A Political History of Uganda*. Nairobi: Heinemann.

Karen, E. Fields, 1985, *Revival, Rebellion in Colonial Central Africa*. Princeton: Princeton University Press.

Karogo, Tabitha, 1987, *Squatters and the Roots of Mau Mau*. Nairobi: Heinemann (K) Ltd.

Kasozi, A. B. K., 1994, *The Social Origins of Violence in Uganda, 1964-1985*. Montreal & Kingston: McGill-Queen's University Press.

Ki-Zerbo, J., and Niane, D. T., eds., 1988, 1997, *General History of Africa IV: Africa from the Twelfth to the Sixteenth Century*. California, UNESCO: James Currey.

Klein, A. Martin, ed., 1980, *Peasants in Africa*. London: Sage Publications.

Kroeber, A. L., 1953, *Anthropology*. Chicago: Harcourt Brace & World.

Lane-Poole, Stanley, 1886, 1990, *The Story of the Moors in Spain*. Balitmore: Black Classic Press.

Lenin, V. I., 1986, *Imperialism, the Highest Stage of Capitalism*. Moscow: Progress Publishers.

Leys, Colin, 1975, *Underdevelopment in Kenya. The Political Economy of Neo-colonialism, 1964-1971*. Berkeley and Los Angeles: University of California Press.

Louis, de Lagger, 1959, *Premiere Partie Le Rwanda Ancien.* Kadgayi: Imprimatur.

Louis, Roger, W., 1963, *'The Diary of Kivu Mission'* Uganda Journal, 24.

Macamo, Elísio Salvado, 2005, *Negotiating Modernity: Africa's Ambivalent Experience.* London: Zed Books Ltd.

Maina, Wa Kinyatti, 1986, *Kenya's Freedom Struggle: The Dedan Kimathi Struggle.* London: Zed Books Ltd.

Mamdani, Mahmood, 1976, *Politics and Class Formation in Uganda.* London: Heinemann.

---------,1996, *Citizen and Subject: Contemporary Africa and the Legacy of Late Colonialism.* Princeton: Princeton University Press.

Mamdani, M., Mkandawire, T. and Wamba-dia-Wamba, 1988, *Social Movements, Social Transformation and the Struggle for Democracy in Africa.* Dakar: CODESRIA Working Paper.

Mamdani, Mahmood and Oloka, Onyango Joe, 1994, *Uganda: Studies in Living Conditions, Popular Movements and Constitutionalism.* Kampala: JEP and Centre for Basic Research.

Mann, Kristin, and Roberts, Richard, eds., 1991, *Law in Colonial Africa: Social History of Africa.* London: James Currey.

Marx, Karl, 1973, *Grundrisse.* London: Penguin Books.

Marx, Karl, and F. Eagles (1969), selected works Volume II Moscow progress, Publishers.

Marx, Karl, Engels, Friedrich and Lenin, V. I., 1972, *On Historical Materialism.* Moscow: Progress Publishers.

Mandelbaum, May, Edel, 1957, *The Chiga of Western Uganda.* New York: Oxford University Press.

Mazrui, A. Ali, 1993, *General History of Africa VIII. Africa Since 1935.* California, UNESCO: Heinemann.

Mendlovitz, II. Saul, and Walker, R. B. J., eds., 1987, *Towards a Just Peace, Perspectives from Social Movements.* London: Butterworths.

Mishambi, G. T., 1980, *'Uneven Development and the Rise of False Consciousness in Colonial Uganda.'* Revised Version of a Paper entitled 'Divide and Rule: the British Policy in Colonial Uganda, presented to the History Seminar, University of Dar-es-Salaam, Aug. 7, (Unpub.)

Mokhar, G., ed. 1981, 1990, *Ancient Civilizations of Africa,* Volumes I, II, III & IV. Geneva: UNESCO.

Mudimbe, V. Y., 1988, *The Invention of Africa: Gnosis, Philosophy, and the Order of Knowledge.* London: James Currey.

----------, 1994, *The Idea of Africa.* London: James Currey.

Mukasa, Selestino, 1912, *'Olugendo Olw'Abakulu Abe Mbalala mu Kigezi ne mu Rwanda,' Journey of Feb. 8 - March 28.* Kampala: Munno.

Mukherjee, Ramkrishna, 1984, *Uganda: An Historical Accident? Class, Nation, State Formation.* Trenton: Africa World Press.

Murindwa Rutanga, 1991, *Nyabingi Movement: People's Anti-colonial Struggles in Kigezi 1910-1930.* Kampala: CBR Working Paper No. 18.

----------, 1996, 'A Historical Analysis of the Labour Question in Kigezi District', in Mamdani, Mahmood, ed. *Uganda: Studies in Labour.* Dakar: CODESRIA, pp 53-135.

----------, 1996, "'Have You Killed Your Tutsi Today ...The Graves Are Half Empty?': An Analysis of Rwanda's Horrendous Holocaust 1990 – 1994",* Jadavpur Journal of International Relations*, Jadavpur University.

---------- 1994, 'People's Anti-Colonial Struggles in Kigezi Under the Nyabingi Movement, 1910-1930' in Mamdani, M. & Oloka Onyango J., eds., *Uganda: Social Movements: Studies in Living Conditions, Popular Movements and Constitutionalism.* Kampala: Centre For Basic Research & JEP.

Museveni, Y. Kaguta.1997, *Sowing the Mustard Seed: The Struggle for Freedom and Democracy in Uganda.* London: Macmillan.

--------- 1985, *Selected Articles on the Uganda Resistance War.* Kampala: NRM Publications.

--------- 1975, 'Fanon's Theory of Violence: Its Verification in Liberated Mozambique', in Shamuyarira, N. M, *Essays on the Liberation of Southern Africa.* Dar es Salaam: Tanzania Publishing House.

Mushemeza, E. D., 2007, *The Politics and Empowerment of Abanyarwanda Refugees in Uganda 1959-2001.* Kampala: Fountain Publishing House.

Nabudere, D., 1980, *Imperialism and Revolution in Uganda.* Dar es Salaam: Tanzania Publishing House.

Ngorogoza, P., 1969, *Kigezi and its People.* Nairobi: East African Literature Bureau.

Nkrumah, Kwame, 1974, *Neo-colonialism: The Last Stage of Imperialism.* London: Panaf.

Nyangabyaki, Bazaara, 1985, *'The Food Question in Colonial Bunyoro Kitara: Capital Penetration and Peasant Response'.* M. A. Thesis, Makerere University.

Nzula, A. T., 1979, *Forced Labour in Colonial Africa.* London: Zed.

Ogot, B. A., ed., 1992, 1999, *General History of Africa: Africa from the Sixteenth to the Eighteenth Century.* California, UNESCO: James Currey.

Okumu-Wengi, Jennifer, 1997, *Weeding the Millet Field: Women's Law and Grassroots Justice in Uganda.* Kampala: Uganda Law Watch Centre.

Petras, F. James, 1981, *Class, State and Power in the Third World.* London: Zed Books Ltd.

Philipps, E. J. T., 1923, *'Mfumbiro, The Birunga Volcanoes in Kigezi-Rwanda-Kivu',* Geographical Journal, Vol. 61, April.

Popper, Karl, 1957, *The Poverty of Historicism.* London: Ark.

Prunier, Gérard, 1995, *The Rwanda Crisis: A History of a Genocide.* Kampala: Fountain Publishers.

Purseglove, J. 1951, *'Resettlement in Kigezi',* Journal of African Administration, Vol. 3, pp. 13-21.

Rabinow, Paul, ed., 1984, *The Foucault Reader: An Introduction to Foucault's Thought.* London: Penguin.

Ranger, Terence, 1985, *Peasant Consciousness and Guerrilla War in Zimbabwe.* London: James Currey Ltd.

Rao, M. S. A., 1984, *Social Movements in India.* New Delhi: Manohar Publications.

Redfield, Robert, 1971, *The Little Community Peasant Society and Culture.* Chicago: University of Chicago Press.

British Colonial Government (1912), *Report on the Work of the British Section of the Anglo-German-Belgian Boundary Commission, 1911,'* London: Darling & Son Ltd.

Rodney, Walter, 1976, *How Europe Underdeveloped Africa,* Dar es Salaam: Tanzania Publishing House.

Roger, L., 1963, *'The Diary of the Kivu Mission',* Uganda Journal, Vol. 27, No. 2, pp. 187-193.

Roscoe, J., 1922, *The Souls of Central Africa.* London: Cassell and Company Ltd.

Rostow, W. W., 1960, *The Stages of Economic Growth: A Non-Communist Manifesto.* Cambridge: Cambridge University Press.

Rwampigi, J. M., 1980, *'The Philosophy of Kiga Religion',* M. A. Thesis, Makerere University (Unpub.)

Said, Edward, 1995, *Orientalism.* London: Penguin.

Sebalijja, Yoana, 1911, *'Olutalo Olwari Mu Lukiga e Rwanda',* Munno, Dec.

Seers, Dudley, ed., 1981, *Dependency Theory: A Critical Reassessment.* London: Frances Printer Publishers.

Sen, Amartya, 2006, 'Our Past and our Present', *Economic and Political Weekly,* Vol. XLI, No. 47, 25 Nov. – 1 Dec. 1, pp. 4877 – 4886.

Sertima, Ivan Van, ed., 1985, *African Presence in Early Europe.* New Brunswick and London: Transaction Publishers.

Shanin, Teodor, 1973 *'The Nature and Logic of the Peasant Economy',* Journal of Peasant Studies, Vol. 1, No. 1 (October).

Shiva, Vandana, 1989, *Staying Alive: Women, Ecology and Development.* London and New Delhi: Zed Books and Kali for Women.

Sunday Times of South Africa Newspaper.

Surana, Pushpendra, 1983, *Social Movements and Social Structure.* New Delhi: Ramesh Jain.

Suret-Canale, Jean, 1988, *Essays on African History: From the Slave Trade to Neocolonialism.* Trenton: Africa World Press, Inc.

Tabaro, Patrick, 2006, *'Rediscovering Africa in the Contemporary Globalisation Epoch',* CBR/ENRECA Occasional Paper Series, Vol. 9.

Thornton, John, 1992, *Africa and Africans in the Making of the Atlantic World, 1400-1680.* Cambridge: Cambridge University Press.

Throup, W. David, 1988, *Economic and Social Origins of Mau Mau 1945-53.* London: Heinemann.

Touraine, Alain, 1981, *The Voice and the Eye: An Analysis of Social Movements.* Cambridge: Cambridge University Press.

Turyahikayo-Rugyema, 1974, *'A History of Rukiga in South Western Uganda and Northern Rwanda, 1500-1930',* PhD Thesis, University of Michigan (Unpub.)

Wallerstein, Emmanuel, 1974, *The Origin of the Modern World Systems.* New York: Academic Press.

Wilson, Richard, 1991, *'Machine Guns and Mountain Spirits, The Cultural Effects of State Repression among the Q'eqchi' of Guatemala',* Critique of Anthropology. London: Sage Publications; Vol. 11, No.1.

Zeleza, P. Tiyambe, 1997, *Manufacturing African Studies and Crises.* Dakar: CODESRIA.

Glossary

Ababaizi	Carpenters, carvers.
Ababirigi	Belgians.
Ababuumbi	Potters.
Abadaaki	Germans.
Abafumu (Sing. Omufumu)	Traditional doctors or healers.
Abagirwa (Sing. Omugirwa)	Priests or priestesses.
Abahaniki/Abajubi	Rain makers.
Abaheesi	Smiths.
Abahuuku	Male slaves.
Abaibiki	Apiarists.
Abairukazi	Women slaves. It also refers to women of the *Iru* ethnicity – a section of the Banyankore of Ankore.
Abakazi/omukazi	Plural/singular of women. Omukazi is related to omukozi – worker.
Abambari	Priests or priestesses.
Abanya-Kigezi	People of Kigezi.
Abaraguzi	People who claim to see into the past, present and future and to prophesy.
Abarangi	Priestesses/priests of a new religious movement that is unfolding in Kigezi.
Abashumba	Male slaves.
Abazaana	Female slaves. It is sometimes applied euphemistically in reference to women.
Aheibanga or Nyakibengo	A cliff over which pregnant girls were thrown. Another infamous form of punishment was to maroon them at the Ahakampene Island, on Lake Bunyonyi. This seems less merciless as the objective was not to kill but to enable men incapable of paying bride wealth to pick wives. This practice is said to have been abandoned after a pregnant girl surprised her brother who had gone to throw her over the cliff by clinging to him firmly and they went down together. It is said that the loss of the son changed the people's attitude to this heinous practice.
Amateeka	Public rallies.

Amatembane	Inbreeding.
Askari	Soldier.
Bakopi	Peasants.
Bakuru B'emiryango	Lineage heads/leaders.
Baraza	From Swahili, meaning Monday. In the colonial context, it was the day of public address, which was Monday.
A/Batwa / Watwa	A people derogatorily termed 'pygmies'.
Ba Nyinamaka (sing. Nyineeka)	Heads of households.
Boma	A town or a place where administration was situated. It is from Swahili and its etymology translates to bombs – implying a place where bombs were kept, controlled or shot from.
Dhanna Bad (Bengali)	Thank you.
Duka	A shop or business premises.
Ebibiina	Cooperatives, people's associations.
Ebinyandaro	Pre-marital pregnancies and children from them.
Eka (pl. Amaka)	Home.
Ebirubi	Forges
Ebitenga	These are provisions from mother-in-law or any other relative or friend.
Ebitooma bya Muhumuza	Site of Muhumuza's homestead.
Emandwa	A religion mainly for the status quo. It was also a state religion.
Emihunda	Sharp-pointed metallic staves.
Emondi	Solanum potatoes.
Endaaro	A shrine.
Endiga	A sword.
Engabo Rugatanga Rutangamyambi	Shields
Enganda (Sing. Oruganda)	A combination of various lineages sharing historical origins, totems, symbols, taboos and so on.
Engisha/orugisha	Talisman
Enkumba	Porridge from raw sorghum.
Enkwatamata	Arms' bearers, warriors, fighters.
Entaara	Trays for winnowing grains.

Enteeko/ Karubanda	Councils or courts in pre-colonial times.
Enturire	A very intoxicating brew from sorghum malt and honey.
Enyama enkuru	Delicacies of meat.
Enyerere, emiringa, entayomba, enjogyera, amajugo	Locally smithed ornaments which glitter, enhance beauty, make particular rhythms as the wearers move, thus reflecting their wealth.
Esente/Empiiha	Money. It is derived from cents, the way empiiha is derived from rupee – the first currency that the colonialists introduced in East Africa.
Ezekibeere	Cows taken by force for free milk contribution.
Kahukeiguru	One of the pre-colonial religions.
Kaj Shesh	Work is finished (from Bengali language)
Kashanju	Forced paid labour.
Mafuka/kateera-rume	A go-between in marriage.
Magaj/magezi	Knowledge, brains in Hindi/Bengali and Bantu languages.
Kuzimuura	The act of paying back the bride wealth after separation or divorce.
Magendo	Smuggling, cross-border trade, illicit trade.
Matama	Swahili name for sorghum.
Mugasya	One of the pre-colonial religions.
Mukaaka	A religious movement that emerged in 1970. It was a precursor to the Abarangi Movement. The word means grandmother.
Muzeire-Kasente	The name that Nyabingi acquired from 1927-1928 when its leadership began mobilising financial resources for the struggle
Nyabingi	A militant revolutionary religion. Its other names included Biheeko, Rutatiina-Mireego, Nyinekyaro, Omukama and Muzeire-Kasente.
Nyakibengo	A cliff over which pregnant girls were thrown.
Obuhemba	Bread kneaded from sorghum. It was derogatorily nick-named *John Kyankarate wanyiha habi* in an effort to undermine and denounce it as unpalatable food only eaten by those in destitution.
Obuhiri/kateera-bagomi	Clubs.
Obushera	Sorghum/millet porridge.
Obwijuranda	Bulging of stomach owing to abnormal circumstances.

Oine obwesigye agongyerera owa Nyinazaara (proverb):	He who has courage drunkenly praises himself in his mother-in-law's compound.
Okubagana	To divide property among the family members; to inherit.
Okubanga	Beautification by shaping teeth with a chisel.
Okubegyera	The practice of leaving part of the cooked food for those who prepared the meal - women and children.
Okucwa	Ostracising or banishing disobedient people from the community. This excessive punishment was practised by elderly people to maintain discipline and their political control over their families.
Okucwa oruganda	Destroying the lineage or nationality by bearing girls only.
Okuha enjeru	The practice of sharing prepared food on a farm with others, especially when they are working in neighbouring gardens, or with a passer-by during a break.
Okujuumba	One of the pre-colonial methods of acquiring a bride.
Okuhereka	Entrusting livestock to someone's care under mutually understood terms.
Okukaraba	A practice of atonement after a person had killed another accidentally.
Okuhindiza/ Okuhingiza	Invoking the gods, spirits or ancestors to punish a transgressor.
Okuhonera omwonyo	Collecting lake salt (from a distance) as a commodity.
Okuhonga	Presenting fines for appeasement of the elders.
Okuhoora enzigu	Revenging.
Okushaba	Marriage negotiations.
Okushaka	Searching for food in times of famine.
Okusigira	A practice by elders of leaving food for children.
(O)kusinda	To avoid calling elders by name as a sign of respect.
Okutaana	Grazing cattle in shifts between households.
Okutamba empazi	Literally: *Treating red ants.* This implies sexual intercourse between a man and his mother-in-law.
Okutanzya ekiiru	Historically, the practice of fining a son-in-law for an unbecoming behaviour. With the coming of colonialism, the marriage arrangements changed to western modes. With this shift, any man who elopes with a girl has to pay this fine to his in-laws.

Okutendera	Working for a man with daughters and receiving a bride as payment.
Okuteekyesa amahega	Giving a new couple some property and freedom to start their own life.
Okuterekyerera	Offering religious sacrifices.
Okutweija	Offering religious sacrifices.
Okuvuumba	The act of seeking free alcohol. People who do this are known as abavuumbi.
Okuzira	A practice in which a man refuses his wife's food or refuses to enter her room because of a disagreement.
Okuzimura	Paying back the bride wealth after a marriage has failed.
Okwaruka	Celebration to mark the end of Okwarama.
Okwarama	The time (three months or more) when a bride stays in her mother-in-law's house immediately after marriage.
Okwevuga	Reciting individual heroic successes.
Omukama	King or ruler. In Kigezi's context, this referred to Nyabingi.
Omukazi	Woman. It comes from *Omukozi* – a person who works. In Bengali it is *kaj*. Moreover, in Bengali like in Rukiga, the imperative, do work is *Kola kazi*. *Kola*, to do or perform and *kazi,* to work.
Omukimbo	Tributes or payment to Abaraguzi or doctors for their services.
Omuraguzi/ abaraguzi	Prophets and prophetesses, prognosticators, seers.
Omuramba	A potent brew from sorghum.
Omuryango	Lineage
Omwari	Bride, newly married woman.
Oruganda	Clan, community, people. This concept is used in many parts of Africa to mean people of the same blood, clan, community, and so on. Variations of this concept do exist because of linguistic and spatial differences but the stem and meaning remain the same. For example, the word is *Jouganda* among the Alur in the Democratic Republic of Congo; *Oganda* among the Jaluo in Kenya; *Oluganda/ oruganda* among the different nationalities in the GLR. These constructions might have led the British colonialists to name the country Uganda as the concept was all-encompassing and inclusive.
Orupikya	A locally invented language formed by mixing words for defence purposes.

Otaine Munyanya tashwera	He who lacks a sister (to bring in bride wealth) can never marry. This is a proverbial song.
Potoro	A corrupted version of patrol aimed at netting tax defaulters and criminals.
Ruharo	Forced unpaid labour.
Rukiiko	Council or meeting.
Rutatiina-Mireego	Another name for Nyabingi because of its militancy and courage. It means *One who is never scared by bows and arrows*.
Ruvaivuro	A religious movement that emerged among the converts of the Protestant Church in early 1930s.
Wimbi	Swahili word for millet.

N.B.

Unless otherwise mentioned in this work, PC refers to Provincial Commissioner of Western Province; DC refers to District Commissioner of Kigezi; ADC refers to Assistant District Commissioner of Kigezi; and Governor refers to the Governor of Uganda. Given that there was no alphabet other than Arabic in this region prior to colonialism, the author acknowledges the contribution of the colonialists and their train for putting the local languages in alphabet for the first time. This is regardless of their imperialist motives. This book acknowledges Partha Chatterjee's exposé on colonial politics which enhanced the status of certain languages over others and made them official by putting them in print; codifying them and transforming them into languages of instruction, education, writing, administration and the court, and so on (Chatterjee, 1993). Out of this objective limitation and the failure of the colonialists and their train to grasp correctly the sounds and pronunciations of the local words, those who first captured the names in writing spelled them the way they seemed to sound. Those written by the British were spelled differently from those by the Germans in Rwanda-Burundi and so were those by the Belgians in Belgian Congo. As such, the following names should not be taken to refer to different personalities or places.

1. Abatutsi - Watussi
2. Abatwa - Watwa
3. Basebya- Bassebya - Basebja - Basebia.
4. Bufumbira - Ufumbiro - Mufumbiro - Mfumbiro
5. Kinkizi - Chinchizi.

6.   Kaigirirwa - Kaigirwa.

7.   Katuregye - Katuleghi - Katulegi Katuleggi.

8.   Makobore - Makubirri.

9.   Muhabura - Muhavura.

10. Muhumuza - Muhumusa - Nyamuhumuza - Muhumusa - Mumusa & Mamusa.

11. Muginga - Mginga.

12. Mukiga - Mkiga.

13. Mutabuka - M'utabuko.

14. Ndochibiri - Ndochibiri - Ndochimbiri - Knochibilillis - Ndochi-biri - Ndochi-mbiri - Ndochimbili - Ndochi-mbili - Ndochikembiri - Ntochibiri - Ndocki-mbili - N' docki-bili - Bichubirenga.

15. Ndungusi - Ndungutsi - Ndungutzi - Ndunugutzi - Ndunguse.

16. Nduraiana -   Ruhayana

17. Nyabingi - Nabingi - Nya-Bingi - Nya Bingi - NyaBingi.

18. Nyindo - Nido.

19. Ruanda - Rwanda

20. Rizizi - Rusisi

21. Rizirakuhunga - Luzira - Kalinga

22. Bufumbira

23. Urundi   - Burundi

Index